Dedicated to the
loving memory of my mother
whose perseverance and
talents gave me something
to write about.

Mrs. Polly Wee nee
Cheang Siew Geok Neo
(1930—2001)

Kueh Bungkek

1 kat. sugar
3 coconuts
3 bowls of water
8 eggs
Flour (starch)

Method

Boil water, coconut and sugar. When cool, add in b...
Then add flour which has been fried on the pa...

Candy

3 cups of coconuts
3 cups of sugar
1 cup of milk
1 tabspn. of butter

Method

Mix all ingredients. Put over fir...
Add vanilla essence.

Kueh Embun

1 bowl egg
1 bowl tepong sago
1 bowl sugar
1 bowl cooked coconut
20 cts. raw bread

Method

Mix raw bread and sugar. Leave ov...

Kueh sipot

1	kati tepong gandom
1/4	ozs mentega
2	biji telor
1/2	" kelapa ambil san
10	" bawang kechik

gaul telor mentega
bawang geling, tarok
tepong gaul tarok
santan, belakan buat
bentok sipot

INGREDIENTS

3 lbs butter
30 egg yolks
10 egg whites
1 lb sugar
20 ozs flour
Bunga Chengkek
Kayu Manis
Buah Pelaga
Bunga Pekak

20 egg yolks
5 egg whites (separate from egg white)
Beat sugar and egg yolks
1 small cup flour
12 ozs butter
1 lb sugar minus a bit

KUEH BOLU

INGREDIENTS

1 bowl egg
1 bowl sugar
1/2 teaspoon baking powder
1 1/2 bowl flour

KUEH EMBUN

INGREDIENTS

1 bowl egg
1 bowl tepong sagu
1 bowl sugar
1 bowl cooked coconut
20 cts raw bread

METHOD

Mix raw bread and sugar. Leave overnight. Put colouring.

KWAY BIJI GAJUS

INGREDIENTS

2 lbs butter
2 lbs sugar

INGREDIENTS

900	Katis	KETUMBAR
300	"	DRIED CHILLI
225	"	JINTAN PUTEH
1,200	tah	LADA
1,800	"	JINTAN MANIS
1,200	"	CASCAS
150	Katis	KUNYIT
300	Tah	KAYU MANIS
5	Katis	BUNGA CHINKAY
5	"	BUA PELAGA
	"	BUA PAL...

225
75
56
17 1/2
28
17 1/2
37 1/2
4 1/2
5

Growing Up in a *Nonya Kitchen*

Singapore Recipes from My Mother

Sharon Wee

Marshall Cavendish
Cuisine

Our Daily Fare

Sweet Rewards

Preface

During her lifetime, my mother had filed away hundreds of recipes. She had our family heirloom recipes, orally passed down for generations, transcribed many times by daughters and maids. When I was growing up, I was tasked with reading aloud my mother's recipes just before she cooked those dishes, so I knew the favourite versions that she referred to most often.

Like my mother, I enjoy food and love to entertain. I was often motivated enough to wake up at 3 am to cook for family and friends and soon realised that perhaps, I should compile her recipes for posterity.

During Chinese New Year in 2001, I came up with a simple idea of a spiral bound compilation for my nieces, consisting of my mother's most popular recipes. I vividly remember as we sifted through stacks of paper as I scanned the 'trusted' copies with a vintage machine. Armed with the bulging plastic folder of scanned documents, I flew back to New York, back to my MBA classes for the next few months, putting aside this personal project for when I had the time.

I delayed returning to Singapore that summer, assuming that I could pick up my mother's techniques a few months later over Christmas. Perhaps then, I could also combine the baking lessons as she geared up for Chinese New Year. Nonetheless, I enrolled in the first of many cooking classes at the end of August 2001 because I wanted to sharpen my basic skills, like how to make the perfect French omelette! It was during that fateful period that I had to rush home to Singapore because my mother had become seriously ill. She passed away three months later. I was never to learn alongside her.

Like many Nonyas of her generation, my mother took many of her best-kept cooking secrets to her grave. And like many Nonyas of my generation, I was more fixated on studies and a career than tapping those tips from my mother. I could not boast that I had learnt to cook under my mother's tutelage.

Still shocked by her passing, my sisters and I rummaged through her belongings and documented all her cake moulds, pots and pans and collection of cookbooks. I hurried through her decades-old recipes, stripping them out of their plastic files and lumping them into storage boxes. Then I hand-carried them all back to New York, with the plan that someday I would study them more closely.

By the time I graduated from business school in 2003, the option of going back to work full-time became a dilemma in light of some medical reasons that my baby had. Moreover, I had grown up with a mother who stayed at home all the time. I did not know any different and wanted to do the same for my children. But my education would have been wasted so I decided that perhaps, the little spiral book should become more ambitious. Her passing meant that I was left to fill in many gaps before I could complete this book. More problematic was the fact that I had put all her recipes into a box and now needed to catalogue them once again. The project took a backseat many times during those years, as we welcomed another baby, moved to a new home and fulfilled commitments associated with raising a young family. Yet, the drive to publish this book never went away as more friends and family egged and encouraged me on.

It faced its many challenges along the way. It first started with converting her handwritten recipe measurements from *katis* and *tahils* (old Chinese measurements) and learning the different *daun* (or herbs) and *rempah* (spice pastes). Recipe testing in New York could be challenging. Shopping for ingredients necessary for our cuisine often entailed trekking down to Chinatown by subway with a large shopping trolley, sometimes in the wake of a snowfall. It was not as easy as driving to the nearest NTUC to stock up on *sago* flour or obtain freshly grated coconut from the wet market. Fresh chillies also seemed to be seasonal and could not be found easily during wintertime. Gradually, I grew fearless with what I could bring back to the US. I literally began to smuggle in ingredients that were hard to find and even got caught once.

In the process, I got reacquainted with my Nonya heritage which I had taken for granted. I interviewed older relatives and family friends and inadvertently forged a closer kinship with them that was unexpected, given all those years of growing up around them.

Researching techniques, deconstructing and reconstructing recipes meant that I had to study the Baba Malay vocabulary, Nonya ingredients and food descriptions. It opened up a whole new appreciation of this culture and a love for its beautiful legacy and rich history. In short, as a fifth generation Nonya from both sides of my family, I became a more genuine Nonya by choice, not just by birth.

This project did not only benefit me. Many who helped work on this book were flooded with nostalgic memories of the cooks in their own families. As they tried the recipes in this book, they recognised that they too could reproduce some of the old dishes which they had enjoyed long ago but were often daunted by just the thought of cooking. In an effort to resuscitate such memories, I began a blog to share what I remember of my childhood, hoping that others would be reminded of theirs as well (http://www.memoriesofanonyakitchen.com).

This cookbook memoir reflects my mother's life and passion... a passion that infected me in the process. I hope that you too will tap into your own self-discovery and remembrances of things past as you enjoy this book.

"He has made everything beautiful in its time."

Ecclesiastes 3:11

My mother, Polly, was born in 1930 in British colonial Singapore, in a seaside bungalow along Pasir Panjang. In our family, we nicknamed this area 'Long Beach' since 'Pasir' and 'Panjang' were Malay words for sand and long respectively.

Halcyon Baba Days

Then, Pasir Panjang was a small-scale equivalent of the romantically fabled setting for *The Great Gatsby*. It was a residential area for many affluent Peranakan Chinese families. The estate she was born at had a special name. It was called 'Riviera' and it had the distinction of being one of the few in Singapore to have a sea pavilion jutting out into the water.

My mother's family, and my father's as well, belonged to a distinct group of Chinese settlers now known as Peranakans. They traced their ancestry from the earliest wave of Chinese immigrants to arrive in Southeast Asia, particularly in Malacca. Their men were known as Babas, and their womenfolk, Nonyas. Although I cannot explain factually how the men became known as Babas, I do know that in many cultures, fathers are affectionately called 'Baba'. 'Nonya', on the other hand, originates from the Portuguese word for lady—'dona'. This is not unexpected considering that the Portuguese occupied Malacca very early on. It is assumed that these Chinese migrants were men who left the mainland and ventured

Clockwise from top left: 'Maidstone' at 42 Cairnhill Road, where my grandfather threw parties to celebrate his mother's birthday; Cheang Hong Lim, my mother's great grandfather; Mrs Cheang Hong Lim née Yeo Bee Neo; Cheang Jim Chuan, my mother's grandfather; Chan Kim Hong Neo, wife of Cheang Jim Chuan; Chia Gin Tee, mother of Chan Kim Hong Neo.

to this unknown region to seek their fortune from as early as the 15th century.

There is a romantic legend that these men had originally escorted a Chinese princess who sailed to this region to marry a local prince. I personally think that these men who came hundreds of years ago bore the same strong Chinese predisposition for seeking a fortune and improving their lot in life. Most of these men hailed from Fujian province (hence, they are called Hokkien); they did not bring with them the women from China as it was illegal to do so. They concentrated on building their livelihood; their foremost need was to earn money first. As they settled, they married the local slave girls from the Indonesian islands and formed a community that intermarried frequently. I would not be surprised if some Portuguese and Dutch blood got thrown in along the way, given that Peranakans sometimes display European physical features.

Having put their roots down early on, the Babas capitalised on their knowledge of the land and their loyalty to the British Crown, serving as a a conduit between the colonial administrators and the locals. They acquired wealth through farming rubber and other commodities, shipping and trading. They were highly Anglicised and were among the first to draw the benefits of higher education, often

enrolling in the schools established by the British and the Christian missionaries, working in the Civil Service and thus further entrenching their status in the establishment. Ultimately, the Peranakans forged a unique culture of their own. This included a distinct patois, architecture, sense of fashion, decorative arts, its own furniture, its own romanised translations of Chinese classics and most famous of all, its cuisine.

The *Babas* and *Nonyas* are also often termed as Straits Chinese in reference to the British Crown settlements of Malacca, Singapore and Penang formed by the East India Company in 1824. Many Babas moved from Malacca to Singapore after 1819, the year that Singapore was founded.

My mother's paternal great grandfather, Cheang Hong Lim made his fortune in Singapore by running a government-tendered monopoly processing raw opium

Clockwise from top: Article in *The Straits Times*, 29 June, 1936, detailing a birthday party thrown for Cheang Jim Chuan; one of three identical houses built by Cheang Jim Chuan for his children, next to his house at 233 Pasir Panjang Road; Tan Im Neo and Cheang Theam Chu, my mother's parents; Standing outside the Pasir Panjang house on Chinese New Year's day, the four children of Tan Im Neo: *kuku* Mike, *kuku* Bock, Aunty Mabel and my mother Polly (*kuku* is a term used for a mother's elder brothers).

imported from British India, a business started earlier by his father Cheang Sam Teo. It was no coincidence that years later, 'Riviera' was situated at the foot of Bukit Chandu which in English, means 'Opium Hill'. Cheang Hong Lim was a philanthropist, a Justice of the Peace and was elevated by the British Governor to one of the four pioneer leaders of the Hokkien community for all his charity work. He had set up a fire brigade and a temple among others. The Straits Times reported that he even took a voyage to Southern China in the 1880s to assess the political and commercial situation of his ancestral homeland. Today, there still remain a green park and a few streets named after him and his descendants in Singapore's Central Business District. He also contributed land for the poor in an area called Bukit Ho Swee. In the 1960s, a great fire razed the *kampong* (village) to the ground. It was from this incident that stimulated the government's ambitious public housing programme. To underscore her family's standing in society, my mother was given a four-character name when she was born—Cheang Siew Geok Neo—as opposed to the more common three-character name that most Chinese families bestow on their children. The four-character name supposedly imparted some form of highborn status. Her name was also characteristically Nonya as it ended with 'Geok' and 'Neo', names frequently used for girls.

Her grandfather, Cheang Jim Chuan, parlayed the family's fortune into shipping and land ownership and became landlord to some two thousand plus properties in Singapore, primarily along Robertson Quay by the Singapore River, between the Orr and Read bridges. It seemed that the family, as with many prominent Peranakan families of the day, mingled with their colonial counterparts, a trend not readily embraced by other locals during that era. My mother's father and uncle hosted an annual birthday party for their mother. These events were reported in the local media, not least because it mentioned that Westerners attended the party. The Malay *kampong* (village) was not forgotten. A *ronggeng* (song-and-dance festivities) was held for them to enjoy.

The multi-generation clan then moved out after the matriarch's death to the centre of town, to a mansion at 24 Nassim Road, and later to another on Cairnhill which they called 'Maidstone'. My mother loved to tell me stories of how haunted it was, what with the servants waking up in the garden because the 'ghosts' had transported them there. Perhaps because of these scary tales, the family

returned to Pasir Panjang once again. This time, to a row of houses built by her grandfather. The Big House (*Rumah Besar*) was situated at 233 Pasir Panjang Road, followed by three smaller houses next to it. Grandfather occupied the Big House with his new wife, along with his unmarried daughters. He reserved the middle of the three smaller houses for my mother's father.

Grandfather was an imposing figure who observed the Victorian edict that 'children should be seen, not heard'. Only my mother's stepsister, Eng, was allowed to stay in the Big House because she was the favourite grandchild. All the other grandchildren were only allowed to visit the Big House on Chinese New Year to receive their *ang pow* or red packets.

As a little girl in the 1930s, my mother witnessed glorious days of riding in an open-top convertible and visiting the horse racing tracks. Chinese New Year meant a new set of clothes and jewellery for the first three days. The house she lived in had two black-and-white maids (indentured domestic help from Southern China, who usually wore black-and-white outfits), a cook and a driver. Her father did not have to work, relying instead on income from the tenants of the two hundred properties which he inherited from his father. He was a dapper dresser with a penchant for walking canes, hats and three-piece suits. His passion was gambling *chap jiki* (an illegal betting game) daily and he was notorious for utilising his telephone (an expensive gadget then) to mostly retrieve the winning numbers.

When the Japanese invaded Singapore and World War II broke out, my mother vividly remembered how the Sikh guard by the Big House was blown off by a bomb. Her father moved the children to Serangoon to live with a Japanese relative who could protect them. Grandfather later died. By the time war ended, much of the life as my mother had known, was to change forever.

My mother's mother, Tan Im Neo, died from cancer in 1947 at the young age of 36. She was the third wife. Wife Number One had been barren, forcing my mother's father to take on a second wife whom we later referred to as Mama Katong. Wife Number Two bore three sons and two daughters but was not accepted by the mother-in-law because she was Cantonese and therefore, not a 'refined Nonya'.

A Married Woman's Life

This led my mother's father to take on Tan Im Neo when she was barely in her teens and 12 years younger than him. She came from a family of 16 children and it must have seemed such good fortune to be married off into a wealthy Baba family even if it meant being Wife Number Three. She went on to have two sons and two daughters. Her new husband was a seeming wastrel and philanderer. My grandmother often cursed her lot in life. She urged her children to study so that they could have a life far better than her own. My mother was the elder daughter and was discouraged from going to school by her father who thought that it was more genteel to stay at home. She did, however, briefly attend Katong Convent when the family moved to the East Coast.

Initially the holiday bungalow for the nuns of the Holy Infant Jesus Order, the new school was an offshoot of the main school in town. Katong became a popular area for Peranakan and Eurasian families. The school was set up to accommodate girls like my mother who lived in that area so that they did not have to travel far. My mother attended the school briefly and dropped

Left: My parents' wedding day—January 31, 1948. Standing outside 73 Lorong K, Telok Kurau.

out right after the school relocated to Ceylon Road during the war. She learnt to write rudimentarily and recognised words visually. At least, she knew how to count and that was crucial for running her future household.

From then on, that was how my mother endured living in a world that would soon transform significantly in her lifetime. It was hard to envision how she could cope when it was the norm to read the newspapers, watch television, decipher advertisement messages, and converse with friends who, unlike her, went on to a higher education. She made up for these shortcomings by being very observant—she deduced information from news images; analysed and memorised everything mentally. She would 'make do' sometimes, such as with the church hymnbook. She simply hummed and mumbled along with the tune.

The language or more accurately, the patois that I spoke with my mother was Baba Malay, with a smattering of English thrown in. Many of my friends these days assume that I grew up speaking Mandarin. That was not the case. By the time I went to school, Mandarin was a compulsory second language. Yet, it became a

constant struggle for pupils like me who mainly spoke English at home. During my older sisters' time in school, Malay was actually the second language as Singapore, part of Malaya then, strove to build a common identity with the hinterland. So even my sisters could not help me with Mandarin. The Baba patois is a Malay-based language incorporating several Hokkien words. I would use the Malay words '*baju*' (clothes) or '*obat*' (medicine) and be more comfortable saying '*makan*' than '*chifan*' (Mandarin for 'let's eat'). Built largely on root words, I could not use it to communicate with those who spoke the more elegant Bahasa Indonesia or more formal Malay. By the same token, I could not speak Hokkien fluently. That, in short, was what I acquired of my "mother tongue". It was the way I communicated with her.

When her mother died, my mother and her sister moved to Kuo Chuan Avenue to be taken care of by their maternal uncle. He brokered the marriage between my mother and father.

My parents had never met before the two families came together for a 'viewing' at the old Wing Choon Yuen restaurant situated at the Great World Amusement Park. It was customary then for the two families to have a banquet so that the prospective groom and bride could meet each other. The conclusion proved favourable and my parents were married in January 1948. As was common then, my mother had been given a dowry by her

....

Clockwise from top: My father's family. He stands on the far left; My mother's portrait, used by the matchmaker, taken when she was 16; The bride arrives at the groom's home, assisted by the '*sangkek um*' or wedding mistress of ceremonies; The wedding bedchamber; My parent's wedding portrait; A young mother on an outing to Haw Par Villa.

late grandmother. This came in the form of a property in Chin Swee Road. Sadly, my mother was forced to dispose of it quickly to pay off her father's ever mounting gambling debts.

By their teens, most Nonya girls would have had some sort of strict tutelage on domestic skills, particularly cooking. This would have been the time for prospective mothers-in-law to go about judging a girl based on her pounding skills with the mortar and pestle. Catered for by servants, compounded by the mental absence of a dying mother, my mother did not have any housekeeping skills or know how to cook when she married. This was considered quite disgraceful when she first went to live with her in-laws in a multi-generational home at 73 Lorong K in Telok Kurau. It became all the more intimidating because she was about to move in with an old lady who was renowned in the neighborhood as a culinary expert and who taught other Nonyas to cook.

This old lady, my father's blind maternal grandmother, decided to teach my mother the essentials of Nonya cuisine in the strictest way imaginable. My mother had to observe the cooking techniques and note the ingredients used, commit to memory and then repeat the process all over again. If the finished product was sub-par in standard, this blind grandmother-in-law would spit the food out. The process would be repeated until the dish was perfected. Almost 60 years later, while riding the bus to visit my dying mother, my father quietly recalled the tears and heartache during this grueling phase in their marriage. Three years into their marriage, exhausted from having to cook all the time for an extended family and impress her in-laws, my mother miscarried her third child. It was a boy that the family had so longed for and would never have.

My mother went on to have six daughters. While my father worked, she stayed at home to raise the children and to care for the in-laws. While a charlady cleaned the house and did the laundry, my mother pursued hobbies such as sewing and baking. She honed her domestic skills—sewing our party dresses, pyjamas and school uniforms, planning and cooking all our meals, and running the household. As a strict disciplinarian, the children were dressed alike and she meted out corporal punishment when necessary. While she could not read, she still went to the flagship MPH bookstore on Hill Street and sought the advice of a bookshop saleslady to buy me my first reading book, by Enid Blyton. I still vividly remember her all dressed up, waiting by the gate as I came home from school one afternoon, rushing me off to the Odeon to see "The Sound of Music" so that I could experience the thrills of watching a movie.

In the 1960s and 1970s, my mother took many cooking classes to widen her repertoire. She befriended like-minded housewives and they began to exchange cooking tips and attend cooking classes together, often at the old Siglap Community Centre. The classes were such an outlet for these housewives in their otherwise, mundane routine. Many of them, including my mother, took the trouble to visit the hairdresser to set their hair and put on their best *cheongsam* (a figure-hugging

Chinese dress) just so to make a big occasion out of attending demonstration classes by master chefs Sin Leong and Tham Yui Kai. These chefs introduced the kind of Cantonese cuisine one nostalgically associates with 1960s Singapore, dishes including paper-wrapped chicken and shark's fin omelette. My mother also took classes at the private homes of fellow housewives. I actually remember, as a child of five, accompanying her to one such cooking class by the mother of our first Prime Minister. Because they were all Nonya ladies, they spoke in Baba patois. My mother knew the elder Mrs. Lee and her sister, Mrs. Leong Yee Soo well. Both sisters were at the forefront of publishing Nonya cookbooks. Aunty Leong used to drive us around in her Volkswagen Beetle to visit her sister, and to the old CK Tang to hunt around for kitchenware.

During many balmy nights, the ladies would sit out in the patio, armed with glue, scissors and files, exchanging and cataloguing their own recipes. My mother had a passion for collecting cookbooks and later in life, had the nearby MPH store call her whenever a new publication was launched. As a child, I often accompanied her to CK Tang and Robinsons and we would check out the latest appliance demonstrations. She was one who thoroughly enjoyed buying and testing these.

Right to the very end of her life, my mother frequently called these lifelong friends and older grandaunts. They had forged a genuine bond of friendship derived from picking up the phone and chatting about recipes, the latest gadgets, cooking tips and why their cookies turned too brown or their cakes, too dry. It is a lifestyle that hardly exists now.

Clockwise from top left: My mother making a *popiah* roll; Standing with my sister, dressed in a *samfoo* which was fashionable then; Sewing into the night; A young mother posing with her young daughters (and a niece in a different outfit) one Chinese New Year; Graduating from a sewing course, wearing her project; Posing in a fashionable Anneke Gronloh-style kebaya, named after the famous singer; With my sister and my paternal grandmother.

My mother's kitchen was the centre of her universe. Much of her life revolved around planning meals, prepping, cooking, baking, chatting with the grocer and nagging at the maid, all within the confines of her kitchen. It was around the dining table that neighbours and relatives often came to chit-chat with my mother.

Preparation

Memories of Our Old Kitchen

The cacophony of chatting, gossipy whispers, laughter, scolding, temper flares, hollering amidst a range of intonations and volumes is very characteristic of a Nonya's kitchen and dining table. While I am about to elaborate on the main tools and ingredients associated with Nonya food, I do have to delve into how intimate the connection could be between Nonya culture and food. No more apparent can it be than with the nicknames given to friends and relatives behind their backs. Nonyas were known for being sarcastic gossips. My mother and her peers had a nickname for almost everyone. Many of these were derived from food nomenclature. For example:

Si pantat kuali—She who has the derriere the size of a wok.

Si hitam sotong—She whose complexion is as dark as that of squid ink.

Udang dalam tanggok—Flirtatious like a jumping shrimp caught in a basket.

Si katek ayam—The short one, like the pygmy chicken.

Si otak lembu—The dumb one with the cow's brain.

Anak kepiting—Baby crab, implying a restless and naughty child.

On the more serious side, many old houses in Singapore had two kitchens. The indoor dry kitchen displayed cabinets for dinnerware, cutlery, food containers, biscuits and beverages. It might have included a sink, an oven and even a stovetop, but that was rarely where the action took place. The outdoor wet kitchen was indeed the hub for cooking, with its own sink and stovetop. All the prepping, chopping, pounding, frying and cleaning took place there.

In our old house at 22 Yarrow Gardens, my mother's passion as a cook meant that we divided our kitchen into three parts, not just two. Of course, the divisions and layout of the kitchen and position of storage cupboards, equipment and appliances evolved over many years based on my mother's cooking needs and habits.

The kitchen closest to the centre of the house, with its cabinets, was where we had our daily meals. We ate at a dining table lined with clear plastic to catch all the food spills. To prevent flies and geckos, if any, from attacking our food, we had dome-shaped food covers (*terong sading*) made of rattan which we placed over plates of food kept at room temperature. We also had a more formal extendible dining table outside the living room area, which was reserved for grand occasions such as Chinese New Year. In this particular kitchen, my mother also had a refrigerator where she kept jugs of chilled boiled water, medicine, picnic ham, butter, jam, snacks and fruits. It was the 'lightweight' fridge. She also had her Baby Belling oven and Kenwood cake mixer placed here which she used during her Chinese New Year baking season. In one of the cabinets, my mother stored a variety of canned food, such as condensed milk, baked beans, corned beef, luncheon meat, sardines, fruit cocktail and sausages. Her experience during the war years where food was in short supply led her to stock up on food throughout her life.

For a long time, we also had an old-fashioned pantry cupboard commonly found in Nonya homes. The doors had fine wire mesh windows and the legs stood in bowls of water. These bowls of water served as mini moats to deter ants from climbing up the cupboard legs.

Next came the middle kitchen. It was indoors but it had a continuous open vent, curtained by a wire mesh and plastic sheath, along the length of the back wall to let out the cooking fumes. The middle kitchen had several wooden plank shelves and drawers to contain her baking trays, Nonya cake moulds, *tingkat* (tiffin carriers), and other items which needed more protection from outdoor dust. She also hung her large *nyiru* bamboo trays here, some of which were about a metre or three feet in diameter. These circular trays were meant to sun-dry foodstuff, including spices prior to grinding them into curry powder.

A few shelves were set aside for my mother's appliances. She bought a number in her lifetime as she was always on a quest to find the best blender and mixer. They were neatly covered in plastic sheets and it was a chore to take the heavy machines out just to use them!

My mother also installed a second refrigerator for meats, vegetables and vacuum sealed plastic bags of spice pastes (*rempah*). This refrigerator played an especially important role during the Chinese New Year period because it could hold all the food we needed to serve over many days. My mother also had her prep table here on which she chopped and sliced. It was positioned close to her utility sink, knives, measuring tools and a cabinet full of spices and sauces. We also had a large and heavy earthenware jar called a *tempayan* to store our rice, the staple of an Asian kitchen. The jar was rarely empty of rice as it was considered inauspicious for a household to run out of rice. The stovetop was stationed here to cook our daily meals.

The third kitchen was outdoors but it had concrete flooring and a zinc roof. Because this open kitchen could be seen from the road, it was a perennial eyesore for my neighbours even though my mother tried to hide her pots and pans behind rattan chick blinds and tarpaulin. Such was the extent to which her hobby of collecting kitchenware manifested itself. My mother installed another huge rack to store army-sized pots and pans and other large and heavy items such as the mortar and pestle (*batu lesong*), *batu boh* and *batu giling* (pages 45–46). It was here that we pounded with the *lesong* (mortar and pestle); or set up the portable charcoal stove to boil her *kueh chang* (page 179). During the *kueh chang* season, the 'shed' became steamy and oily with the boilers going at full strength and the dumplings strung along bamboo poles, waiting to be cooked. We had a wash area to do our laundry and clean the huge pots, as well as slaughter the occasional chicken from the nearby village (*kampong*). This kitchen also featured a huge water dragon pot, about a metre or three feet tall. This distinctive brown jar, decorated on the outside with images of dragons and phoenixes, was carried over from the pre-war days when water had to be drawn from a well. It was placed here to catch rainwater. This was once again a result of my mother's experience during the war years, to ensure that we had a constant supply of water if there was ever a shortage.

Ever a true Nonya, when my parents decided to move to a smaller apartment, a key criteria was a spacious kitchen area to store the paraphernalia. Needless to say, the maid's quarters became a second kitchen and my father made 20 car trips just to transport the kitchen items.

Clockwise from top left: The outdoor third kitchen in our old house at Yarrow Gardens; The dry first kitchen in the house; An old-fashioned pantry cupboard. The legs stand in bowls of water to deter ants from climbing up; Packing into tiffin carriers (*tingkat*) leftover food from a party; Hard at work wrapping *ati babi*.

Essential Nonya Ingredients

These days, the modern home does not afford the luxury of space and the Nonya cook may not always have the little garden patch where she can pluck a handful of *laksa* leaves, snip a stalk or two of *pandan* leaves or pick the blue clitoria (*bunga telang*) flowers off her fence. Rarely also would she be slaughtering chicken in the confines of her wet kitchen. Yet perhaps, she might still retain the same display of condiments beside her stovetop. My mother, like many of her friends, placed their most frequently used condiments and ingredients within easy access while they cooked. That often meant a plastic tray beside the tabletop double gas cooker where there were small bottles of soy sauces, sesame oil, and jars of minced garlic, salt and sugar. In the past, there would also have been a metal container to hold used cooking oil for reusing.

Perhaps under the sink or on an open shelf under the counter, there would have been shallow baskets of garlic, shallots and dried chillies with a mortar and pestle (*batu lesong*) resting nearby on the floor. The refrigerator would have had a drawer full of fresh chillies, kaffir lime (*lemo kesturi*), *belachan*, dried shrimps (*udang kering*), coriander leaves (cilantro) amongst other ingredients. With the humid air, the smells lingered in the kitchen to create a very distinct pungent aroma in the Nonya kitchen, at once fishy, spicy and sharp. I have listed the components and ingredients that typify a kitchen like my mother's. Do note however that the more one cooks, the more comprehensive the pantry and the kitchen tools would be. With my mother, it was a lifetime of acquisitions, trial and error and experience. You may prefer to source the fresh ingredients on the day of cooking. My sister Maggie has the habit of going marketing every morning to get the freshest ingredients for dinner. She also goes to three different supermarkets clustered near one another, as she believes that one sells fresher vegetables while another sells cheaper canned items. There are also some items that can only be found in the wet market. In my mother's time, savvy housewives knew when the fresh fish or fruit came in and that the best time to shop for fresh ingredients was early in the morning.

Dry Spices

My thrifty mother stored spices in the refrigerator for years but that is not a practice one should observe as most spices lose their aroma beyond a year. While the shelf life of each spice varies from six months to two years, as a rule of thumb, clean them out after six months. When buying spices, get a conservative amount of each spice even if buying a large quantity may seem more economical. The best way to store spices is to pack them in small airtight containers marked with the date of purchase and kept in a drawer or corner of the refrigerator. Generally, whole spices retain their flavour better than ground spices, so the preference is to use the whole spice itself.

Fresh Herbs and Vegetables

Asian vegetables, unfortunately, do not stay fresh beyond a day in general. This applies especially to bean sprouts (*taugeh*) and coriander leaves (cilantro). Leafy greens also shrink to half their volume when cooked so it is recommended that you buy more to allow for the shrinkage and the need to pluck off some dulled, yellowed or rotten leaves before cooking.

Dried Ingredients

Many dried ingredients, for example for those used in *chap chai* (page 61), can be purchased from Chinese medicinal shops. These are often of better quality than the pre-packaged ones in the dry goods section of supermarkets.

Canned Food and Condiments

My mother often bought canned food that was "Made in China" by state factories such as Ma Ling. Times have changed and there are now many better brands to choose from. With packaged or canned ingredients, the fewer preservatives and artificial flavourings, the better. My mother kept a good quantity of these items in her dry pantry together with bottles of HP Sauce and Maggi Chilli Sauce, symbols of the Western influence from colonial times. In the refrigerator, she would have oyster sauce, preferably of the Lee Kum Kee brand, and rice wine vinegar. Other essentials include:

Cooking oil—Peanut oil (preferably Knife brand) is favoured for deep-frying. Vegetable oil (made from soy) and canola oil are healthier alternatives.

Cornflour—A ready ingredient for making a quick slurry to thicken sauces, also known as cornstarch.

Dark soy sauce—Not to be confused with Kikkoman sauce which is made using a higher percentage of wheat and less of soy itself. Chinese-style dark soy sauce is usually made with the addition of caramel or molasses for colour as well as flavour.

Light soy sauce—Preferably Pearl River Bridge, Koon Chun or Amoy brands.

Pepper—Unless otherwise specified, ground white pepper is used whenever a recipe calls for pepper as a seasoning.

Salt—My mother used standard table salt but I prefer using coarse sea salt.

Sesame oil—Used as a seasoning (preferably Kadoya brand). Sesame oil is not used for frying because its low smoking point will result in an off, burnt taste.

Techniques

Sequence of Ingredients for Pounding or Blending

Whether by pounding with the mortar and pestle or blending with an electric food processor, adding ingredients in the right sequence will contribute to a finer paste. The harder and drier ingredients such as candlenuts, fennel, cumin and coriander seeds are pounded first, followed by sliced up galangal, turmeric and lemon grass in that order. And then red chillies and finely sliced shallots.

Soaked dried chillies are then added. Having been reconstituted in water, the chillies provide some moisture, which helps to bind the spice paste. *Belachan,* or dried prawn (shrimp) paste, is added last, its pasty texture enhancing the consistency of the pounded spices further. As *belachan* is salty, you may want to stagger the amount added to control the saltiness of the spice paste.

Frying Spice Paste (*Rempah*)

After all that hard work of pounding the spice paste, it is crucial that you do not scorch it when cooking and hence unwittingly introduce a burnt taste to your dish. This is the part in the cooking process that requires the most patience and precision. The wok or Dutch oven should be heated. Oil is then added until it glistens. If the oil begins to smoke, turn down the heat and let the oil temperature come down, even if this means removing the wok from the heat for a while. Add the spice paste and begin to stir gently so that the paste does not burn at the bottom. As the paste cooks, a warm, fragrant aroma will be released. The paste will also begin to deepen in colour, sizzle slightly and *keluar minyak* (literally 'oil arises'). The last term means that a spicy oil will start oozing, taking on the colour of the red chilli or the deep yellow hue of the turmeric (*kunyit*) and galangal. This whole process depends on the amount of paste that you are frying so you need to be patient. Turning up the heat does not always speed things up and you may end up burning the paste instead.

Basic Spice Paste and All That Follows

After my mother passed away, my sister Molly and I did an inventory check of all that she left behind— her clothes, jewellery, sewing threads and fabrics and of course, everything in the kitchen—tools, dinner sets and cutlery. In fact, we did not dare dispose of her spices and food colourings for years. While we were going through everything, we stumbled on numerous sealed plastic bags of spice paste (*rempah*) in the bottom drawer of the fridge. Looking at the orange paste, we assumed that they were for making our favourite *ikan nanas* (page 222) soup and we eagerly distributed these bags to our other sisters as well. We happily consumed them. In retrospect, the paste might have been the basic *rempah titek*—the mother spice paste by which all other spice pastes are derived.

It was many years later, when I had almost completed writing this cookbook, that I learnt about the foundational spice paste known as *rempah titek*. It is used in recipes like *kang kong belachan* (page 247) and *sambal titek* (page 249). This particular paste consists of three to four key ingredients— shallots, *belachan*, red chillies and optionally, candlenuts. Individual families had their preferred recipe for this paste with varying amounts of each of the three or four components. For example, some families may prefer the paste more salty and therefore include more *belachan*, while another family may include candlenut for a thicker consistency, or more chilli for more heat.

By adding turmeric, galangal and tamarind and oftentimes lemon grass, the basic *rempah titek* thus became a *garam assam* which formed the spicy foundation for dishes like *ayam buah keluak* (page 66) and *udang garam assam* (page 231).

Building on this, the addition of coconut milk and ground coriander seeds—the latter for added flavour—progressed the paste further to *rempah lemak* which was used for *satay babi* (page 70) and *otak otak* (page 130). An experienced Nonya cook would have the confidence to make these *rempah* in bulk to dole out for cooking the relevant dishes. Unfortunately, I do not. I still make these pastes from scratch for each dish according to the proportions dictated by the recipe. Perhaps, with time and experience, I will be able to do so.

The Agak-Agak Philosophy

Traditionally, the Nonyas engaged all their senses when they cooked—it was important to gauge the colour of the gravy, smell the aroma of the spices, feel the warmth of the charcoal heat, listen to the rhythm of the pounding and most importantly, taste the final product when the cooking is finished. As such, recipes passed down the generations were inexact. Cooking was by estimation or what the Nonyas called *agak-agak*.

The cook was emboldened to adjust the taste by adding more salt or sugar or both, redden the curry with more dried chillies, kick up the flavour with more shallots or turn down the heat to thicken the gravy. As the quality of ingredients changed through the decades—a result of farming technology or change in supply source—the cook did not hesitate to calibrate the recipe to produce the same taste she remembered from previous years. My mother made such changes over the years and it was challenging for me at times to clearly assess which recipe was most accurate. I soon realised that she made these adjustments to suit the times, to reflect the fact that some of these ingredients did not carry the spunk that she was used to. I have since learnt to embrace this philosophy—that one should be in control of the cooking process and hence, tweak the ingredient amount of each recipe if necessary, according to one's preference.

Therefore, if you sense that you need more salt or less chilli for the dish than stated in the recipe, take the liberty to 'agak' how much more or less is needed. You may choose not to add salt or sugar until just before serving because the flavours brew over time and may end up more salty or sweeter than you expect. This is especially so for dishes that employ prawn (shrimp) stock, *belachan* or fermented soy bean (*taucheo*).

Ingredients

Basil Seeds (*Bijik Selaseh*)

Agar Agar Strips

Bean Curd, Deep-Fried (*Taupok*)

Agar Agar Strips/Powder

Agar is extracted from a variety of seaweed—through an intensive process of washing, sun-drying and boiling until the seaweed dissolves into a gelatinous substance. The substance is then dried and trimmed into raffia-like strips, or ground into powder.

Alkaline Solution (*Ayer Abu/Abu* Water/ Potassium Carbonate)

Alkaline solution is used in *kueh ko swee* (page 268) to give it its chewy and springy texture. It is the same ingredient that is found in yellow noodles, contributing to its hue; as well as in dim sum items such as *cha siew bao*. It is available in bottled form as potassium carbonate often under the Koon Chun brand name. In the past, Nonya cooks obtained *ayer abu* by adding a whitish 'rock' to boiling water. The solution was stored in large glass bottles for use when required.

Bamboo Shoots

I cheat by buying the tinned version. The best bamboo shoots apparently come from China's Zhejiang province and the most flavourful are the small, young winter shoots. Study the label on the tin to see if you can find these two qualities. It is best to boil them first before they are julienned for p*opiah* (page 144) and *pong tauhu* (page 56). A hallmark of a meticulous Nonya cook was to be able to slice them *halus* (fine).

Banana Leaves

Banana leaves are a common sight around Asian snacks (*kueh*) and desserts, serving as wrappers as well as trays for displaying the various colourful treats. The supple leaves are naturally non-stick and are ideal for holding the many gooey glutinous rice flour desserts. Morever, the leaves impart a lovely, sweet banana fragrance.

Banana leaves are also famously seen in South Indian restaurants where they are used as disposable plates on which rice and curries are served.

Basil Seeds (*Bijik Selaseh*)

They can be found in Indian provision shops under the name of *takmaria*. After soaking, basil seeds take on a gelatinous coating. In Asia these are usually used in drinks or desserts.

Bean Curd, Deep-Fried (*Taupok*)

These are derived from extracting the water content from the curd and then deep-frying to produce a 'puff' that is dry and crispy on the outside. We use the rectangular or square pieces and quarter them for *chap chai* (page 61). These first need to be soaked in water to reconstitute to obtain a moist, sponge-like texture.

Firm Bean Curd (Taukua)

Bean Curd, Firm (*Taukua*)

Firm bean curd is a pressed bean curd which therefore explains its firm texture. It is fried and then sliced finely to garnish *popiah* (page 144) or fried and cubed as a *gado gado* (page 138) component. Fresh ones can be found in wet markets while those with a longer shelf life are commonly found in the refrigerated section of supermarkets. Unseal the latter just prior to cooking.

Bean Curd, Medium or Soft (*Tauhu*)

Medium bean curd lends some springiness to the meatballs in *pong tauhu* (page 56). My mother, and now my sister, would buy the traditional round balls of bean curd one can only find in wet markets. These round ones are not super soft but are medium firm. Alternatively, medium bean curd found in supermarkets would be a good substitute. For the low-key pork and meatball soup which we sometimes cooked for our daily meals, we often used the soft silky type of bean curd.

Bean Curd Sheets

These sheets are sold dry and paper-thin. They should be gently wiped with a moist cloth to make them more pliable and to remove excess saltiness. Bean curd sheets are used for wrapping *ngo hiang* rolls (page 73).

Bean Sprouts (*Taugeh*)

In primary school, I used to throw small, green mung beans in the garden soil and watch them grow into sprouts. Make sure to buy perky, earthy smelling sprouts. Older shoppers tend to pluck a sprout or two, a quick snap indicating freshness. Sprouts soaked in water do not necessarily indicate freshness. After purchase, the root ends of bean sprouts are plucked off and any green-black hulls are fluffed off. This can be painstaking and often a good chore passed on to a young child keen to learn to cook! Bean sprouts are most often blanched before serving with *laksa* (page 125) or *gado gado* (page 138).

Belachan

Almost every dish in this book requires a pat of this slightly moist and brown paste. It is made from dried, salted, then fermented tiny shrimps which are ground further into a smooth paste and later dried in the sun. An old lady used to deliver to our home round slabs of pungent home-made *belachan* (pronounced blah-chan) wrapped in cloth. These round discs are still available in shops in Malacca but *belachan* is more commonly available in rectangular blocks wrapped in plastic and paper.

As *belachan* is salty and fishy, adding too much of it in any one recipe would overpower the overall taste of the dish.

When pounding, the firm paste should first be chopped into smaller cubes.

To arouse its aroma and make it more 'crisp', some cooks would toast the paste in a dry pan, sometimes using a spatula to break up the paste into a powdery fine texture. I prefer Malaccan *belachan* which I find less salty than that from Penang. To store, keep it sealed in an airtight container in the refrigerator, so that the smell will not pervade.

Black Glutinous Rice (*Pulot Hitam*)

This rice is actually purplish in colour and needs to be soaked overnight before preparing the dessert *pulot hitam* (page 296).

Belachan

Black Glutinous Rice (Pulot Hitam)

Black moss

Brinjal

Buah Keluak

Candied Melon (Tang Kueh)

Candlenuts (Buah Keras)

Black Moss

This is actually a dark green algae. It is expensive (which probably explains why there are numerous, cheaper counterfeits on the market) but can be kept for a long time. Thought to have a cleansing effect on the body, black moss can be found in Chinese medicinal shops. The Chinese word for black moss, '*fa cai*' bestows this ingredient a venerated status as it sounds like the word for prosperity.

Brinjal

Known as eggplant in the US and aubergine in England and France, these dishes were cooked using the long, slender purple variety. Believe it or not, eggplants are supposedly a member of the potato family! It was believed that old brinjals may harbour worms. Therefore, when selecting brinjals, choose those that are not too soft to the touch to ensure they are young. It is also important that the brinjal is not too light or the flesh may be dry.

Buah Keluak

Any Peranakan will stop to wax lyrical about *buah keluak*. The dark pasty meat found within the nuts is an acquired taste no doubt, but it is definitely a mark of identity for the community. Derived from the *Pangium edule* tree native to South East Asian mangrove swamps, the fruit which produce these nut seeds are poisonous. However, a process of fermentation removes the toxicity. *Buah keluak* are sourced from Indonesia. It is the weight of each seed, and not the size, that one should feel for as it is the meat within that is needed for cooking. The nuts have to be scrubbed clean, soaked for a few days to remove the grit and earthy smell. The best way to crack and pry open the nuts is to use a cleaver to knock cracks on the surface of the shell.

Cabbage

My *kohpoh* (grandaunt) explained to me that cabbage was frequently used in Nonya dishes because it was affordable. We tend to discard the first two layers of leaves and the core stem, and cut the leaves into quarters. Cabbage should be added at the end for *chap chai* (page 61) and *hee pio* (page 58), otherwise the leaves will overcook and produce a bitter aftertaste.

Calamansi Lime (*Limau kesturi*)

These limes are squeezed over *sambal belachan* (page 75) to offset the fishy taste. It is also used as a garnish for *mee siam* (page 133), lending a tart edge to the gravy. The limes are small, about twice the size of marbles. Half the lime crosswise before squeezing. If these are not available, you may substitute with key limes.

Candied Melon (*Tang Kueh*)

This is chopped finely and cooked in *kueh chang* filling (page 179), lending sweetness and a level of bite. Candied melon can be found in the dry goods section of supermarkets and better quality ones can be found in Chinese medicinal shops.

Candlenuts (*Buah Keras*)

These nuts provide a creamy texture to dishes they are used in, serving as a thickener. A relative of macadamia nuts, they are pounded whole and raw. However, unlike macadamia nuts, candlenuts must be cooked before they can be eaten as they are slightly toxic. Avoid dry nuts that look like they are flaking on the surface. Buy only what you need. Candlenuts can turn rancid quickly. Store them in the refrigerator.

Cardamom (*Buah Pelaga*)

Cardamom was known in ancient times to relieve indigestion. It gives a warm and sometimes smoky flavour. We use green cardamom pods here. Pound and grind as fine as possible before using.

Cassia Bark (*Kayu Manis*)

Cassia is often wrongly assumed to be cinnamon. Actually, it all depends on the history of the dish. Both give a sweet yet spicy woody scent. Cinnamon was more commonly used in Indian dishes, while cassia lent its fragrance to Chinese recipes. Cassia also happens to be more pungent and would therefore produce a more fragrant *kueh bumbu* spice powder (needed for *lapis spekkoek*, page 114). Then again, cinnamon, in its stick or powder forms, is more readily available and makes a convenient alternative. To distinguish between cinnamon and cassia bark sticks, the cinnamon bark rolls in one direction like a cigar while both sides of the thicker sides of the cassia bark curl towards each other.

Castor (Superfine) Sugar

The more refined type of sugar is suggested for baking many of the cookies in this book because it dissolves faster and also contributes to a smoother texture.

Cauliflower

Cauliflower is rumoured to cause body odour! In Peranakan cooking it is used to make *achar* (page 81). The florets are sliced away from the core stem and then trimmed to match the size of the other vegetables so that they all cook uniformly.

Chicken

My mother once regaled that as a young wife shopping for freshly slaughtered chicken, she did not know how to describe a male chicken in Hokkien to the Chinese vendor, calling it a *tapor kuey* (boy chicken). Like many Nonyas, myself include, we call chicken by its Malay equivalent—*ayam*.

An old-fashioned wedding custom dictated that both a hen and a rooster were to be placed under the marital bed on a couple's wedding day. Guests would then coax the fowls to come out. The fowl that emerged first would indicate the gender of the wedded couple's firstborn. Interestingly, it took a long time for the rooster to come out from under my sister's marital bed, foretelling the 12 years it took her to conceive her son.

I once grumbled to my sister's Indonesian maid that she had chopped the whole chicken into 'toy' pieces, unlike the bigger pieces I had become accustomed to in the US. She giggled and said that the smaller pieces cooked more efficiently and were easier to dig into. There was some sense in her reply. Indeed, many dishes in this book would suggest "cut into serving pieces". The rule of thumb is to cut the whole chicken, preferably not more than 1.5 kg (3½ pounds), into 16 even-sized pieces. Doing so, you should get 4 drumsticks, 2 wings, 4 thighs and 6 cuts of the breast portion. The Chinese tend to find more flavour in the dark meat but some, like myself, fight over the boneless and meaty breast meat. If you plan on frying serving pieces of chicken (as with paper-wrapped chicken, page 154), you can divide the breast meat into four bigger pieces instead of six.

Chillies, Dried (*Cili Kering*)

Dried chillies contribute to the redness of a dish, essential for dishes like *laksa*. This was important for my mother and my *kohpoh* (grandaunt) who would gently fry the spice paste (*rempah*) until it exuded the prized red oil that would ultimately give the deep earthy hue to the gravy.

Dried chillies should be soaked in hot water for a few minutes to reconstitute, and then sliced into half inch pieces, discarding the stalk. We normally leave the seeds intact but if you prefer to remove them, you could do so before soaking by tearing the tail end of each chilli and shaking the seeds out.

Dried Chillies (Cili Kering)

Chinese Lettuce

Fresh Red Chillies

is also used to tease the lions during the Chinese New Year lion dance in a ceremony to scare away evil spirits and to summon luck and fortune. The Chinese word for lettuce also sounds like the word for fortune.

Chinese Sausage (*Lap Cheong*)

Chinese sausages are steamed and sliced when served as a garnish for fresh *popiah* (page 144). It is readily found in local supermarkets and in Chinatowns elsewhere. I once made the bad mistake of packing some in my luggage, and I got caught at US Customs.

Clitoria (Pea Flower/*Bunga telang*)

Much has been written about this special flower. Peter Wee of Katong Antique House used to direct me to the Holy Family Church a few doors down to pluck the flowers off the vine creeping along the fence. The flowers need to be sun-dried before they can be soaked in hot water to extract the signature colouring that contributes to the vibrant and distinct indigo blue found in *kueh chang* (page 179) and *putri sarlat* (page 265). No commercial blue colouring can quite match this shade but can be best settled as a convenient alternative. The dried flowers will keep in a refrigerator for a long time, so grab them if you can find them, even if it means standing by a stranger's house with his dog barking at you as you furtively pluck the flowers.

Cloud Ear Fungus

Like all dried ingredients, cloud ear fungus should be soaked in hot water for at least 20 minutes to reconstitute before prepping. Once softened, you could slice the fungus as desired.

Chillies, Fresh, Red

My husband grew up in New Mexico, one of the 50 American states. Chilli is prevalent there and was first used by the Native American tribes. They in turn introduced chilli to the Spanish conquistadors who then brought chilli back to Europe and subsequently all the other lands they conquered, including Asia.

The fresh long and bright red chillies we refer to as red chillies are also called Holland chillies. This particular type had been developed in Holland so that the Dutch could replicate their favourite Indonesian dishes back in their homeland, far away from their previous colonies. Indeed, Holland is reputed to have some of the best Indonesian restaurants in the world.

My mother believed that fresh red chillies were hotter than the dried ones. The smaller fresh type, the bird's eye chilli (*cili padi*), is especially fiery. It is thus no surprise that pint-sized aggressive people are nicknamed '*cili padi*'... scary things sometimes come in small packages.

The chilli seeds and the membrane they lie on, contain capsaicin, the ingredient that gives chilli its hot sensation. We never removed the seeds when we cooked. But if I have to accommodate my guests, I would slice along the length of each chilli to remove the seeds. My mother also always threatened to smear our lips with chilli paste if we ever told a lie. It was an effective tactic.

Chinese Lettuce (Asian lettuce)

The leaves of the Chinese lettuce are longer and greener than those of the iceberg lettuce. The leaves can be used to line the *popiah* skin before spreading the condiments, or after, when making *popiah* (page 144). To avoid tearing the *popiah* skin, it is better to remove the rib of the leaf. Chinese lettuce

Clitoria (Bunga Telang)

Cloud Ear Fungus

Cloves (*Bunga Chingkay*)

These four-pointed studs are actually dried flower buds. They are super integral for us when making pineapple tarts because they lend their sharply sweet-peppery pungence to the jam. Discard the tiny round knob at the top as these are actually the dried unopened petals and do not contain any aroma.

Cloves are native to Indonesia, hence the prevalence of the famous *kretek* cigarettes made from cloves. While I avoid second-hand cigarette smoke, I do not mind inhaling the intoxicatingly sensuous whiff of the *kretek*, thought to be more harmful than the average cigarette. Indeed, I once had an Indonesian maid who used to smoke *kretek* like a chimney and I can still recall vividly how she would puff away as she hung clothes on the line to dry. Cloves are also used in a special oil for body massages and to relieve aches and pains.

Coconut Milk

Traditionally, coconut milk for cooking was derived from soaking freshly grated coconut flesh in plain water (volume according to recipe) for an hour or so and then squeezing it in muslin to extract the milk. The first extraction was thicker and often termed as milk number 1. The process was then repeated using the same batch of grated coconut and additional water. The thinner extraction was then called milk number 2. During cooking, the creamier milk number 1 was usually added to the simmering gravy after the thinner milk. This was to prevent curdling which can take place when the cooking temperature is too high.

Recipes using milk number 1 and milk number 2 can be utterly confusing. Besides, these days, it can be challenging to source for freshly grated coconut although one can find frozen packs at the supermarket. Refrigerated coconut milk would be great if you can find it. Alternatively, a good can of coconut milk is a viable substitute, especially if it is of an organic variety. Be sure to read the ingredients list as many brands add flour, which often results in a thicker gravy. Undoubtedly, using canned coconut milk is a sell-out from the traditional method, something my father laments and disapproves of because it results in a thicker gravy without the natural oily sheen.

A good can, without having to shake too much before opening, should have all-white milk, with a layer of cream at the top. Reserve that layer as your milk number 1 which you add in the later part of your cooking.

Compressed Rice Cakes (*Lontong*)

In this cookbook, I have used 'lontong' interchangeably with 'ketupat'. These refer to the compressed rice cakes which are the staple for *gado gado* (page 138), *lontong* (page 208) and soto *ayam* (page 212). 'Ketupat' refers to compressed rice locked in square-shaped dumplings wrapped in a criss-cross matrix of coconut leaves. 'Lontong' is more easily achieved by cooking rice in specially designed metal cylinders lined with banana leaves. The cylinder of rice would be sliced like a loaf of bread and then each slice is quartered before serving. Nowadays, you also find plastic packets of measured rice, technologically designed for quick boiling and then served as 'ketupat'.

Coriander Leaves (Cilantro)

This is my favourite herb. Coriander leaves are commonly used as a garnish in many Nonya dishes as Italian parsley is for many Western dishes. Yet, a few find the pungent aroma too rubbery for their liking.

I used to toss tiny coriander seeds on my garden patch and watch the tender leaves grow. Once harvested, coriander leaves wilt very quickly. In Chinese or Nonya cooking, the leaves are used for garnish while the stems are discarded. However, the Thais use the stems and roots for cooking as they believe that these add more flavour.

Coriander Seeds (*Ketumbar*)

I have always assumed that *coriander* was an Asian spice since it was used for curry powder (page 65), *itek sio* (page 69) and *ati babi* (page 76). Interestingly, coriander (cilantro) was first grown in Southern Europe and is believed to have been introduced to Egypt and Europe by the Roman soldiers. The more frequently used light brown seeds give a sharp, almost citrusy aroma. Most times, coriander is

Compressed Rice Cake (Lontong)

Coriander Seeds (Ketumbar)

Dried Lily Buds

Dried Anchovies (Ikan Bilis)

Dried Fish Maw (Hee Pio)

ground as fine as possible. Alternatively, you can use ground coriander powder for a smoother texture if the ground seeds seem too gristly.

Cumin (*Jintan Puteh*)

Sometimes confused with caraway seeds because they look similar, cumin is used for the various spice pastes and curry powders in this book. It is earthy, counterbalancing the heady spiciness of dishes it is used in. Yet, cumin can also be bitter, so be sure not to add more than is required.

Dried Anchovies (*Ikan Bilis*)

These are served along with *nasi lemak* (page 127). They can be bought in packets or sourced from open sacks at dry goods stores. The better ones are not too skinny while the big ones become more chewy and less crispy when fried. To serve them crispy, fry in hot oil, skim off the surface and transfer to a plate lined with oil-absorbent paper. The dried anchovies will become crispy when cooled. You could also sprinkle some sugar to balance the saltiness.

Dried Fish Maw (*Hee Pio*)

This key ingredient for *hee pio* soup (page 58) is sponge-like and gives the soup its distinctive characteristic. *Hee pio* gets especially expensive towards Chinese New Year, with the better quality ones snapped up quickly. My mother, and now my sister, would be sure to order them well in advance.

Sold in dried form, fish maw needs to be soaked in hot water before cooking. It is best to add this to the soup only just before serving, otherwise it will overcook and make the soup cloudy.

Dried Lily Buds

These are soaked in hot water to soften. I trim them into shorter lengths for easier consumption. Dried lily buds are said to have diuretic properties.

Dried Mung Bean Noodles (*Tang Hoon*)

An ingredient for *chap chai* (page 61), the noodles need to be soaked in hot water first to soften before cooking. A small packet is sufficient and, depending on the brand, may require some snipping to make it shorter and more manageable when serving.

Dried Mushrooms

The best in quality are plump flower mushrooms, worth purchasing as a gift for older Chinese relatives. Soak the mushrooms in hot water for at least 20 minutes, remove from the water and squeeze out the excess moisture before prepping. The stems are usually discarded as they are too woody to eat.

Dried Shrimps (*Udang Kering*)

Dried shrimps are best prepared this way: rinsed with water to remove some saltiness, soaked in hot water for a few minutes to soften and then patted dry before being pounded or processed into a coral-coloured floss.

I used to buy plump and bright pink dried shrimps, assuming these were of better quality. Apparently, the bright pink is derived from preservatives and artifical colouring to deceive folks like me. And the bigger ones may be too fishy and salty, distorting the taste expected from the recipe measurements in this book.

Dried Mung Bean Noodles (Tang Hoon)

Dried Shrimps (Udang Kering)

Dried Tamarind Fruit
(Assam Poey)

Fennel (Jintan Manis)

Fermented Soy Bean Cake (Tempeh)

Fermented Soy Bean Paste (Taucheo)

Dried Soy Sticks

Similar to the film or skin that forms on the surface of milk when it is heated, this comes from heating soybean milk instead. The skin is lifted and dried. The sticks need to be soaked in hot water till softened and pliable before cooking.

Dried Tamarind Fruit (*Assam Poey*)

This dried fruit gives a sour tang to dishes it is used in. Also known as *Assam Gelugor*, it is a fruit native to Malaysia. It is used for *itek tim* (page 55). The better ones are found in Chinese medicinal shops.

Duck

Because duck is fatty and gives off a gamey flavour, the skin is usually pricked to render excess oil while cooking. For *itek sio* (page 69), my mother tended to cut the duck up into serving pieces beforehand.

Fennel (*Jintan Manis*)

Fennel is sometimes assumed to be anise, which is from a different plant from the same family. The latter is more commonly used in India. Fennel seeds have a faint sweetness to them, hence the word '*manis*' which means 'sweet' in Malay. Interestingly, this plant originated in the Mediterranean and ended up in India by way of Arab traders. It is used to make many of the spicy gravies and contributes a kind of refreshing flavour to the dish.

Fermented Bean Curd Cake (*Tempeh*)

This originates from Indonesia and is used as a component in *gado gado* (page 138). The cakes can be found in the fresh food section of supermarkets. They are fried and cubed before serving.

Fermented Soy Bean Paste (*Taucheo*)

This paste lends saltiness and depth of flavour to a dish. Some bottled versions have whole beans while others are more mashed up. It is better to mash the bean paste to a finer paste before cooking. In this book, fermented soy bean paste refers to the standard version and not the hot or spicy type.

Fish

Regardless of where you live, it is advisable to buy the freshest fish there is. Lime is sometimes squeezed on the fish to offset the smell or taste. Below are a selection of fish popularly used in the recipes in this book:

Dorab or Wolf Herring (Ikan Parang)

Spanish Mackerel (Ikan Tenggiri)

Horse Mackerel (Ikan Gelair)

Chubb Mackerel (*Ikan Kembong*)
This is often used for *ikan sumbat* (page 244) where a cavity is sliced along the back fin and stuffed with chilli paste.

Dorab or Wolf Herring (*Ikan Parang*)
Long enough and suitable for cutting up into shorter pieces for *ikan nanas* (page 222).

Horse Mackerel (*Ikan Selair*)
This is the fish popularly used for *ikan sumbat* (page 244). It is oily and fleshy and goes well with the chilli paste.

Silver Belly Bream (*Ikan Kekek*)
The smaller fish is sometimes used for *ikan nanas* (page 222) but is less easily found these days.

Spanish Mackerel (*Ikan Tenggiri*)
This meaty fish is used to make *otak otak* (page 130), *ikan garam assam* (page 231) and *ikan gulai* (page 232).

Stingray (*Ikan Pari*)
The fillets of the stingray are frequently used for *ikan gulai* (page 232).

Yellow Snapper
I tend to prefer snapper which I personally think is more fleshy and less fishy than mackerel, for making *otak otak* (page 130) and *ikan gulai* (page 232) or *ikan nanas* (page 222).

Five-spice powder

The concoction that lends its name to *ngo hiang* (which means five fragrances in Hokkien), is gound from star anise, cassia bark, fennel, cloves and Sichuan peppercorns. Sometimes, there might be two additional spices, from coriander, ginger, dried orange peel or cardamom. As a result, each source of five-spice powder is unique based on the basic ingredients and the proportion used. Stick with one that you personally like and which is not too overpowering. The fresher and higher quality powders can be found in Chinese medicinal shops.

Galangal (Lengkuas)

Galangal (*Lengkuas*)

This is a root, almost identical to ginger. It is also known as blue ginger. Because it is so hardy and fibrous, it needs to be skinned and sliced across its sinews, and then sliced once again into fine matchsticks before pounding. It is best to find fresh ones to slice thin before freezing, than to purchase frozen chunks of galangal to use. If you do the latter, it is best to thaw the galangal first as it is almost impossible to slice when frozen.

Ghee

In this book, *ghee* is used in the Indian dish *nasi biryani* (page 201). This clarified butter is often used in Indian cooking. Traditionally, Indian *ghee* might have been made from the milk of water buffalos and certain brands might be too overpowering in taste.

My Indian friend prefers to make her own clarified unsalted butter to ensure the best quality for herself. My mother always used the QBB brand with its signature green tin.

Ginger

Ginger is an ingredient used in many Asian dishes. The younger ginger has a thinner skin which can be peeled away by scraping with the back of a teaspoon. This is the best way to retain the sweet-spicy flavour which is most concentrated directly beneath the ginger skin.

Ginger is said to *pukol angin* ('beat the wind' out of the body). Slices of ginger were rubbed on the back, leaving red streaks. The more streaks the better as it was considered that more of the cold dampness that caused aches and pains was released.

Glutinous Rice (*Pulot*)

This rice makes up the sticky part of many Nonya snacks (*kueh*). The younger grain is preferred as it has a higher starch content.

Gula Melaka (Palm Sugar)

Traditionally found as slightly moist, reddish-brown firm cylinders, it goes without saying that my favoured ones come from Malacca. This is purely delicious with a unique sweet taste. *Gula melaka* needs to be scraped or grated before gently heating it to attain the syrup that coats many Nonya snacks.

I have been warned that there are 'fake' ones out there that include a high percentage of white sugar as opposed to the sugar palm sap from which *gula melaka* is traditionally made of. A telling sign is that it is harder to slice through and not as soft and crumbly as pure *gula melaka*.

Glutinous Rice Flour

In the past, glutinous rice grains were soaked in water and later ground using the stone mill (*batu boh*) into fine rice. The 'paste' was then wrapped in cloth and weighed under a heavy granite slab to extract the excess water. When dried, the rice flour was produced.

These days, glutinous rice flour is readily available and is used to achieve a sticky, doughy consistency.

Hong Kong Flour

This is a super-milled wheat flour with an extra light and fluffy texture.

It is the preferred choice for making *cha siew pao* (barbequed pork buns), a popular *dimsum* item.

Jicama (*Bangkuang*)

Imagine my excitement when I saw jicama in the US for the first time, in a supermarket outside of Chinatown! It is used in Mexican food and the jicama is crunchy and requires longer simmering to soften the texture. In Singapore, jicama is known as turnip although the two are different. Jicama is used as an ingredient in the filling for popiah (page 144). To remove the tough outer skin, I use a paring knife or a potato peeler.

Kaffir Lime Leaves (*Daun Limau Purut*)

The West has been a little slow in discovering the delights of this fragrant citrus scent, but it is now sought after these days as a scent in soaps and hand lotions. I used to pluck fresh leaves off my sister's thorny plant and smuggle them into the US where they would keep in my freezer for months until I needed them. To use these leaves, characterised by double leaves along one stem, slice off the middle rib, then roll the leaves and slice finely.

Ladies' Fingers (Okra)

These green pods resemble long slender fingers, hence their name. Also known as okra, ladies' fingers are popular in the southern part of the US where it was introduced by African slaves. When cooked long enough, ladies' fingers produce a glue-like substance that thicken the sauce. Do not buy pods that are too long as they may be tough and fibrous.

Laksa Leaves (*Daun Kesom*)

Not always easy to find, these narrow, dainty, point-tip leaves are gently split and torn to release their sharp fragrance. They contribute to a certain intoxicating zing when added to *laksa* (page 125) as a garnish. They are also known as Vietnamese mint.

Jicama (Bangkuang)

Gula Melaka

Kaffir Lime Leaves
(Daun Limau Purut)

Ladies' Fingers (Okra)

Laksa Leaves (Daun Kesom)

Laksa Rice Noodles

Laksa Rice Noodles
These white noodles are a signature ingredient of *laksa* (page 125). The noodles are best bought fresh no more than a day before cooking. Blanch in boiling water briefly before serving with the gravy.

Lemon Grass (*Seray*)
This is one of the most essential ingredients in the Nonya repertoire. It lends a sharp, lemony tang when used in dishes. It also happens to be more easily found in Western supermarkets, given the spread of the South East Asian immigrant community and the popularity of lemon grass for aroma- and homoeopathy.

The thick and tough outer layer and top third of each stalk are discarded. If the lemon grass is reserved for pounding, it should be chopped into very fine slices, about 0.25 cm or $^1/_8$ inch thick. Lemon grass is so fibrous that you must try to grind them as fine as possible, otherwise the fibres in the gravy may choke you. Sometimes, the whole lemon grass stalk is left in the gravy when simmering. In this case, the lemon grass stalk can be bruised with a pestle or a cleaver to release the flavour.

Long Beans
The correct type of long beans to use are the particularly long ones that live up to their name. The beans are then chopped into shorter pieces before cooking. The more common ones, about 10 to 15 cm (4 to 6 inches) have a higher water content and can make a stir-fried dish too soggy.

Lotus Seed Paste (*Lengyong*)
This almost golden paste is the main star of mooncakes. The smoothest, finest paste is desirable. Thankfully, manufactured seed paste can be found in the refrigerated section of supermarkets especially near the Chinese Mid-Autumn Festival.

Mace
Mace comes from the membrane that covers the nutmeg seed. It has a less potent form of the same warm and spicy aroma.

Mixed Spice Powder (*Bumbu Kueh*)
Ground from a combination of cassia bark, cardamom, star anise and cloves, this powder is what makes *kueh lapis spekkoek* (page 114) so alluring. As each Nonya has her own secret recipe for the spice mix, you may also want to make your own fragrant concoction. Commercial bottles are available in the baking section of supermarkets.

Mung Beans
These beans are used to make bean paste filling. To do so, the beans are soaked in water first to reconstitute, as well as to loosen the green outerskin, before being steamed and mashed. The beans can also be cooked with their skin on, as in *kachang hijau* (page 298).

Mung Bean Flour (*Tepong Hoon Kueh*)
An ingredient for *kueh pisang* (page 286), this flour is derived from ground mung beans. An Indonesian specialty, they are packaged in cylinders wrapped in white paper and can be found in the baking section of the supermarket.

Nutmeg (*Buah Pala*)
The spice gem native to Indonesia that pit colonial powers against one another, nutmeg is also reputed to have prevented the spread of the plague in medieval Europe. Nutmeg's warm and spicy flavour can turn on both sweet or savoury dishs. To use, you can grate the amount needed from a whole nutmeg or simply use ready ground nutmeg.

Mung Bean Flour (Tepong Hoon Kueh)

Pandan Leaves

Pisang Rajah

Popiah Skin

Popiah Skin

Fresh *popiah* skin in Singapore, the best one can be found in the famous store at 421 Joo Chiat Road. Otherwise, frozen *popiah* skin is available in supermarkets. Those that closely resemble the round fresh ones in terms of texture and the frayed edges are preferred. The frozen ones need to be thawed by either steaming or heating in a microwave oven with a damp towel on top to keep the skin moist. The damp towel should stay on the skin for the entire duration of the meal.

The square frozen type is suitably thick for *popiah goreng* (page 153) and may make a better alternative than the fresh *popiah* skin in this case.

Pork

Pork is a staple meat in Nonya dishes. In fact, so utilised is pork that a leg of pork, decorated with intricate red paper cutouts, would be sent to a bride's home as a gift from the groom's family.

There are many ways in which pork is used, depending on the different cuts:

Belly Pork (*Samchan Bak*)

This is the ideal cut for *tauk yu bak* (page 235) as the gelatinous layer gives the sauce a certain flavour and smoothness. Further, slow simmering results in a velvety texture when the fat and meat seem to melt in the mouth. My kids love it.

Caul lining

This is a fat membrane that is integral to *ati babi* (page 76). This has to be specially ordered from the butcher to ensure you get the freshest available. It should be washed thoroughly under cold, running water and then soaked in slightly salted cold water before preparing the meatballs.

Fillet

Pork fillet would be assumed to be the most tender of all cuts of pork meat, suitable for stir-frying.

Ground or minced pork

This is used for many dishes including *ngo hiang* (page 73), *ayam buah keluak* (page 66) and *pong tauhu* (page 56). I prefer mine to have a percentage of fat for some flavour, moisture and softness. I believe that my mother sometimes chopped her own minced pork using belly pork so that it included the fat.

Pandan Leaves

The pandan essence derived from the leaves is the Asian counterpart to vanilla essence. Yet it is no plain vanilla as it gives a sweet yet heady fragrance to many Nonya desserts, as well as to dishes such as *nasi lemak* (page 127). The *pandan* plant serves to repel mosquitoes and rows of them can be found in outdoor venues like the Jurong Bird Park.

For cooking, fresh leaves are preferred. They are commonly tied into a knot, gently crushed to release the essence and thrown into the pot. The leaves give a green colouring to various snacks like *putri sarlat* (page 265) and *kueh talam hijau* (page 272). To extract the colour, the leaves are cut into half-inch pieces, and then crushed in a mortar to extract the green colouring and flavour.

Frozen leaves are a frequent subsititute, as well as *pandan* essence in a bottle. With the latter, be sure to pick a brand that does not smell too synthetic.

The *pandan* leaves used for *kueh chang* (page 179) are of a larger type. Yet, the leaves still impart a similar fragrance.

Pisang Rajah

This is a specific type of banana used for Nonya *kueh*. The flesh is firmer than the other varieties of banana and hence more suitable for the steaming process.

Pork Hind Leg (*Twee Bak*)

The better marbling of meat and fat makes this cut popular for braising or chopping into minced pork.

Prawns (Shrimps)

There is sometimes confusion over which term to use. In Singapore, shrimp is specifically small-sized while prawns refer to the medium to larger ones (see also Dried Shrimp). The white medium prawns are used for the porkball paste in *pong tauhu* (page 56) or *ngo hiang* (page 73), the discarded shells boiled for flavourful stock. The larger prawns are expensive and used for the stir-fried dishes.

My mother used to add a teaspoon of sugar to a bag of medium prawns to keep them 'fresh', especially if she was going to freeze them for later use.

Rice

It goes without saying that rice is a staple to go along with many Peranakan dishes. It is cooked plain, made into *nasi lemak* (page 127) and *nasi minyak* (page 203) and boiled into *bubor* (page 257).

Rice is woven into the Peranakan psyche with notions that if you do not clean off the loose grains of rice on your dinner plate, you will definitely end up marrying a person with a pock-marked face! My mother also had a favourite saying '*tambar nasi*' meaning 'to exaggerate'. My older relatives also swore by the tiny square box of compressed ground rice powder called *bedak sejuk*. They used it as a face powder and they attributed their smooth and fair skin complexion to it.

The preferred type of rice is the Thai *hom mali* jasmine rice. The name is a misnomer because the rice does not have the strong floral jasmine scent. Because fluffy white rice accompanies so many of the wonderful dishes in this cookbook, it is worth making sure that you get the best quality rice. Like buying diamonds, do not settle for a cheap bag of rice assuming that the commodity is the same across the board. I once did and my father could instantly tell the difference.

To cook rice, I use a trusty Japanese electric rice cooker. Rinse the rice grains with water until the water runs clear. (The water from rinsing the rice is great for nourishing your houseplants.) To cook the rice, I always add enough water to come up to the first segment of my pinky finger, with my fingertip resting on surface of the rice.

Rice Flour (*Tepong Beras*)

This is traditionally made the same way as glutinous rice flour using a stone mill (*batu boh*). Rice flour is also readily available in packs in the dry goods section of supermarkets.

Rice Vermicelli

The basic component of *mee siam* (page 133), these noodles come in dried form and need to be reconstituted by soaking in hot water prior to cooking. My mother swore by the Chilli brand.

Rosewater (*Ayer Mawa*)

Rose water essence is popular in the Middle East and India as a flavouring. It is distilled from rose petals and differ from rose essence which is more concentrated.

Sago Flour

Sago flour is not easy to find although it is used to make many of the *Nonya kueh*. To date, many shopkeepers would direct you instantly to tapioca flour, its popular substitute. If you like to stick to originality, you could look around for the Sunflower brand available in a bright yellow plastic packaging.

Salted Mustard Cabbage (*Kiam Chai*)

Also spelled as *kiam chye,* there are actually two varieties of salted mustard cabbage. One is more sour, less salty, and has leaves as well as stems; the other is more salty, less sour, and has only thick stems. Use the latter. These are sold in packs, largely containing the stems and not much of the leaves. The salted vegetable is used in *itek tim* (page 55) to offset the strong taste of duck. It is best to soak the salted vegetable first to rinse off the saltiness. As a result, avoid overseasoning the soup as the vegetable might lend more saltiness at the end of the simmering.

Salted Mustard Cabbage (Kiam Chai)

Semolina (*Sugee*)

Sugee is derived from durum wheat that has not been as finely ground as wheat flour. It is used to make *Sugee* cake and cookies. Eurasians, famous for their *sugee* cake, recommend the King's brand.

Sesame Seeds (*Bijan*)

These tiny seeds form the filling for *kueh bijan* (page 116). Yet, unlike the Mediterranean *tahini* which is a ground sesame paste, the *kueh bijan* filling consists of individual seeds which will get pasty as you consume this savoury treat. To bring out the nutty flavour, toast the seeds beforehand.

Shallots

Shallots in Asia are much smaller than the ones found elsewhere. They are also more intense in flavour and heat. In the US, shallots are expensive and the smaller variety is more commonly found in farmers' markets. How you prep shallots depends on how you use them. As an ingredient for spice paste (*rempah*), you could peel and chop them into smaller cubes, then add to the blender along with the other ingredients. Shallots can also be peeled and sliced finely, then shallow-fried in oil until light brown and skimmed out of the pan. The sliced shallots will darken and turn crispy, for use as a garnish.

Slaked Lime Powder (*Kapor*)

Kapor was my mother's secret ingredient for ensuring that her *achar* vegetables remained crunchy. It is similarly used as a stir-fry ingredient in Thai cooking to keep vegetables crunchy. Its chemical name is calcium hydroxide, and it has many industrial uses which make it questionable for cooking due to health concerns.

In the past, *kapor,* areca nut, betel leaf and gambier were hand rolled together to form the addictive *sireh* which Nonyas used to chew and spit as a leisurely pastime.

Sour Plums

These can be found in Chinese medicinal shops and are used for *itek tim* (page 55). Made from unripe plums, these are usually pickled in vinegar and salt.

Spring Onions (scallions)

Fresh stalks are often sliced or chopped finely and used as a garnish for soups. The white bulbous ends of the stalks are usually discarded, and only the green portion is used. For *pong tauhu* soup (page 56), chopped spring onions are added to the porkball paste for added flavour.

Squid (*Sotong*)

Squid was used in the daily repertoire of home-cooked meals. My mother discarded the head and ink sac, and washed the cavity clean of the dark ink.

Star Anise

A beautiful, flower-like dried spice, star anise is integral in five-spice powder. Because it is native to South China, it has lent itself to many Indochinese dishes including Vietnamese *pho* (a rice noodle soup). Star anise gives a warm, heady, almost sticky fragrance and should be used sparingly. Many cooks prefer to pluck one of the eight petals, saying that it is sufficient for whatever dish they are preparing.

Sweet Potato

This tuber is popular in the US where it is served as sweet potato pie or mashed sweet potato, amidst others. The orange-fleshed sweet potato is more commonly found there. Sweet potato traveled from the Americas to Asia by way of explorers. In Asia, sweet potato is frequently used in desserts. I recall purple-fleshed sweet potato being used for *bubor cha cha* (page 301).

Tamarind (*Assam*)

Tamarind pulp lends a sour plum-like tang to dishes it is used in. The tree from which the pods come from are native to Africa but are prevalent in India where there is even a state called Assam. The preserved pulp, made up of several seeds

Sour Plums

Shallots

Tamarind (Assam)

Water Convulvrus (Kangkong)

Turmeric (Kunyit)

Yellow Noodles (Hokkien Noodles)

coated with gelatinous flesh, is soaked in hot water (volume according to recipe) for at least
10 minutes. The pulp is then squeezed in muslin or pressed dry in a sieve (using your hands or a spoon) to extract its concentrate. The juice is sometimes combined with more water for volume.

Tapioca (Cassava/*Ubi Kayu*)
Tapioca is venerated for feeding those who lived through the Second World War, along with yam. Choose the young, more tender types for baking.

Treacle (Dark Molasses)
Treacle is another name used to describe dark molasses, a thick and gooey by-product of sugar refining. It is used in fruit cake to give it its dark colouring. Its slightly bitter tinge offsets the sweetness of the candied fruit in the cake.

Sometimes, light molasses, also known as golden syrup is used instead. This is what contributes to a lighter coloured fruit cake.

Turmeric (*Kunyit*)
This is now thought to be a cancer-prevention agent. Turmeric lends a bright yellow colour to dishes it is used in, similar to the deep red hue produced by dried chillies. It has an earthy, mustardy flavour. Peel the skin and slice into fine matchsticks before blending into spice paste (*rempah*). The best way to skin turmeric is to use the back of a teaspoon to scrape off the skin.

Vanilla Essence
A cooking teacher who taught me liked 'rounding off' the flavour of a cake by adding a tiny bit more of vanilla essence. Vanilla is the second most expensive spice, after saffron, due to its labour-intensive process of extraction. The best essence come from Madagascar and the most trusted brand is Nielsen-Massey. Avoid using imitation vanilla essence which will make your cakes taste plastic.

Water Convolvulus (*Kang Kong*)
Used in various South East Asian dishes, *kang kong* first originated in India. Note that the leaves shrink to almost half the volume when cooked and the leaves do not keep well in the refrigerator.

White Pepper
Unless specified, the book uses ground white pepper where it is required. White pepper is actually hotter than black pepper and is produced from soaking black pepper in water until the outer black skin disintegrates, thus exposing the inner white core with the more intense flavour. Pepper is frequently used to enhance the flavour of a dish, and it also aids in digestion.

White Poppy Seeds (*Kas Kas*)
These seeds are now discouraged from use because of its relation to opium. How ironic given that my mother's family fortune was derived from opium farms. It is worth noting that the poppy seeds used in cooking, e.g. sprinkled on bagels, are mature seeds and not the unripe seeds that produce morphine. *Kas kas* was used as a gravy thickener.

Yellow Noodles (Hokkien Noodles)
These glossy, yellow noodles are made of flour, eggs and water. They are considered 'fresh' although packaged ones with longer shelf lives are now easily found in the refrigerated section of supermarkets.

It goes without saying that these noodles are the main ingredient of Nonya Hokkien noodles (page 86), Hokkien *mee* soup (page 136) and interestingly, also *mee rebus* (page 134)! The first dish is a testament to the fact that many Peranakans are descended from Hokkien immigrants.

The noodles are actually parboiled but are cooked or boiled once again before serving. My mother always believed that noodles would get bloated and soggy, so she would often blanch the noodles just before serving.

A well-outfitted kitchen is the first step to overcome the perception that Nonya cooking is laborious. It is better to invest in high quality tools, pots and pans than to buy the cheap-sale toys that are bought on impulse. My mother was a culprit herself as she wandered into the kitchen department at Tangs frequently and bought many different gadgets. Fortunately, she acquired some heavy duty appliances that still last three decades later, such as her faithful Kenwood cake mixer.

Cooking Utensils

Knives and Peelers

My mother often got impatient with me when it came to cooking, blaming it on my left-handedness. She was deft with her chopping skills although there was the odd occasion when she would accidentally cut herself. She alternated between the clunky cleaver and the large chef's knife. Much as an old-fashioned *hausfrau* would skin apples with a paring knife, she did likewise.

I cannot function without a good set of sharp carbon steel knives, preferably German. A personal favourite is Wusthof. It is worth investing in the following as they will set you off for a lifetime of pleasant cooking:

6-inch chef's knife—This versatile knife is used to slice meat, dice onions, smash and mince garlic, chop vegetables and separate chicken joints.

3.5-inch paring knife—This knife is especially good for the peeling and slicing of shallots, ginger and the cutting up of smaller vegetables.

Bread/Serrated knife—A serrated blade comes in handy for slicing through stubborn textures such as fish meat, cooked meat, as well as the soft insides of vegetables like the brinjal.

Prawn (shrimp) deveiner cum peeler—The hook-shaped deveiner saves the day when you need to peel lots of shrimp and remove the unsightly entrails.

Potato peeler—This T-shape peeler helps to peel off the tough skin of jicama effortlessly.

I am faithful to a wooden chopping board. The wood absorbs the slicing 'shock', does not blunt the blade nor let the knife slide off course.

Mortar and Pestle vs. Electric Blender

Many Nonya dishes require spices to be blended into a fine paste before cooking. For years, I ground my spices with an electric blender. However, after trying out the traditional mortar and pestle to pound a spice blend, I could discern the difference in the taste of the dish. There was a more pronounced kick and tighter fusion of spices brought about by the pounding. Therefore, while the electric blender is more convenient and practical, use the mortar and pestle as often as you can.

Olden-day Nonyas could not live without their mortar and pestle. Mothers-in-law often judged the cooking proficiency of prospective brides by the pounding rhythm and fineness of their spice paste. The Nonyas called the mortar and pestle the *batu lesong*. Pounding was called *tumbok-tumbok* (pronounced toom-boke). With a new mortar, my mother pounded dry grated coconut to absorb the grit tucked into the micro fine crevices of the new mortar. You should pound the coconut until it leaves a shine to the surface of the mortar and pestle and it replaces the smell of granite. The mortar would eventually achieve a smooth surface after pounding many times over. This is essential so that bits of a spice paste would not get stuck in the tiny cracks and crevices. These days, new mortars come with smoothened surfaces. Some of these new ones are also made from a more inferior granite and therefore not held with the same regard by older cooks. A Nonya superstition is that you should stop using your *batu lesong* if the mortar base is wearing thin. You must not crack it, otherwise it would be bad luck. Whether it is to avoid the risk of wasting paste that required a chunk of time to pound or truly, to avoid ill fortune, another superstition admonishes you not to cross or walk over a *batu lesong*. The Nonyas would scream "*jangan langga!*" (don't knock it over).

With electric blenders, the blender cup size should not be too large. Otherwise, the spices will scatter about, making it harder to blend them into a fine paste. Many cooks use a coffee bean grinder but that may be too small. Another good option is the stick blender and its accompanying container about the volume of a good-sized mug.

Middle Eastern and Indian cuisines tend to prefer to prepare their spice blend on the day of cooking. Perhaps this was also done by the Nonyas of old. My mother began to make various spice pastes in bulk, divide them into cooking portions and vaccum seal them in double plastic bags which she would then freeze up.

When pounding or blending, stop periodically and use a spatula or spoon to press down the paste, and then resume the process. Sometimes with a blender, a few spoonfuls of water could 'lubricate' the blending process to produce the desired fine paste. It is important to grind down the fibrous texture of galangal, ginger and lemon grass, as well as the grist of fennel, cumin and coriander. Otherwise, it makes for a rough and bristly gravy later on, which is not good.

The food processor has also made it more convenient for shredding jicama for *popiah* (page 144). Obviously, you will require the larger cup for this. However, if you have time, use a mandolin to shred, which results in finer and more uniform strips for the *popiah* filling.

Grinding Stone Slab (*Batu Giling*)

The *batu giling* is a heavy rectangular granite slab with an accompanying granite rolling pin used to grind or refine large batches of spice paste. It is very hard to find. I managed to seize one in Serangoon and shipped it back to New York, only to have it break everything else in the crate.

Stone Mill (*Batu Boh*)

The *batu boh* is a heavy two-tiered cylindrical granite grinder, not unlike a stone mill. It was used to grind wet and previously soaked glutinous rice in the days when rice flour was not readily available. The ground product was put into sacks and topped with heavy granite blocks overnight to press out the excess water. These days, the only *batu boh* you would see are antique ones which descendants flaunt in their home décor.

Spoons and Such

I have adapted my wooden spoon, initially used for Bolognese sauce, to prepare my curry gravy. The wooden spoon is sturdy and well-designed to scoop off the lumps of paste that might still stick to the base and sides of the pot. In addition, the following tools are recommended:

Chinois (Cone-shaped strainer, preferably with fine mesh)—This is a handy strainer to clarify soup stock while extracting the most flavour out of the source. With an accompanying cone-shaped wooden hammer you can press down prawn shells or chicken bones right to the base tip to squeeze out every single drop of flavour.

Noodle Strainer—To hold bean sprouts, yellow noodles and such for a quick dunk in boiling water to blanch.

Slotted Spoon—Essential for skimming fried foods out of hot oil.

Strainers—Versatile for a quick blanch and for skimming off impurities from soup stocks.

Soup Ladles—Essential for serving soups.

Tongs—In place of long chopsticks, I prefer to use tongs as they are less clumsy. Tongs are versatile and useful. You could use them for turning over pieces of chicken in hot frying oil, lifting up *popiah goreng* from the deep frying, or transferring pieces of *kueh* to a tray.

Wok (*Kuali*)
Most Singapore homes cook with a traditional, concave, cast iron wok, rounded at the bottom. It is called a *kuali* by the Nonyas. A wok is very versatile and can be used for swift stir-frying, deep-frying, blanching and steaming.

In the olden days, a black cast iron wok was most preferred because it lasted for decades. But it was heavy and if not cared for properly, susceptible to rust. A carbon steel wok is the next alternative and a good one will outlast a cheap non-stick wok.

These days, the modern kitchen has one major difference that makes the use of concave woks difficult and dangerous. The electric stove is a flat surface and the gas stove ring is set closer to the flame; both stoves do not fit a concave wok snugly. The wok will not spread heat properly and can easily tip over, especially dangerous if you have hot oil in the wok. Therefore, I suggest a flat bottomed wok. A 36-cm or 14-inch wok (measured using the outer rim) is ideal for its cooking versatility and portion size.

A new wok has to be seasoned. My mother's explanation for this was that food would not stick in a well-seasoned wok. She would typically heat the new wok over a low fire and then fry grated coconut until the coconut dried out and left a thin shiny layer of grease on the wok's surface. Sometimes, she would fry a solid lump of pork lard around the wok to coat it. These days, it would suffice seasoning a new wok by pouring a cup of corn or peanut oil and stir-frying for 10 minutes to coat the inner surface of the wok.

It is also suggested that a wok is never scrubbed with detergent after use. It would gradually spoil the wok's surface. I use a nylon-netted sponge and warm water (with minimal or diluted liquid detergent if necessary) to rinse the wok.

For the first 20 uses, I would also suggest coating the wok with a thin layer of oil before storing away. The wok would eventually become shiny and darkened, indicating that it is well-seasoned.

Stockpot or Dutch Oven
A large pot is necessary for the various gravy dishes. While the Le Creuset cast iron Dutch oven is wonderful for braising *beef rendang (page 216)*, it is also heavy. My sister swears that it permanently hurt her back when she carried it for me when I purchased it. An All-clad heavy bottom version is good enough and will be large enough to contain all the soup or gravy necessary for a particular dish.

Batu boh

Batu giling

Mortar (batu lesong)

Apom bokuah mould

Curry puff moulds

Jelly moulds

Kueh bolu mould

Kueh koya moulds

Kueh ku moulds

Mooncake moulds

Pai ti moulds

Pineapple tart moulds

Other unique kitchen equipment

My mother cultivated special relationships with the supply stores that specialise in Nonya cookware. The following items can be found at Hup Soon in Joo Chiat and at Ghim Hin Lee. A few of these moulds are best described by referring to the photo illustrations.

Apom bokuah mould

Similar to the Scandivanian *ebelskiver* pan but with a more shallow cavity, the moulds should be lightly oiled before making the pancakes.

Cake tins

Buy the light coloured aluminium tins. My mother tended to use the 23 to 25 cm (9 to 10 inch) round trays for her *kueh*. The non-stick tins, particularly for baking, darken the cake.

Chiffon cake mould

The cake tin with a funnel in the middle is still the best way to achieve the light and fluffy chiffon cake.

Cookie cutters

Various shapes can be found although my mother used those that produced cookies about 2.5 cm or 1 inch in size.

Cookie sheets

These come in handy for baking cookies and for spreading spices to sun-dry or sort.

Crimper

Like a mini pair of tongs, these pinch and crimp *kueh bangket* (page 101) cookies to form the delicate bumps on the surface.

Curry puff mould

The plastic bifold mould produce semi-circular curry puffs in a jiffy. Traditionally, curry puffs were moulded by hand and expertly sealed and crimped around the edges by dexterous fingers. My mother did them like a factory machine. When using the plastic mould, first flatten the ball of dough on a separate surface. Lightly flour the surface of the mould before laying the dough on top. Heap a modest amount of filling onto the cavity. Dab some water along the edges of the dough before folding over.

Jelly mould

The classic moulds for *agar-agar* were white porcelain containers made in England. They often came in the shapes of rabbits and fish. These are now hard to find and moulds made from aluminium are more easily available.

Kueh bolu mould

The old-fashioned moulds were cast in brass but they are now made of a light metal alloy. Each cavity has a deep flower shape and should be lightly oiled before baking.

Kueh koya mould

The *kueh koya* moulds I grew up with were wooden. They are not so easy to find and my sisters and I often contemplated driving up to Malacca to find 'authentic' ones. These come in slender 3 cm or 1-inch wide blocks with about five cavities. The designs often depict animals (rabbits or birds) or flowers. As with all other moulds, like that for mooncake and *kueh ku*, the cavity should be deep and the carving sharply contoured so that the product would produce a well-defined shape.

Kueh ku mould

Look out for deep beautiful carvings inside the mould. If you purchase a wooden mould, be sure to dry it completely (in the sun) so that the wood does not warp or crack.

Mooncake mould

A new plastic version in two components punches out the mooncake speedily. This is more convenient than the traditional wooden moulds whereby you might need to tip the side of the mooncake with a paring knife to coax it out.

Pineapple tart mould

I could only find the heavy, industrial-looking cast metal stamping mould from Hup Soon. These are specially ordered from Hong Kong. Most times, a plastic mould would do.

Pai ti mould

Look for a lighter aluminium mould as the heavy brass one will tire you out.

Serrated cutter

For cutting Nonya *kueh* and giving a pretty zig-zag edge to the sides.

Chinese New Year

Chinese New Year was the most important celebration in our family. It was marked with many traditions.

Snack platter laid out for Chinese New Year.

Months before, my mother would purchase brand new curtain fabrics from Katong Shopping Centre or Arab Street and sew the trimmings herself. We had to get our hair cut and buy new clothes and shoes, including underwear, something that always tickled my children and their friends when I explained these old customs. Sometimes, my mother went as far as getting all of us up early in the morning of January 1 to start repainting the entire house! It was a dreadful thing for any brother-in-law who might be living with us temporarily during that time.

By Chinese New Year's Eve, the home would witness a flurry of activities. The maid would be mopping the floor several times, the last time right after our family's reunion dinner. This was in anticipation of the need to put away the broom. It was believed that to sweep the floor on the first day of the Chinese New Year would be to "sweep away good luck" coming in. We would be sure to put out brand new bed linens, curtains and towels. My sister Molly would be fluffing the cushions and laying out the home-baked cookies into their Corningware containers. The rice jar had to be filled to the brim to ensure a year of bounty. My favourite task was to slip the crisp, new dollar notes into the little red *ang pow* envelopes. My mother had different dollar amounts set for children, grandchildren, nieces and nephews and distant relatives.

Some of us went as far as going swimming on New Year's Eve to 'wash away' bad luck, or what we called *buang suay*. While we lived at Yarrow Gardens, my mother made sure to hang a long, red banner, called a *chai ki*, across the front porch. We even had discreet little hooks knocked into the wall just for this banner to hang on. On the morning of Chinese New Year, it was also important that the main door was only opened by a family member whose animal sign did not clash with that representing the New Year. All these customs were instilled in us from young—steps to control our fortunes for the future. Honestly, they were superstitions that can be very hard to shake off.

In the days leading to Chinese New Year, my mother made sure to order the groceries in advance. She did most of the purchases through a vendor, Ah Seng. Men like Ah Seng rarely exist these days with the onslaught of supermarkets and convenience stores. He had worked with my mother and my father's mother since the 1950s to deliver groceries on a daily basis. In the 1970s, Ah Seng drove around in a white van. He took orders from housewives who could not make the time to visit the wet market. Ah Seng took down orders by telephone and while making his rounds. He would then shop for and deliver the produce in the morning, gathering the different fresh items from several markets but primarily from the old Joo Chiat, Katong and Siglap markets. Whenever Ah Seng opened the back of his van, which was lined with damp old newspapers, the air would be filled with the smell of coriander leaves (cilantro), fresh meat and fish. Ah Seng would carry all the goods into our house, sit down and take out his tiny notebook to tally up my mother's total bill. Then they would discuss the orders for the next day; and in the case of Chinese New Year, order well in advance sought-after goods like shark's fin, dried fish maw and *buah keluak*.

Chicken was a major ingredient in many of the New Year dishes and it was important to have plump chickens, as

I learnt early on in life. One year, my mother got our maid to bring over her two best chickens from her *kampong* (or village). The two ladies then adjourned to the back of our house where they slaughtered the chickens in the area where we washed clothes. It must have happened when I was about nine years old and studying farm animals at school. These creatures were therefore dear to my heart. That morning, I could hear the screaming and crying of these two birds as they were getting slaughtered. Then a bizarre thing happened. Our maid came out to the front of the house with a plastic bag containing one of the freshly killed birds. Apparently, after plucking out all the feathers, my mother judged that the bird was too skinny to serve up for the New Year. It seemed to me then that the bird had died in vain. I thus began my 'chicken strike' by boycotting chicken in my diet. A few months later, my mother tried to pacify me by letting me purchase two little chicks. I named them Hanky and Panky. Naturally, the chicks started to grow and caught the attention of the neighborhood stray cat. One day, the cat crept in and tried to hunt down the chicks. Hanky and Panky were quickly sent off to the *kampong* of our maid to grow up in supposed safety. I should have known better. The following Chinese New Year, when we were all tucking into our delicious chicken curry, my sister Beng turned to me and asked if I liked the curry. I nodded my head. Then she smiled gleefully and asked me, "Do you know who they are...?" My heart broke and I went back on my chicken strike.

The family always came together for Chinese New Year. My mother would wake up at the break of dawn to complete the cooking of our customary Chinese New Year dishes. Waking up to the aroma and warmth of my mother's cooking will always remain in my memory and is a very special part of my childhood.

It was a custom for my married sisters to visit their in-laws first thing in the morning. They would then head over to my parents' home and have lunch there. My parents, considered senior members of an extended family, would remain at home for the first two days to receive guests. These could include their nieces and nephews or in earlier times, their younger siblings. That meant that we would

welcome relatives to our place who would then join us for lunch too. Upon entering the home, my parents were paid respect to by children and grandchildren kneeling down one at a time to *soja* (the act of paying respect). My oldest sister Beng set the procedure going, annually asserting herself as fearless leader of the pack. I would have had to kneel down, clasp my hands up and greet them with the saying: "*Panjang panjang umor*" (a wish for long life). In return, I would get my *ang pow* or red packet.

Lunch was a *tok panjang* which literally meant long table. The term itself reflects the intermingling of Malay and Chinese vocabularies since *tok* is a Hokkien (or Fujian) word for 'table' and *panjang* is a Malay word for 'long'. Peranakan Chinese families often owned an extendible table specifically for the *tok panjang* feast. In fact, it is a habit I have kept. I own one such table and conveniently extend it when I throw dinner parties. On this most important occasion—Chinese New Year—my mother used the formal extendible table to seat several people at a time.

On the table, we laid out a full spread of the soup and gravy dishes, pickles and sides, served on our best china. The main features included *ayam buah keluak* (page 66), *hee pio* (page 58), *pong tauhu* (page 56), chicken curry (page 66), *ngo hiang* (page 73), *sambal timun* (page 84) and *itek tim* (page 55). The china came in various sizes. The smaller plates were used for the *ati babi* (page 76) and *ngo hiang*, the shallow bowls for gravy dishes such as *buah keluak* and soup bowls for *hee pio* and *pong tauhu*. There

were also tiny dishes for *sambal belachan* (page 75). Unlike Chinese families, Babas never used chopsticks and instead, adopted the Anglo-Indian custom of using forks and spoons, with the exception of Chinese soup spoons to accompany the soup bowls. While big platters are used for dishes on a Western dining table and passed around, we placed two or three of the same offering spread at intervals across the table. In a typical *tok panjang*, the table continually turned over to serve a meal to family members and visitors. Old family friends and relatives would join us for lunch. Of course, my father, being the patriarch, ate first, along with more senior relatives and guests. There was surely a pecking order as the brothers-in-law and finally the youngest ones took their place after the elders got up from their seats. The dishes were continually replenished. My sisters and the maids were always rushing about the kitchen bringing full plates out and taking empty ones back in while my mother was on hand to control the warming up and dishing out of her precious soups and gravies. Without question, we had to place *sambal belachan*, chilli *chuka* (page 160) and *achar* (page 81) around different parts of the table to ensure everyone had access to them. This *tok panjang* would go on throughout the afternoon and by dinnertime, the whole process would repeat once again.

Most of the *tok panjang* dishes required a few days of advance preparation. The preference was to cook most of the food by the eve of Chinese New Year. Some of that food could then be served at the reunion dinner, leaving most for the big day itself. This took away the burden of trying to cook everything in time for our *tok panjang* lunch on New Year's Day. Furthermore, most Nonya dishes, being so flavourful, would often blossom better in taste if cooked a day or two in advance. My mother never ate a full meal on that first day, often saying that the cook rarely ate her own food because she felt so full from just preparing it. One year, my mother kept complaining loudly for days that she was fed up with having to cook and bake for the New Year, grumbling that it was a thankless job. Nonetheless, she proceeded to prepare and cook as with every year. To our dismay, relatives and friends caught wind of her complaints and did not show up on that first day, leaving us without anyone to entertain.

Because of such aches and pains, many families resorted to catering in the past, and wealthy families had their own chefs to cook these dishes. These chefs, whom we called *chong po*, were in a class of their own. They traced their roots to Hainan island and were synonymous with Nonya and colonial British cooking. These days, savvy chefs who trained in such Baba homes and British army barracks have set up their own restaurants and catering services with signature dishes such as *babi panggang* (roast pork), *sayur kuakchai* (pickled mustard greens) and shark's fin omelette. *Babi panggang* was best prepared outdoors on a charcoal grill. My mother specially ordered this for the *tok panjang* from our long-standing caterer, Ah Heng.

To cater for our Muslim friends who visited but could not consume pork and lard, we also ordered food from another old family friend who owned the Jubilee Restaurant near Arab Street. The catering trucks from Jubilee would arrive with trays full of yummy *nasi biryani* (page 201) and beef *rendang* (page 216), which only added to the vast array of dishes to be served on that big day.

In addition to celebrating the first day of the New Year, we kept the tradition of coming together on the eve, for reunion dinner. We had steamboat, fried Nonya *mee* (wheat noodles), paper-wrapped chicken and symbolic dishes of *fatt choy* (black moss fungus). The family reunion dinner would sometimes become a testy affair if steamboat was the main feature. For a start, my mother always used this occasion to test out a new steamboat, be it electric, charcoal or a portable gas stove. We could spend what seemed like hours stoking the fire while literally steaming away in the humid weather, waiting for the fishballs and meat to cook. Then my hungry, impatient father would get all grouchy and keep asking if the

fishballs were done. By then, everyone would get testy too. Although no major quarrels ever broke out, the steamboat fiascos seemed to diminish the whole spirit of having a family reunion as everyone would go away in a bad mood.

Interestingly, what we as a Baba family were accustomed to eating for Chinese New Year bore little resemblance to what a typical Chinese family would have. One year, my oldest sister Beng arranged a family reunion dinner at a coffee shop bordering Chinatown. Every dish had *fatt choy* and some form of dried seafood, leading my brother-in-law to remark that the *fatt choy* fishballs resembled bulls' testicles. We argued with the coffee shop owner that it was such an awful dinner because we had no idea how to eat anything! The manager curtly replied, "All for good luck". Remarkably, that year was bullish indeed and it was a prosperous year for several family members.

We also ended the 15-day run of the New Year with another reunion which could be as simple as a barbecue. Nonetheless, our barbecues were spectacular. We had seasoned chicken wings, pork and beef fillet, squid or calamari, along with sausages, *otak otak* (page 130), satay, prawns (shrimps), corn, potato salad and green salad. It was a barbecue to end all barbecues and I get so excited just thinking about it.

Many years after my mother's passing, gathering to cook for Chinese New Year's Eve became more challenging. It became apparent that even with six daughters splitting the work, we could not fully replicate what one mother served up for decades. While she almost single-handedly churned out five soups, a myriad of gravy dishes, pickles and sauces, we could neither meet her challenge nor exact standards.

Itek Tim

Soup with Simmered Duck and Salted Mustard Greens

The one unusual thing about this soup is the inclusion of brandy. It amazed me when I first studied this recipe. Most of the old Nonya *bibiks* (grandaunts or senior ladies) would drink 'a bit' of brandy each night before they went to bed. Benedictine DOM was a favourite. They claimed that it was a tonic that kept them strong and healthy. No wonder, since many of them lived past 80 years of age and remained mentally alert and physically robust.

makes 8 to 12 servings

1 whole duck, about 1¼ kg or 2¾ pounds

1 tablespoon brandy and more for seasoning if preferred

450 g or 1 pound salted mustard greens (*kiam chai*), including the leafy greens

6 cups water

450 g or 1 pound pork ribs

3 dried tamarind fruit (*assam poey*)*

3 preserved sour plums*

3 large tomatoes, sliced lengthwise into quarters

2 teaspoons salt

* Dried tamarind fruit (assam poey) and preserved sour plums are best sourced from a Chinese medicinal shop.

1. Rinse and pat dry the duck. Trim off excess fat. Chop into parts, about 6 to 8 pieces. Pour 1 tablespoon of brandy over the duck and toss to coat evenly.

2. Rinse the salted mustard greens under cold water. Then soak in a pot of cold water for no more than 10 minutes. Strain and pat dry. Slice into 5 cm or 2 inch pieces.

3. Fill a pot with enough water to cover the duck, pork ribs, dried tamarind fruit and sour plums, about 6 cups. Bring to a boil and then lower to simmer, skimming off the surface every so often to remove excess gristle and oil. (To remove gristle and oil from the surface of the soup, stir the ladle in the middle of the pot to direct the gristle to the sides of the pot. This makes it easier to scoop the gristle off.)

4. Cover to simmer for at least an hour to ensure that the duck meat becomes very tender.

5. Add the salted mustard greens and cook for an additional 15 minutes.

6. About 10 minutes before serving, add the cut-up tomatoes. Season with salt and a bit more brandy if you prefer.

Pong Tauhu

Soup with Pork and Prawn (Shrimp) Meatballs, and Bamboo Shoots

This is truly my favourite meatball soup. Children love it too. It is important to prepare your stock well to obtain a rich, wholesome flavour.

makes 6 to 8 servings

meatballs
310 g or 11 ounces minced pork
170 g or 6 ounces minced prawns (shrimps), retain shells for stock
170 g or 6 ounces firm bean curd (*taukua*), cut into small cubes
1 teaspoon salt
½ teaspoon white pepper
¼ teaspoon dark soy sauce
1 egg
1 bunch spring onions (scallions), discard white portion, chopped finely
1 tablespoon chopped coriander leaves (cilantro)

soup
450 g or 1 pound pork bones
10 cups cold water (to make stock and add to the soup)
Prawn shells from prawns used in meatballs
4 tablespoons oil
200 g or 7 ounces canned bamboo shoots
1 teaspoon minced garlic
½ teaspoon sugar
1 tablespoon salt, more or less according to preference
Chopped coriander leaves for garnishing

1. Combine the meatball ingredients in a bowl and mix well into a paste. Leave to season for at least an hour.

2. Rinse the pork bones. Bring the pork bones and 5 of the 10 cups of cold water to a boil, then lower heat to a simmer for an hour. Keep pot partially covered and skim the surface of the stock from time to time.

3. Rinse the reserved prawn shells and drain. Heat a pot and pour in 2 tablespoons of the oil. Fry the shells until they turn orange and fragrant. Add the remaining 5 cups of water. Boil and then simmer for at least half an hour, skimming off froth and gristle from the surface. Strain and reserve the prawn stock.

4. Place the bamboo shoots in a small pot of cold water and bring to a boil for about 20 minutes. Discard water and leave to cool. Then julienne finely into thin strips.

5. Heat a deep pot over medium heat and pour in the remaining 2 tablespoons of oil. When the oil is glistening, add the minced garlic, making sure not to burn the garlic. Fry the minced garlic until light golden brown. Add half of the browned garlic to the meatball paste and reserve the other half for the soup stock.

6. With the remaining garlic in the pot, add the sugar and stir. Toss in the sliced bamboo shoots and pour in the prawn stock and pork stock. Turn up the heat and bring the soup to a boil.

7. Using your hands, roll the meatball paste to form balls about 3 cm or 1½ inches in diameter. (To ensure that your meatballs are all even in size, you may choose to roll out the meatballs first and place them on a tray. You can then pinch and add to adjust the size of each meatball. Do this early instead of doing them on the spot and tossing into the soup.)

8. Toss the meatballs into the soup. Add a few more cups of water if necessary to cover the meatballs. Lower the heat and bring the soup to a simmer. The soup is cooked when the meatballs rise to the surface. Add salt to taste.

9. Garnish with chopped coriander leaves and serve in individual soup bowls or a large serving bowl.

Hee Pio

Soup with Fishballs, Meatballs, Fish Maw and Cabbage

To serve this soup authentically, you will need some intricate fish paste rolled in egg omelette. I have included the preparation technique for them. However, you could also simplify the soup, but the absence of the cut-up fish paste omelette roll would be well noted in a fastidious and traditional Baba family.

Hee pio soup derives its name from the dried fish maw in it. Apparently, the best ones are large and straight, not too curled up. When I inspected the ingredients list on a packet of fish maw more closely, it indicated that these better fish maw often come from eels. I personally do not use these.

The soup is best cooked on the day of serving. You can prep the individual components and assemble a new bowl for each serving. Warming up leftover soup too many times breaks up the fish maw and cabbage and may make the soup cloudy. In fact, throw in the cabbage just 10 minutes prior to serving your soup so that it does not overcook.

makes 8 to 12 servings

fish omelette rolls
4 eggs
1 tablespoon oil
1 teaspoon salt
450 g or 1 pound fish paste

soup
450 g or 1 pound pork rib bones
600 g or 1¼ pounds minced pork
350 g or ¾ pound minced
    prawns (shrimps)

15 g or ½ ounce cloud ear fungus,
    soaked in hot water for 10 minutes,
    then chopped (optional)
2 teaspoons salt
1 teaspoon white pepper
½ a chicken, chopped into
    serving pieces
1 large packet dried fish maw (*hee pio*),
    soaked in cold water until soft
1 packet fresh white fishballs
1 head large cabbage, stem discarded,
    leaves cut into 5 cm or 2 inch squares

to make fish omelette rolls

1. Beat the eggs together with the oil and salt.

2. Heat a non-stick omelette pan over high heat. Add some oil to coat the pan. Pour in the beaten egg mixture, just enough to coat the pan. Flip over to fry the underside. When the omelette is formed, remove from the pan. Repeat the process with the remaining egg mixture. Leave the pieces to cool completely.

3. For each omelette, spread a layer of fish paste. Then roll tightly such that each fold is 2.5 cm or 1 inch thick and pressed down. Roll until you form a long ovoid roll.

4. Prepare a steamer. You can use a covered wok filled with roughly 5 cm or 2 inches deep of water, set with a wire rack in the middle of the wok.

5. Place the fish rolls on a heatproof plate. Place the plate on the steamer rack and steam the fish omelette rolls for 5 to 10 minutes until the fish paste is opaque white.

6. Leave the rolls to cool completely. Then, using a bread knife, carefully slice each roll into 1.5 cm or ¾ inch pieces, taking care not to undo the delicate egg omelette.

for soup

1. Rinse the pork rib bones under running water. Place the bones in a large stockpot and cover with just enough cold water. Bring the cold water to a boil, then cover and simmer for 2 hours until you obtain a tasty stock. Skim occasionally to remove froth and gristle.

2. Remove the pork rib bones and strain the stock to clarify it, if necessary.

3. Mix the minced pork and prawns (shrimps)—also chopped cloud ear fungus, if using. Season with salt and pepper. Scoop out the paste and roll into meatballs, each about 2.5 cm or 1 inch in diameter.

4. Add the chicken pieces to the pork stock, followed by the meatballs, fishballs and fish maw. Boil gently and season with more salt and white pepper, if necessary.

5. Ten minutes before serving, add the chopped cabbage, followed by the slices of fish omelette roll. Serve with *sambal belachan* (page 75).

Chap Chai

Vegetable Stew with Sliced Pork and Prawns (Shrimps)

You can prepare this hearty stew a day beforehand. It only gets tastier, especially if kept overnight before serving. This is best served with white rice and *sambal belachan* (page 75).

makes 6 to 10 servings

1 small head cabbage

30 g or 1 ounce glass vermicelli (*tang hoon*)

5 dried Chinese mushrooms

30 g or 1 ounce cloud ear fungus

30 g or 1 ounce dried lily buds

30 g or 1 ounce dried soybean sticks

30 g or 1 ounce black moss fungus *

140 g or 5 ounces small- to medium-size prawns (shrimps)

4 tablespoons oil

5 to 6 cups water

3 cloves garlic, peeled and finely minced

110 g or 4 ounces fermented soy bean paste (*taucheo*), pound finely if whole beans are used

110 g or 4 ounces belly pork strip, sliced into 0.5-cm or ¼-inch pieces

1 teaspoon dark soy sauce

4 pieces firm bean curd (*taukua*), quartered

½ teaspoon salt

½ teaspoon sugar

* There has been some suggestion that the black moss fungus is counterfeit if it appears black. The real moss is dark green in colour. Furthermore, while the real moss is elastic after being soaked in water, the fake ones stick together when squeezed. I have never seen the dark green type of moss and because I use so little of it in the first place, I have no qualms settling for the so-called fake ones.

1. Remove the outer leaves of the cabbage. Discard the stem and tough white portions. Cut the green leaves into 5-cm or 2-inch squares.

2. Place the vermicelli, Chinese mushrooms, cloud ear fungus, dried lily buds, soybean sticks and black moss in a bowl and soak with just enough hot water to cover. Leave aside for at least half an hour to soften. When the mushrooms are sufficiently soft, remove the stems and slice them into halves. Discard the water in which these ingredients were soaked.

3. Shell and devein the prawns and keep aside. Rinse the shells.

4. Warm a pot over high heat and then add 2 tablespoons oil. Stir-fry the prawn shells until the shells turn orange and fragrant. Pour in the water. When the stock begins to boil, lower the heat and simmer for at least half an hour, covered. Then strain the stock by discarding the prawn shells.

5. Next, place a Dutch oven or stockpot over high heat. Add the remaining 2 tablespoons of oil and when glistening, add the minced garlic. Stir-fry until fragrant, pour in the fine soy bean paste, stir, and then add the sliced pork and prawns. Next, add the dark soy sauce for flavour as well as colour.

6. Pour in the reserved stock. Turn up the heat. When the soup is boiling, add the cabbage, firm bean curd pieces and all the previously soaked ingredients. Add more water, if necessary, until all the ingredients are covered. Continue to boil until these last ingredients are soft before you serve. It is not necessary to simmer as this may overcook and break up the contents of the stew.

7. Just before serving, taste and add salt and sugar as necessary. Depending on whether you have prepared this a day or two beforehand, the fermented soy beans may lend some saltiness to the stew and you may not need to add any more salt.

NOTE: To prevent your cabbage leaves from disintegrating (because they become too soft), add them only when you warm up your stew prior to serving.

Chicken Curry

This chicken and gravy dish was our comfort food. My father loved to eat leftovers of this curry for breakfast, scooping up the remaining gravy with slices of French loaf (baguette).

One of my mother's trademark specialties was her curry powder which she made herself. For a brief period, she also made it in large quantities for an instant noodle manufacturer. The curry powder went into the little sachet found in the noodle packet. My mother kept large round rattan trays to contain the various dry spice ingredients. She would first painstakingly inspect the different grains to weed out tiny pebbles and grit. Then, she would rinse the dry spices and lay them on the rattan trays to dry in the sun. She would then fry the spices in her large iron wok, in dry heat, until a fragrant aroma indicated that the spices had 'bloomed'. The spices were then combined into large brown paper sacks and taken to the Indian miller for grinding. The powder returned still warm and highly aromatic. My mother would painstakingly divide the powder into several plastic bags and vacuum seal each bag to retain the freshness of the powder.

I still have a bottle or two made by her. Along with my wedding cake, my curry powder occupies a little corner of my refrigerator as a legacy. Years ago, an American friend passed on a recipe for roasted butternut squash for my baby. The recipe called for a quarter teaspoon of curry powder and a dash of maple syrup. I added some of my mother's curry powder. In a very touching way, I was passing down a small token from my mother to her grandchild whom she had never met.

When cooking curry, adjust the amount of curry powder added depending on how spicy you want the dish to be. Also, as with many other Nonya dishes, this curry always tastes more flavourful the day after cooking.

makes 8 to 10 servings

1.4 kg or 3 pounds chicken parts, preferably thigh meat and drumsticks

5 tablespoons curry powder, of which 1 tablespoon is used to marinate chicken

1½ teaspoons salt or more, to taste

2.5 cm or 1 inch ginger, skinned and julienned

2 cloves garlic, peeled and chopped roughly

3 shallots, peeled and diced

4 tablespoons oil

3 cups coconut milk

4 medium potatoes, boiled, peeled and quartered (Idaho potatoes preferred)

4 hard-boiled eggs, peeled

1 cup coconut cream

1. Rinse and pat dry chicken parts. Marinate them with 1 tablespoon of curry powder. Add some of the salt. Massage well and leave chicken aside to season for at least an hour.

2. Mix the remaining curry powder with a few tablespoons of water, just enough to form a wet paste.

3. Pound or blend the ginger, garlic and shallots in that order, until a fine paste is formed. Set aside.

4. Heat a Dutch oven and add the oil. When the oil is glistening, fry the ground paste of ginger, garlic and shallots until fragrant and golden brown. Make sure that the heat is not too high so as to avoid burning the spices. Then add the curry paste.

5. Next, add the chicken pieces. Use a pair of tongs to turn and coat the chicken pieces with the spice paste. Continue frying for 5 to 10 minutes until the chicken pieces are cooked.

6. Slowly pour half of the coconut milk into the pot. Stir and bring to a boil for about 10 minutes until a thin layer of oil surfaces. Add the remaining coconut milk and simmer covered, stirring occasionally until the chicken is tender, about 30 to 45 minutes.

7. Mix in the boiled potatoes and eggs. Finally, add the coconut cream. Stir well. Turn off the heat. Taste gravy once again and add more salt if preferred.

8. The curry is best served with rice or a French loaf (baguette).

Curry Powder

makes about 900 g or 2 pounds

450 g or 1 pound coriander seeds
    (*ketumbar*)

110 g or 4 ounces cumin (*jintan puteh*)

60 g or 2 ounces fennel (*jintan manis*)

15 g or ½ ounce cassia bark
    (*kayu manis*)

6 cloves (*bunga chingkay*)

40 g or 1½ ounces white peppercorns

110 g or 4 ounces dried chillies,
    stems removed

75 g or 2½ ounces dried turmeric
    (*kunyit*)

1 piece nutmeg (*buah pala*)

5 cardamom pods (*buah pelaga*)

150 g or 5½ ounces white poppy
    seeds (*kas kas*) (optional)

1.   Pick out tiny pebbles and other impurities from the coriander, cumin and fennel.

2.   Rinse all the spices separately and leave them to dry on large trays, preferably made from rattan. Place under direct sun to dry over three to four days, stirring occasionally to ensure even sunning.

3.   Warm up a large wok. Dry-fry the coriander for 4 to 5 minutes until it is fragrant. Set aside. Then dry-fry the cumin and the fennel (you could do this together) for about 2 minutes until fragrant. Be careful not to burn the spices.

4.   Add the remaining spices and dry-fry altogether for about 5 minutes until the mixture is warm and fragrant.

5.   Grind the combined spices into a fine powder (a coffee grinder does the trick). Dry-fry it once again until it is warm and has a strong spicy whiff. Leave aside to cool completely on a large metal tray. Then store the powder in an airtight bottle.

Ayam Buah Keluak

Chicken in a Spicy Gravy with *Buah Keluak*

These nuts may look peculiar but the contents are even more alarming. Officially, the nuts are derived from the *Pangium edule* tree native to South East Asian mangrove swamps. More alarmingly, the fruit which produce these nut seeds are poisonous. However, the fruit and nuts can be made edible by fermentation. We assure ourselves that over several generations, we have not heard of any Baba who has died from *buah keluak* poisoning!

I once tried to smuggle them into the US and got questioned by the customs officers. They took half an hour to go through a Permitted Foods directory and could not find the nuts on the list. My husband had never before seen these until he visited Singapore to meet my parents for the first time. He relished the home-cooked dish and it so impressed my mother. There was then no doubt that my parents would accept him into our family.

Some Nonya families leave the contents as they are, without combining the nut flesh with ground meat and prawns (shrimps). The former has a more bitter aftertaste.

When you pick the nuts, be sure that they are heavy, even if they sound hollow when you shake them.

preparation of nuts

A few days before you serve this dish, the *buah keluak* nuts (about 12 for this recipe) need to be soaked in water for two consecutive nights. Each night, scrub the nuts under running water to remove dirt and grit. Rinse and soak again in fresh water. On the third day, use a pestle to pound the smooth mouth of each nut to crack them open. Alternatively, you can also use a cleaver or a sharp tool to chip along the edges to crack the mouths open. Use a tiny spoon (a caviar spoon would be even better!) to extract the flesh. Taste the flesh, toss those that are too bitter and reserve the rest. Brush the empty shells clean under running water.

Sun them until they are dry, the shells placed with the mouths facing downwards to drain the cavity. You will need both the shells and the nut flesh for the dish.

makes 8 to 12 servings

spice paste
150 g or 5½ ounces galangal (*lengkuas*), skinned and diced finely
45 g or 1½ ounces turmeric (*kunyit*), skinned and chopped
90 g or 3 ounces lemon grass (*seray*), upper stalks and outer layers removed, sliced thinly
45 g or 1½ ounces candlenuts (*buah keras*), diced
3 red chillies, deseeded
215 g or 7½ ounces shallots, peeled and sliced
7 dried chillies, deseeded and soaked in hot water
30 g or 1 ounce *belachan*, chopped

buah keluak filling
12 *buah keluak* nuts, reserve the extracted flesh from the nuts
60 g or 2 ounces prawns (shrimps), deveined and minced

75 g or 2½ ounces chicken or pork, minced
½ tablespoon sugar
Pinch of salt

main dish
5 tablespoons oil
1 whole chicken (about 1.4 kg or 3 pounds), cut into serving pieces
½ tablespoon sugar
1 tablespoon salt
2 stalks lemon grass (*seray*), discard top half, smash remaining parts
140 g or 5 ounces tamarind (*assam*), soaked in 7 cups hot water
1 tablespoon thick coconut milk
1 tablespoon cornflour, mixed with water to form a slurry (optional)

1. Pound the reserved *buah keluak* flesh into a fine paste and set aside.

2. Blend or pound the spice paste ingredients in the order given until you get a fine texture.

3. Warm a large pot or Dutch oven over high heat and then add the oil. When the oil is glistening, lower the heat and add the spice paste. Stir the paste constantly for about 5 minutes until fragrant, taking care not to burn the paste.

4. Set aside 3 tablespoons of the fried spice paste.

5. To the remaining spice paste in the pot, stir in the chicken pieces and fry lightly, then add the ½ tablespoon of sugar, 1 tablespoon of salt and smashed lemon grass.

6. Strain the tamarind juice and discard the seeds and fibre. When the chicken pieces are half-cooked, pour the tamarind juice into the pot. Simmer for another 10 minutes.

7. Meanwhile, for the *buah keluak* filling, mix the minced prawns and chicken (or pork) with the 3 tablespoons of fried spice paste, as well as the sugar and salt. Blend well and stuff the empty shells with the mixed paste. Add the stuffed shells to the pot.

8. Stir the coconut milk into the pot.

9. Continue to simmer for another 30 minutes until a fine layer of oil surfaces and the chicken is tender. Add a bit of cornflour slurry to thicken the gravy, if necessary.

Itek Sio

Braised Duck in Thick Tamarind Gravy

Before my mother became a Christian, as a dutiful daughter-in-law, she would prepare dishes to offer at the ancestral altar. From a child's eyes, I associated *itek sio* with ancestral worship. I suspect it was an appropriate dish because it could be left out in the open for a longer time and kept for days without refrigeration because of its preservative ingredients which included tamarind, sugar and spices. We also had *itek sio* during Chinese New Year. The thick, dark gravy is sweet yet tangy and when done well, the duck will have a pretty glaze. Interestingly, and for reasons I never got to ask my mother, she also added pork. This dish can be made about two days in advance. I find that the longer it keeps, the tastier it is.

makes 8 to 12 servings

½ a duck

450 g or 1 pound pork (belly pork)

120 g or 4 ounces ground coriander (*ketumbar*), toasted until fragrant

90 g or 3 ounces sugar

½ tablespoon salt

1 tablespoon white pepper

1 tablespoon white vinegar

2 tablespoons thick black soy sauce

90 g or 3 ounces tamarind, soaked in 1 cup hot water

Oil for frying

140 g or 5 ounces shallots, peeled and pounded fine

1 bunch coriander leaves (cilantro)

1. Rinse the duck and pat dry. Using the tip of a paring knife, make about 20 insertions into the skin of the duck. Because duck is very fatty, these cuts will release excess oil while cooking. Cut the duck into serving pieces.

2. Slice the strip of pork into 1.5 cm or ½ inch pieces.

3. Marinate the pork and duck with the ground coriander, sugar, salt, pepper, white vinegar and thick black soy sauce. Leave to season for at least 6 hours.

4. When ready to cook, heat a wok and add the oil. Fry the shallots until fragrant, being careful not to burn them. Add the duck and pork. Use tongs to turn the pieces so meat is cooked on all sides. Use a ladle to scoop out excess oil.

5. Strain the tamarind juice and discard the seeds and fibre. Add the tamarind juice. After it has boiled briefly, bring the heat down to a simmer and cover the wok until the gravy thickens. While the dish simmers, scoop gravy over the duck and pork frequently to keep them moist. This will also help a nice glaze to develop on the duck and pork skin. Simmer until the gravy thickens.

6. When ready to serve, garnish the dish with chopped coriander leaves.

NOTE: If you find duck too gamey for your liking, you could also substitute with chicken. In that case, it would be called ayam sio.

Satay Babi
Sliced Pork Stir-fried in Spicy Coconut Gravy

When I began studying the techniques of cooking Nonya food, I started with *satay babi*. The ingredients make up the foundation of most Nonya dishes. Besides, the dish provides an opportunity to learn how to pound these core ingredients in the right sequence, beginning with the tough sinewy rhizomes, such as galangal, and ending with reconstituted dried chilli and *belachan*.

I sought the tutelage of my dearest 90-year-old *kohpoh* (grandaunt) Beng Neo, then, who insisted that I came to learn from her after 3 pm when the kitchen was not too hot from the afternoon sun. She sat at the table and had her tea and Marie biscuits, while waiting patiently for me to pound the spices into a fine *rempah* (spice paste) with much sweat and persistence. She reminded me that in the old days, young girls had to learn to pound well and with a good rhythm because potential mothers-in-law would come around to judge them on these skills. Well, for modern day wives, there is always the food processor, although I must agree that pounded spice paste tastes much better.

makes 6 to 10 servings

450 g or 1 pound pork (fillet or leg meat)

2 stalks lemon grass (*seray*), upper stalks and outer layers removed, sliced thinly

5 candlenuts

5 red chillies

140 g or 5 ounces shallots, peeled and quartered

1 teaspoon *belachan*

1 tablespoon vegetable oil

1¾ cups coconut milk

¾ teaspoon salt

1 teaspoon sugar

1. Rinse the pork and pat dry. Slice the pork into very thin stir-fry slices, about 2.5-cm or 1-inch wide.

2. Pound or pulse grind the spice paste ingredients as follows: lemon grass, candlenuts, red chillies, shallots and *belachan*. Continue to pound or pulse grind until you obtain a smooth paste.

3. Heat a wok and add the oil. Lower the heat and stir in the spice paste. Cook till spice paste is fragrant and the oil separates from it.

4. Add the sliced pork and toss to coat with the spice paste. When the pork is mostly cooked, stir in the coconut milk. Bring to a boil and then simmer, uncovered. Continue to cook over low heat until the gravy thickens.

5. Add the salt and sugar, adjusting the amount according to taste.

Ngo Hiang

Pork with Five-Spice, Rolled and Fried in Bean Curd Sheets

Ngo hiang was one of my mother's specialties. My sister Angela takes pride in making them now, but they are never enough for the entire family. You see, when my mother made them, she seemed to have an endless supply at every party, and for days and days during Chinese New Year. We ate our *ngo hiang* with chilli *chuka* (page 160) or *sambal belachan* (page 75).

Ngo hiang literally means five fragrances and refers to the five-spice powder that gives the meat rolls their signature aroma. The five spices used are: cassia bark, Sichuan peppercorns, fennel seeds, star anise and cloves. The best quality five-spice powder is actually sourced from Chinese medicinal shops. Alternatively, you could settle for the bottled powder found in supermarkets.

My mother's *ngo hiang* differ somewhat in that she cut them up before frying, so that both sides of each small piece were evenly browned. I find that hard to do at times—the individual pieces could fall apart. So I fry them as long rolls, slice them with a bread knife and keep them warm and crisp in an oven.

My mother preferred to chop or grind the individual ingredients first and then mix them together by hand, refraining from using an electric blender. This retained the crunchiness of the water chestnuts. She also steamed the rolls beforehand so that the filling cooked and stayed moist, thus shortening the frying time before the outer bean curd skin charred.

I have chosen to stick with the original recipe portion for several reasons. The quantity may seem plenty but *ngo hiang* is a great buffet item and can feed many guests. Besides, the *tok panjang* meal usually accommodates 10 to 12 guests per seating and over many seatings throughout the day. My father often preached that nothing was more embarrassing than to run out of food for your guests. Should you have too many rolls, you could always freeze the extra for as long as three months, and fry them for other occasions.

makes at least 12 servings

900 g or 2 pounds minced pork

450 g or 1 pound prawns (shrimps), shelled, deveined and minced

230 g or ½ pound peeled water chestnuts, fresh preferred, otherwise canned

1 medium yellow onion, diced finely

10 shallots, diced finely

1 bunch spring onions, discard white portion, sliced finely

2 tablespoons five-spice powder

1 teaspoon ground coriander (*ketumbar*)

1 teaspoon white pepper

2 teaspoons salt

2 tablespoons sugar

2 tablespoons plain flour

1 tablespoon dark soy sauce

2 tablespoons sesame oil

2 eggs

8 to 10 bean curd sheets

2 tablespoons cornflour, mixed with water to form a slurry

2 tablespoons water

Oil for frying, preferably peanut oil *

* Peanut oil (of an Asian brand) imparts a nice flavour to the *ngo hiang*. It also has a high smoke point and is especially suitable for deep-frying.

1. Place minced pork and prawns (shrimps) in a large mixing bowl.

2. Dice water chestnuts finely into cubes with sides about 0.5 cm or ¼ inch. [For the water chestnuts, slice midway across horizontally, hold them together and slice into strips, then dice the strips.]

3. Toss the water chestnuts, yellow onions, shallots and spring onions into the bowl of minced pork and shrimp.

4. Add the five-spice powder, coriander powder, white pepper, salt, sugar, plain flour, dark soy sauce, sesame oil and eggs. Mix this filling well and leave to marinate for at least 20 minutes.

5. Meanwhile, use a damp cloth to wipe both sides of each piece of dry bean curd skin. This removes the saltiness and makes the dry skin more pliable, which is important in ensuring that the skin does not crack and expose the filling.

6. Lay down a sheet of beancurd sheet flat on the table. Scoop 3 to 4 tablespoons of the *ngo hiang* filling and shape it into a line about 3 cm or 1½ inches thick, a third of the way from the baseline of the skin. Fold the baseline flap over the filling, continue to roll tightly into a log. Dab the cornflour slurry along the edge of the skin to seal the *ngo hiang* roll tightly.

7. Wrap the other rolls.

8. Set up a steamer. You can do so with a wok or a Dutch oven by placing a pot rack in the middle and filling with enough water to reach the base of the pot rack. Turn on the heat to boil the water. Cover the pot.

9. Place the rolls on a heat-proof dish and steam in the pot, covered, for 5 to 10 minutes.

10. Remove the *ngo hiang* rolls to let them cool completely. At this point, you can freeze any excess rolls you may have.

11. Discard the water from the wok or Dutch oven. Wipe clean and fill with peanut oil, sufficient for deep frying. Heat the oil until it reaches a temperature of 180 degrees C or 350 degrees F, smoking hot.

12. Fry a few rolls of *ngo hiang* at a time. Turn occasionally to brown evenly. Scoop out with a perforated ladle and rest the rolls on grease-proof paper. With a bread knife, slice each roll into 2.5-cm or 1-inch pieces. Keep warm in an oven at 120 degrees C or 250 degrees F.

13. Serve with sliced cucumber garnish, and accompanied by chilli *chuka* (page 160) and *sambal belachan* (page 75).

Sambal Belachan

Belachan Blended with Lime Juice and Chilli

No Nonya would be worth her salt (or *belachan*) if she could not concoct this at home, a key ingredient being *belachan*. An old lady used to deliver to our home round slabs of pungent home-made *belachan* wrapped in cloth. Nowadays, you can find packaged *belachan* in supermarkets. In my experience, I prefer those made in Malacca, which I find less salty than those made in Penang. Every family has its own secret method of making *sambal belachan*. This accompaniment brings out the flavour of the Chinese New Year soups and dishes. It can also be used as a stuffing for fried mackerel (see recipe for *ikan sumbat*, page 244), or as a marinade for fried chicken.

makes about 90 g or 3 ounces

60 g or 2 ounces *belachan*

3 red chillies

1 kaffir lime leaf (*daun limau purut*), stem and midrib removed

Sugar to taste

Salt to taste (if necessary)

2 small calamansi limes (*limau kesturi*) or substitute with key limes

1.   Cut up the *belachan* into cubes and toast them in a frying pan over medium heat. Use the back of a spatula to rub down the *belachan* paste against the surface of the pan. Continue to toast until it is fragrant, brittle and dry.

2.   Deseed the red chillies if you prefer. Remove stems and chop into short pieces.

3.   Pound or blend the chopped red chillies and kaffir lime leaf. Stir in the roasted powdered *belachan* and continue to pound or blend until you obtain a fine dark paste. It is usually unnecessary to add any more salt; but you may add some sugar if you wish to tone down the pungent *sambal*.

4.   Slice the lime into quarters. Scoop a teaspoon of *sambal* into each sauce dish and place a quarter of lime on the side. Squeeze the lime juice into the *sambal* when the meal begins.

Ati Babi

Pork and Liver Meatballs Wrapped in Caul Lining

To me, these meatballs are a very quintessential part of Nonya cuisine and a dying feature at that. Very few people still make them, let alone know how to buy the caul lining. The trick is to visit a butcher in a wet market and ask him to keep it for you. Be sure that it does not smell bad or feel gooey. In the lead-up to Chinese New Year, it is most important to place your order well in advance too.

makes 6 to 8 servings

40 g or 1½ ounces pork liver

200 g or 7 ounces pork caul lining, soaked in slightly salted cold water

1 cup oil

8 shallots, peeled and minced

1½ tablespoons sugar (or 1 tablespoon sugar and ½ tablespoon *gula melaka*)

300 g or 11 ounces minced pork

1 tablespoon ground coriander (*ketumbar*), toasted until fragrant

1 teaspoon white pepper

½ teaspoon salt

½ tablespoon vinegar

1 tablespoon dark soy sauce

Peanut oil for deep-frying

1.   Rinse and pat dry the pork liver. Cook the liver in boiling water. Remove and run it under cold water to cool completely. Then chop into fine cubes.

2.   Rinse the caul lining under a tap of cold water, making sure to clean it thoroughly. Pat dry.

3.   Heat a wok and add some oil. Fry the minced shallots until light brown. Add the sugar and stir until the sugar dissolves. Scoop out the fried shallots.

4.   Add the remaining ingredients—chopped liver, minced pork, ground coriander, white pepper, salt, vinegar and dark soy sauce. Mash well into a fine meatball paste.

5.   Roll out the meatballs, each about 4 cm or 1½ inches in diameter. To ensure that your meatballs are all even in size, you may choose to roll out the meatballs first and place them on a tray. You can then pinch and add to adjust the size of each meatball.

6.   Place the caul lining flat out on a clean table surface. Place one meatball near the edge of the lining and roll to fully cover the meatball with the lining. Make sure that you double-roll over any part of the lining that has a hole. Trim off with a paring knife or a pair of scissors. Repeat the process until you wrap all the meatballs.

7.   Pre-cook the meatballs by steaming for 5 minutes.

8.   To fry the meatballs, heat a wok and fill a quarter of the wok with peanut oil. The meatballs are meant to be shallow-fried rather than deep-fried. Lower the heat to moderate and fry the meatballs for about 15 minutes until they are dark brown and fully cooked. To test, you can slice through a meatball with a paring knife.

9.   Serve with *sayur kuakchai* (page 80) and *sambal belachan* (page 75).

Ayam Kormak

Mild Chicken Curry

This dish was one of the many sent over on Chinese New Year's day by my father's friend who owned a famous restaurant along Arab Street. He made it a tradition to provide *nasi biryani, ayam kormak* and *rendang* for our Muslim guests.

I remember it to be a less spicy curry with a richer gravy, as opposed to chicken curry which has a thinner consistency. It is delicious and goes well with *achar* (page 81).

makes 8 to 12 servings

spice paste
3 tablespoons coriander seeds (*ketumbar*)
1 teaspoon cumin (*jintan puteh*)
1 teaspoon fennel (*jintan manis*)
1 teaspoon white peppercorns
60 g or 2 ounces ginger, peeled and
    julienned
1 clove garlic, peeled and chopped roughly
10 green chillies, stemmed

kormak
1 whole chicken, about 1.5 kg
    or 3 ½ pounds

30 g or 1 ounce ghee
1 cup thin coconut milk
2 tomatoes, cut into wedges
40 g or 1½ ounces white poppy
    seeds (*kas kas*)*
¾ cup thick coconut milk
2 to 3 teaspoons salt
1 bunch mint leaves, stems removed
1 bunch coriander leaves (cilantro)

* *Kas kas* can be substituted with ground almonds (skinned) or ground cashew nuts.

1. Grind or pound the spice paste, adding the ingredients in the order given.

2. Cut the chicken into serving pieces.

3. Heat a wok and add the ghee. When the ghee melts, add the pounded spice paste and fry until it is fragrant.

4. Add the chicken pieces followed by the thin coconut milk. When the gravy begins to boil, toss in the tomatoes and turn down the heat to a simmer until the gravy thickens and the chicken is tender.

5. Mix the *kas kas* with the thick coconut milk and pour into the curry.

6. Season with the salt according to taste. Then garnish with the mint leaves and coriander leaves before serving.

Sayur Kuakchai
Pickled Mustard Greens

Sayur kuakchai accompanies fried staples such as *ati babi* (page 76) and *ngo hiang* (page 73). I especially remember it as an essential side for *babi panggang* (roast pork). On special occasions such as Chinese New Year or a wedding lunch, my mother would order this delicious *babi panggang* from her Hainanese caterer, Ah Heng. He was a *chong poh*, an in-house chef for a large and affluent Baba family who subsequently catered for Nonya parties. He would therefore have mastered the requisite skills to produce delicacies that were difficult for the average household to prepare on their own, in this case, the spit-roasted pig.

To make *sayur kuakchai*, you will need to find the right mustard greens. These are specifically known as the bamboo mustard cabbage which have longer leaves and are not as tightly bunched up as the Swatow mustard cabbage.

makes 600 g or 1¼ pounds

600 g or 1¼ pounds bamboo mustard cabbage

3 tablespoons salt

5 cm or 2 inches ginger, peeled and finely julienned

2 teaspoons yellow mustard powder

4 tablespoons sugar

2 tablespoons vinegar

1. Rinse the mustard cabbage and slice into 5-cm or 2-inch shreds, including both stems and leaves. Sprinkle 2 of the 3 tablespoons of salt over the greens. Set aside to allow time for the salt to draw excess water out of the mustard cabbage.

2. Add the remaining 1 tablespoon of salt to the julienned ginger and leave aside.

3. Combine the mustard powder, sugar and vinegar and stir together into a paste.

4. Squeeze the mustard cabbage and ginger dry. Toss them into the spice paste.

5. Leave to marinate for at least half a day before serving.

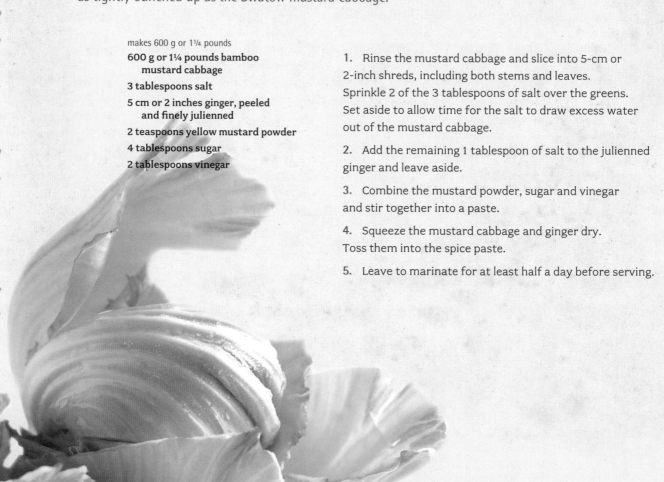

Achar

Pickled Vegetable Crudités in Spiced Vinegar

Achar was one of the last Chinese New Year items to be made, after the cookies and before the cakes. To make the pickles, my mother bought sacks of cucumbers, carrots and cauliflower, in addition to bags of spices and bottles of vinegar. It was a major endeavour as she would selflessly stand for hours to chop the vegetables into the perfect-sized crudités, not trusting many of us around her to cut them into the same shape or size. A bottle of her famous pickled *achar*, along with a selection of cookies, a small *lapis* cake and a pair of tangerines, made up my mother's gift pack to her closest friends and relatives.

She collected glass bottles throughout the year, preferably Horlicks bottles. Soaked and rid of its labels, these glass bottles were filled with the *achar* which could last a year or more because she had added sodium benzoate, a preservative now considered carcinogenic. Its spicy, tangy kick went especially well with other simpler Nonya specialties like *ngo hiang* (page 73) or *chap chai* (page 61).

Many people often asked us how her pickles could stay crunchy past several months in a refrigerated bottle. The secret, apparently, was the addition of slaked lime powder to the water used to soak the cucumbers. I also discovered that this same slaked lime powder was often added to Thai vegetable stir-fries to keep the vegetable crunchy.

makes about 8 kg or 17½ pounds

pickles
3 kg or 6½ pounds cucumbers
230 g or ½ pound carrots
1 large head cauliflower
½ large head cabbage
4 teaspoons slaked lime powder
    (*kapor*)
4 cups salt
1 ¼ cups rice vinegar
2 cups water

spiced pickling solution
120 g or 2 ounces turmeric (*kunyit*)
10 candlenuts (*buah keras*)
450 g or 1 pound shallots, peeled and diced
4 red chillies
30 g or 1 ounce dried chillies, soaked in
    hot water for at least 10 minutes
1 tablespoon *belachan*
340 g or 12 ounces peanut
    brittle (*tow tung*), chopped roughly.*

1¼ ounces salt
3 tablespoons sesame seeds (*bijan*)
2 cups oil
450 g or 1 pound garlic, minced
5 cups rice vinegar
2½ cups water
1½ kg or 3 pounds sugar
140 g or 5 ounces salt

stuffed chillies
150 g or 5½ ounces large green chillies
200 g or 7 ounces dried shrimps,
    soaked in hot water for 10 minutes
5 candlenuts
10 shallots, peeled and diced
1 teaspoon *belachan*
2 tablespoons sugar

* Peanut brittle (*tow tung*) can be substituted with sesame brittle for those who have peanut allergy. .

preparing and blanching pickles

1. Cut the cucumbers lengthwise on four sides, discarding the tips and central core. Cut further into strips, about 1 cm by 5 cm (½ inch by 2 inches).

2. Skin the carrots and discard the head and tip. Cut further into similar strips, about 1 cm by 5 cm (½ inch by 2 inches).

3. Remove the stems of the cauliflower and cabbage, and cut into smaller pieces, about 2.5 cm by 2.5 cm (1 inch by 1 inch).

curing and preparing the vegetables

1. For each type of vegetable, fill a bowl of cold water and add a teaspoon of slaked lime powder. Soak the vegetable in the bowl of water for at least an hour. Discard the water and rub the vegetable with a cup of salt. Wrap the vegetable in a cloth sack or with a dish towel and press it under a heavy object (for example, a pestle on top of a baking sheet). Leave it to press overnight. Do this process for each of the four types of vegetable.

2. The next day, bring the rice vinegar and water to a boil in a large pot. Place the cut cucumbers in a strainer and dip into the boiling pot for a minute. Shock the cucumbers under cold running water and leave to drain. Spread onto a large tray to cool and dry the blanched cucumber.

3. Repeat the process with the carrots, cauliflower and cabbage.

stuffing the chillies

1. Slit the green chillies lengthwise on one side and discard the seeds.

2. Drain the dried shrimps from the hot water and pat dry. Pound or blend finely and set aside.

3. Pound or blend the remaining ingredients—candlenuts, shallots and *belachan*. Add the pounded dried shrimps and stir. Season with sugar.

4. Stuff each green chilli with the pounded paste. Set aside.

preparing the spiced pickling solution

1. Pound or blend in sequence the turmeric, candlenuts, shallots, red chillies, dried chillies (discard the hot water) and *belachan* into a fine paste.

2. Heat a large wok or Dutch oven and add the oil. Fry the minced garlic until light golden brown. Stir in the pounded spice paste and fry until fragrant, being careful not to burn the spice paste. Pour in the rice vinegar and water and stir into a gravy. Season with the chopped peanut brittle (or sesame brittle), sugar, salt and sesame seeds. Bring the gravy to a boil.

3. Add the blanched vegetables. Scoop the vegetables out onto a large tray and spread it into a thin layer to cool. Turn up the heat for the pot of gravy to boil, and then turn down to simmer and thicken. Return the vegetables to the thickened gravy, along with the stuffed green chillies.

4. Scoop the vegetables back onto the tray once again. Spread them out and let them cool completely before bottling.

Sambal Timun

Cucumber Cuts Tossed in Fresh Chilli Paste

My sisters insisted that I should not omit this old-fashioned side dish. It is hard to find this nowadays, let alone have the recipe for it. My mother always had this at the *tok panjang* during Chinese New Year, and I would avoid it because it included gizzards. Nonetheless, its absence at our table now signify that a previous generation of true Nonyas, like my mother, is fast disappearing and with it, some of the more traditional dishes.

My father taught me how to remove the bitterness of fresh cucumbers. You slice off 2 cm or an inch from the stem tip of the cucumber and use the same tip to rub against the cut surface of the longer cucumber. Rub in a circular motion until a froth appears. Repeat the same process with the other end of the cucumber. Rinse or wipe off the froth.

makes 4 to 6 servings

sambal
3 tablespoons dried shrimps, soaked in hot water for 15 minutes, then pat dry
2 red chillies
1 teaspoon *belachan*, roasted until fragrant
2 tablespoons lime juice, preferably from calamansi limes (*limau kesturi*)

2 teaspoons sugar
½ teaspoon salt

salad
2 cucumbers
1 chicken liver (optional)
1 chicken gizzard (optional)

sambal

1. Pound or grind the dried shrimps until it is fine. Set aside.

2. Pound or grind the red chillies until smooth, taking care to stop and scrape the paste from the sides of the bowl back to the middle before pounding again. Then add the ground dried shrimps, followed by the *belachan*, pausing now and then to scrape the sides.

3. Add the lime juice, sugar and salt and adjust the seasoning according to taste.

4. Set aside in a bowl or store in a bottle if you do not intend to use the paste immediately.

salad

1. Rinse and pat dry the cucumbers. Remove the bitterness of the cucumber by repeating the process mentioned at the start of this recipe.

2. You may skin the cucumber or leave as is. Then cut each cucumber lengthwise into two halves. Use a small teaspoon or a paring knife to scrape out the section containing seeds. Slice the cucumber into 1.5 cm or ½ inch pieces.

3. If you include the chicken liver and gizzard, boil them first and let them cool. Then cut them into pieces about the same size as the cucumber slices.

4. Add *sambal* paste and toss together.

Nonya Hokkien Noodles
Stir-fried Noodles in Gravy with Pork and Prawns (Shrimps)

It was customary for my family to serve this at the Chinese New Year's Eve reunion dinner. Today, my sister Nancy has taken over the specific responsibility of making this for our reunion dinner.

The Nonya version differs from the fried Hokkien noodles you would see in hawker centres. For a start, it has more gravy. This noodle dish is a staple in a Nonya feast. It is also worth noting that when the dish is served at a wake or after a funeral, you are supposed to use only preserved ingredients, meaning dried, not fresh, scallops and squid.

In this recipe, I have excluded squid. Most recipes would also instruct you to use *kang kong* (water convolvulus) which my father agreed on. However, I have chosen to use mustard greens which add a bit more crunch and are more refreshing.

makes 4 to 6 servings

noodles
110 g or 4 ounces belly pork strip
 (*sam chan bak*)
110 g or 4 ounces prawns (shrimps)
4 cups water
4 tablespoons vegetable oil
3 shallots, peeled and sliced finely
3 cloves garlic, peeled and minced
110 g or 4 ounces mustard greens
 (*chai sim*), sliced into 5 cm or
 2 inch pieces
450 g or 1 pound yellow noodles
110 g or 4 ounces bean sprouts,
 heads and tails trimmed
1 to 3 teaspoons salt
½ teaspoon white pepper

garnish
2 eggs, beaten
3 red chillies, deseeded and sliced finely
Deep-fried sliced shallots
1 bunch coriander leaves (cilantro)

1. Place the belly pork strip in a large pot filled with the 4 cups of water. Bring it to a boil. Meanwhile, rinse, peel and devein the prawns, reserving the shells.

2. Remove the pork from the stock when it is half-cooked. Leave aside to cool. Slice into thin strips about 5 cm or 2 inches long and 0.25 cm or $1/8$ inch thick. Reserve the pork stock.

3. Heat a Dutch oven. Add half of the vegetable oil. When the oil is glistening, fry the prawn shells until they turn pink. Add the pork stock and stir until the stock begins to boil. Turn the heat down to simmer for at least 15 minutes. Set aside.

4. Meanwhile, prepare the garnishing. First fry the eggs to form an omelette. After it has cooled, roll the omelette and slice it finely into very thin strips.

5. Heat a wok and add the remaining vegetable oil. Fry the sliced shallots until they turn light golden brown. Transfer to a plate lined with parchment paper.

6. Using the same wok and oil, add in the minced garlic and fry until it is fragrant, being careful not to burn it. Then add in the sliced pork and prawns (shrimps). Pour in the stock, but not all at once—scoop enough to form a gravy and add more to dilute if the gravy seems too thick.

7. Leave it to bubble before adding the sliced mustard greens, beginning with the cut stems first since they take longer to soften.

8. Add the green leaves, the yellow noodles and bean sprouts in that order. Season with salt and white pepper according to taste.

9. Dish the noodles onto a large platter and garnish with the sliced omelette, red chillies, fried shallots and coriander leaves (cilantro).

10. The noodles are best served with *sambal belachan* (page 75) and cut lime. The noodles can also be served alongside *rojak chinchang* (recipe below).

Rojak Chinchang
Spicy Cucumber and Pineapple Relish

½ pineapple, cored and diced finely

2 cucumbers, peeled and deseeded, diced finely

Sambal belachan (page 75)
1 tablespoon sugar
½ to 1 tablespoon dark soy sauce

1. Combine the finely diced pineapple and cucumber in a bowl. Add the *sambal belachan* according to preferred taste.

2. Season with the sugar and dark soy sauce.

3. Serve along with the noodles. (You could use the remaining *sambal belachan* as a side condiment, accompanied by a halved calamansi lime or *limau kesturi*.)

Golden Agar Jelly

Each Chinese New Year, I looked forward to visiting *kohpoh* Beng Neo, not least because she served this crunchy golden jelly. I associate this jelly with sarong-kebaya clad matriarchs because they seem to be the only ones who make them best of all.

Kohpoh's secret in the early days was apparently to use rainwater collected in large dragon pots. She said that rainwater produced the clearest and hence most exquisite jelly. Sometimes, crushed egg shells would be added while cooking the agar-agar to gather up the froth from the surface. The shells would clarify the jelly in the same way that consommé is prepared as the calcium helps absorb off-colours.

This agar jelly often came in the shape of rabbits or fish. The classic moulds were made in England from white porcelain which bear a crackled glaze.

To produce the golden colour of the jelly, the jelly syrup was boiled in a brass pot, in the same way that the filling for pineapple tart was cooked to achieve its golden shade. Today there is skepticism in using brass pots, so to produce the golden sheen, you may want to use food colouring instead.

The longer the jelly is kept, the more it crystallises. In fact, the Nonyas would sun the jelly for a few days to help it crystallise. It could then be stored without refrigeration for months.

makes 4 to 6 servings

60 g or 2 ounces *agar-agar* strips (or *agar agar* powder)
7 cups water
450 g or 1 pound rock sugar

1 teaspoon rose syrup
Sugar according to taste
1 teaspoon yellow food colouring
¼ teaspoon red food colouring

1. Cut the agar-agar strips into 8 cm or 3 inch pieces and rinse. Bring the water to a boil in a large pot and add the strips and rock sugar, stirring continuously. Lower heat to a simmer and skim the surface to remove froth. Simmer for at least 3 hours until the syrup thickens.

2. To test how well-done it is, scoop up some jelly syrup and if it hardens in the ladle after a while, it is ready. Add the rose syrup, taste and adjust the level of sweetness by stirring in sugar if necessary.

3. Add a few drops of yellow food colouring first and then sparingly, add drops of red food colouring until you achieve a golden hue. Stir.

4. Pour the jelly syrup into the moulds. You can let the jelly harden at room temperature or in the refrigerator. If you are leaving the jelly to harden at room temperature, place the moulds in a baking tray filled with water to prevent ants from getting to the jelly.

The Housewives Baking Club

*Every year, about eight weeks
before Chinese New Year,
my mother and our neighbour,
Aunty Paddy, would begin
their annual cottage enterprise.*

*My mother (left) and Aunty Paddy
in the kitchen together.*

**Aunty Paddy lived across the street from us at Yarrow Gardens and had
been our neighbour for more than 30 years. The two ladies baked cookies
and sold them to friends and regular customers. They ran their businesses
separately in their respective kitchens but found joy in sharing their daily
'production reports' and labour of love.**

All year round, these same friends, customers and family would collect empty
Horlicks bottles, Marie biscuit and Ovaltine tins and pass them on to my mother
and Aunty Paddy who would soak and rinse them to remove the labels. After
neatly lining the cookies, each layer separated from the next by a trimmed
plastic sheet, the containers were sealed with white masking tape and labelled.
My mother also cut out intricate lattice designs on red paper, which she would
glue to the tops of the containers.

The two ladies produced a range of biscuits but 'outsourced' the more complicated *kueh belanda* or loveletters which were thin 'cigar' rolls of coconut-flavoured wafers. Aunty Paddy had a distant relative who made these. They came in signature boxy rectangular tins printed with reversed cover designs for brands such as Kiwi shoe polish. We could still figure out the logos and hence ponder the odd relationship between Kiwi shoe polish and delicious wafers! *Kueh belanda*, which translates to 'Dutch cake', most probably had its origins in Europe. Indeed, a few years ago, I bought a Scandinavian waffle maker, only to discover that it produced thin, crispy waffles with intricate designs on the surface, similar to our *kueh belanda*.

The most popular item that my mother and Aunty Paddy sold was pineapple tarts (page 94). They produced so many of those that it took several days to jam the fresh pineapples. They personally did this themselves and pricked their fingers several times in due course. Both Aunty Paddy and my mother possessed a large brass deep pan to simmer and jam the pineapples. Aunty Paddy told me that it was the contact with the brass metal that gave a deep golden glow to the pineapple jam. Family members and friends came by to help snip the tart pastry. The old-fashioned tarts were actually not tarts at all, which are defined as open pastry topped with jam. Instead, they were pastry dough enclosing the jam, ovoid in shape with a tip at one end. The ladies snipped the surface of the dough to achieve little needle-like pinches and also inserted one clove at the broad end of the 'tart'. It took some imagination to realise that these were supposed to look like pineapples. In fact, a friend of my sister Beng, once remarked that they looked like porcupines! Because the snipping was so tedious and laborious, the two ladies did fewer and fewer of these 'porcupine tarts' as they got older. The snipping just worsened the unforgiving arthritis affecting the older helpers.

Relatives were also recruited to do other tasks. As a child, I had to arrange the cookies in each bottle. I had to ensure each layer of cookies was lined with specially cut out rounds of tracing paper or thin plastic to fit the base of the bottle.

Tracing paper was also used to line large round metal trays, each about a metre or three feet in diameter. These trays were docking stations for the cookies to rest after they were taken out of the oven. Covered by the large plastic *terong sading* or food protector/covering, they cooled with the aid of a fast rotating fan. The rationale was that if these hot cookies were placed directly into their storage bottles, the condensation caused by the heat would cause them to soften. We were also forbidden from consuming any of these oven-fresh cookies straightaway, for fear of us developing a hoarse throat later on.

While Aunty Paddy focused more on biscuits, my mother spread her efforts to include her *achar* pickles and her cakes. She had a clear time-table of when to make certain items and in what order. The cookies came first, followed by the pickles, the tarts, and lastly the cakes. I suspect this was to preserve the freshness of the goods accordingly, as she prepared the food that could stay fresh over a longer time first.

She also made the traditional *kueh bolu* (page 113). These are like spongy French madeleines but they come in their own distinct shapes. My mother set up a makeshift charcoal stove at the back of our house and would spend a day making them. Using special brass trays that came with several mould cavities, they required a good memory as to which mould had been filled and when; and good judgment as to which *kueh bolu* cakes were ready to be taken out.

One of the hardest Nonya cookies to master was *kueh koya* (page 110). Made from ground green mung beans (*kachang hijau*), these cookies literally melted in your mouth and came in delicate moulded shapes of flowers or animals. The beans were first dry-fried and ground into a fine powder. Mixed with a precise amount of water and sugar, the paste was packed tightly into wooden *kueh koya* moulds. The challenge was to bake the cookies in the mould in the sun until the powder mixture dried, and then to bake these again over slow charcoal fire, with the end result being that the cookies should not crumble when one turned them over out of the moulds. My mother tried making them but the process was difficult and trying. It was not often that she would make them.

Chinese New Year also meant that most Nonyas would make *kueh bakul*. There were elaborate traditions associated with making this, which is a round glutinous rice cake that looks like hardened honey with a glossy surface, the glossier the better in fact. The sides are wrapped with banana leaves and the middle of the surface pasted with one of those intricate red paper cutouts. As a child, my sister, Maggie, observed the older womenfolk fuss over making them. My grandmother would shoo all the little children out of the kitchen, and especially menstruating women. It was thought unlucky for unpurified women to have a hand in making what was considered a sacred offering to the ancestral gods. The *kueh bakul* had to turn out perfectly right, good enough for the gods so as to deserve a good New Year.

In any case, both my mother and Aunty Paddy made a tidy profit from their annual endeavours. Any profit made by my mother almost always went into buying gold jewellery. Eventually, she had a nice collection of gold trinkets and diamond pendants which had been acquired through this hobby of hers.

My mother used to nag at all her daughters for not bothering to learn the tricks of her trade. In fact, she was right. By the time she died, we had no idea how to operate the precious Baby Belling oven which was only used to bake *kueh lapis spekkoek* (page 114). The oven must have given up on us and decided to blow itself out one Chinese New Year morning, a stern reminder of how much we had neglected it that baking season.

General Principles for Baking Cookies, According to Aunty Paddy:

- Use chilled butter.

- Aunty Paddy actually grinds her sugar. So it is not really fine sugar, neither is it truly castor sugar. In most instances, I use castor sugar as a substitute.

- In many of the cookie recipes, she first mixes the butter, sugar, vanilla or almond essence by hand (and eggs if there are any).

- Then, she adds the flour and other dry ingredients, and kneads them into a dough.

- If the dough is too wet, she adds more flour. If the dough is too dry, she adds more butter. Based on her experience, baking in colder climates tend to require less flour.

- She always chills the dough in the refrigerator for a few hours, even overnight. Then she takes it out to let it soften before being rolled and cut. The lead time depends on the weather; longer for a cold climate, shorter if it is hot and humid.

- Do not grease the baking tray. Instead, line with parchment paper. Greasing the tray results in burnt bottoms for the cookies.

- Always cool the cookies completely after baking, then store them in airtight containers.

Pineapple Tarts

My mother was known for making thousands of these tarts. Over time, with fewer relatives to assist her and as she got older, she simply made them into 'apples' topped with a clove that resembled an apple stem. These round 'apples' were made from pastry enclosing the jam. Finally, she made open tarts with the jam exposed. Open tarts resulted in a drier jam tart, as opposed to jam enclosed in the pastry which did not have direct exposure to the oven heat. I have included recipes for both open and enclosed tart doughs.

In the past, the jam was cooked over charcoal in a shallow bronze pot. The bronze gave the jam its golden colour. Unfortunately, these pots are no longer sold because there are fears that the corrosion may cause adverse health effects.

The pineapple used was the common sweet-sour variety which has a greener skin. White sugar was added to make the jam sweeter. Nowadays, you can find sweeter pineapples in the supermarkets, for example, the honey variety which has a more orange-yellow skin. If you prefer to sweeten your jam with natural fruit instead of processed sugar, this is a good option. Note, however, that the honey pineapple is far juicier and produces less pulp for the jam, so you may have to substitute one sweet-sour pineapple with two honey pineapples. It is also important to make sure that your jam does not have too much juice residue as it may leave the tarts mouldy.

makes about 50 tarts

pineapple jam
6 pineapples, skinned and eyes removed
   (about 340 g or 12 ounces grated
   or chopped)
1 petal from 1 star anise
1 cinnamon stick, about 2.5 cm or 1 inch
3 cloves
2 cups sugar, adjust according to taste

open tart dough
450 g or 3½ cups flour
230 g or 8 ounces (2 sticks) unsalted
   butter *
Salt (optional) to add a tinge of
   savouriness to the pastry
2 egg yolks
1 egg white
1 teaspoon vanilla essence
3 tablespoons water (if necessary)

enclosed tart dough
450 g or 3½ cups flour
230 g or 8 ounces (2 sticks)
   unsalted butter *
Salt (optional) to add a tinge
   of savouriness to the pastry
2 eggs
1 teaspoon vanilla essence
3 tablespoons water (if necessary)
50 cloves

egg wash
2 to 3 eggs, beaten

* My mother used the Buttercup brand
of butter which was salted. It gave a slight
savoury edge to the pastry. These days,
unsalted butter is frequently used for
baking, and a little bit of salt can be added
to give a tinge of savouriness.

pineapple jam

1. Squeeze the grated pineapple with a muslin clothbag to extract the juice. Discard or reserve the juice for a different use. Place the pulp in a sieve, layer it with the muslin cloth and top it with a heavy object such as a mortar. Leave it overnight to dry out the pulp from excess juice.

2. Combine the grated pineapple and spices and cook over low heat in a large saucepan. Add the sugar a little at a time, according to taste. Keep stirring the jam to prevent any burning at the bottom of the pan. Continue to cook until the pineapple jam is thick and golden brown. Remove the spices. Remove the jam from heat and let it cool. Do so by putting the bowl of jam in a larger tray with a moat of water to prevent ants from climbing into the jam.

open tarts

1. Rub the flour and butter to form fine crumbs.

2. Beat the egg yolks, egg white and vanilla essence.

3. Create a hole in the middle of the flour mixture. Pour in the beaten egg mixture a bit at a time; knead lightly to form a dough. Do not pour the entire egg mixture if the dough starts to become soggy. Adjust the amount accordingly.

4. If the dough remains dry, add water sparingly until you get a nice consistency. This may happen more so in dry weather. (Note: An alternative to Steps 1 to 4 is to engage the function of your food processor!)

5. Leave the pastry dough in the refrigerator for at least a few hours.

6. When you are ready to bake, take the pastry dough out of the refrigerator to soften, at least 20 minutes prior to working on the tarts.

7. Line baking tray with parchment paper.

8. Roll out pastry dough into a flat sheet about 0.5 cm or ¼ inch thick. Use a good pineapple tart mould to cut out the tart base. Repeat until all the dough has been used up. Lay the pastry out on a baking tray. Refrigerate for about 15 minutes to keep the pastry hard.

9. Preheat the oven at 180 degrees C or 350 degrees F.

10. Remove the pastry from the refrigerator and heap a teaspoon of jam onto each pastry base. Repeat until all the dough or jam is used up.

11. (Optional) To embellish tart, use a paring knife to slice a few thin ribbons of pastry. Top the jam with a ribbon for decoration.

12. Bake in the oven for 10 minutes until pastry is light brown. Remove from oven and brush egg wash on the pastry. Place the tray back in the oven for another 10 minutes until the pastry turns golden brown.

enclosed tart

1. Follow instructions for open tarts to make the dough (Steps 1 to 9). To enclose tarts, just take a teaspoon of jam and roll into a ball.

2. Take each circle of pastry cut-out and enclose a ball of jam, rolling it to form a ball. Pinch into tear-drop shapes (like miniature pineapples). Brush with egg wash before snipping. Use a clean pair of manicure scissors to make angled cuts into the pastry. Insert a clove into fatter end of the enclosed tart. Repeat until all the dough or jam is used up.

3. Bake in the oven for about 20 minutes or till pastry turns golden brown.

Almond Cookies

These almond cookies were popular among the items which my mother sold. They differ from the flat, brown almond cookies you receive at the end of a meal in some Chinese restaurants. Instead, these look like big toes because of the quartered almond pressed in the middle of each pudgy round cookie. Aunty Paddy made them too and gave me a few tips. One essential note is to snip the tips off each almond so that they do not burn during baking.

makes 30 to 40 cookies

115 g or 4 ounces raw almonds, preferably without skin

275 g or 10 ounces butter, chilled

225 g or 8 ounces self-raising flour

115 g or 4 ounces cornflour

170 g or 6 ounces castor sugar

1 teaspoon almond essence

1. If preparing almonds with skin on, scald the raw almonds with hot water to loosen the skin. Cool the almonds, then remove the skin.

2. Snip off both tips of each almond, and then slice each almond laterally into two halves. Next, slice across each lateral half. Set aside the almonds.

3. Mix butter, self-raising flour and cornflour by hand.

4. Add the sugar a little at a time, and then knead. Chill the dough in the refrigerator for a few hours. Thaw for 10 to 20 minutes before using.

5. Preheat oven to 150 to 180 degrees C or 300 to 350 degrees F. Line the baking tray with parchment paper.

6. Shape the pastry into round balls, each about 2.5 cm or 1 inch in diameter. Position one chopped almond quarter into the middle of each ball, press downwards to flatten slightly to resemble thumbprint cookies.

7. Place the cookies on a tray lined with parchment paper. Bake in the oven for 20 minutes until they turn light brown.

8. Remove to cool completely before storing in an airtight container.

Cashew Nut Cookies

The cookies my mother made required a special cutter that followed the kidney C-shape of each cashew nut. If you cannot find a similar cutter, you could use an oval or rectangular cutter, so long as it can accommodate the cashew half in the middle of each cookie.

makes 40 to 50 cookies

230 g or 8 ounces butter
170 g or 6 ounces castor sugar
3 egg yolks
1½ tablespoons evaporated milk
2 teaspoons vanilla essence
310 g or 11 ounces flour

115 g or 4 ounces cornflour
140 g or 5 ounces cashew nuts, halved

egg wash
2 or 3 eggs, beaten

1. Mix the butter with castor sugar, egg yolks, evaporated milk and vanilla essence by hand.

2. Add the flour and cornflour, and knead into a ball of dough. Chill the dough in the refrigerator for a few hours. Thaw for 10 to 20 minutes before using.

3. Preheat oven to 150 degrees C or 300 degrees F.

4. Line a tray with parchment paper.

5. Flour a table surface and a rolling pin. Roll the dough flat into a thickness of 0.5 cm or ¼ inch. Use a cutter to shape out the cookies. Press a cashew half into the middle of each cookie.

6. Place the cookies on the baking tray. Brush with egg wash.

7. Bake in the oven for 20 minutes until light brown. Let the cookies cool completely before storing in an airtight container.

Peanut Cookies

makes 40 to 50 cookies

300 g or 10½ ounces butter
300 g or 10½ ounces castor sugar
300 g or 10½ ounces peanuts (toasted and ground, even with the skin on for colour variation)

450 g or 1 pound flour

egg wash
2 eggs, beaten

1. Cream butter and castor sugar until light and fluffy. Add the ground peanuts and incorporate into the creamed butter.

2. Lastly, fold in the flour. Chill the dough in the refrigerator for a few hours. Thaw for 10 to 20 minutes before using.

3. Preheat oven to 150 degrees C or 300 degrees F.

4. Line a tray with parchment paper.

5. Pinch and divide the dough into balls, each about 2.5 cm or 1 inch in diameter. Press each ball down flat on the baking tray, about 1 cm or ½ inch in thickness.

6. Brush cookies with egg wash.

7. Bake in the oven for 25 to 35 minutes until golden brown. Let the cookies cool completely before storing in an airtight container.

Kueh Bangket

Sago (or Tapioca) Flour Cookies

These dainty, flower-shaped biscuits melt in your mouth. *Kueh bangket*, like *kueh koya* (page 110), *kueh belanda* and *kueh bolu* (page 113), are very traditional Nonya biscuits served during Chinese New Year. Like *kueh belanda*, which literally translates to 'Holland cake', *kueh bangket* has some relation to the Dutch. The word '*bangket*' is close to the Dutch word for biscuit—'*banket*'. The test for quality lies in how firm and pretty it can look while it still melts smoothly in your mouth. More than anything, it should not break up into powdery pieces. It is important to dry-fry the flour and let it cool completely. Therefore, you might want to do this a few days ahead of time. The dough may seem too crumbly, especially if the climate is dry. In that case, you may want to add an additional egg yolk.

I recall my mother's *bangket* to have a lovely vanilla flavour although fussy connoisseurs might insist that there should be some *pandan* flavour as well. If you wish, you could add knotted *pandan* leaves when boiling the coconut milk.

makes 50 to 60 biscuits

450 g or 1 pound *sago* or tapioca flour
170 g or 6 ounces castor sugar
2 egg yolks (3, if climate is dry)
1 egg white
½ teaspoon vanilla essence
½ cup thick coconut milk *

6 *pandan* leaves, tie 3 leaves each
   into a knot
¼ teaspoon bicarbonate of soda
   (optional, for added crispness)

* Some swear by fresh coconut milk , particularly for its flavour which seems fresher and less overpowering than canned milk.

1. Fry the flour and one of the knotted *pandan* leaves over low heat until it is light and fluffy. Keep stirring to prevent the flour from burning at the bottom. Cool completely.

2. Gently boil the thick coconut milk with the other knot of pandan leaves. Let this cool and discard the *pandan* leaves.

3. Preheat oven to 180 degrees C or 350 degrees F. Line a tray with parchment paper.

4. Beat the castor sugar, egg yolks and egg white until the castor sugar dissolves. Add the vanilla essence, bicarbonate of soda (if using) and the boiled coconut milk. Fold in the flour a little at a time, just enough for you to obtain a dough that can be pliable. Remove from the bowl and knead into a firm ball of dough. Cover the dough with a damp cloth, taking small portions of the dough each time for rolling and leaving the rest covered.

5. Reserve the remaining flour for dusting on the table surface and the cookie cutters.

6. Pinch some dough and roll flat into a thickness of 0.5 cm or ¼ inch. Press down a *kueh bangket* cutter to cut the cookies. Use a crimper to pinch the edges of each cookie to give it a delicate design. Repeat until all the dough has been used up.

7. Bake in the oven for 10 minutes. Let the biscuits cool completely before storing in an airtight container.

NOTE: My mother's original recipe, as with those of her peers, called for sago flour. These days, it is rather difficult to find sago flour. It is widely acknowledged that tapioca flour is a fine substitute. I personally tend to disagree. However, in scouring around, I could only locate the Sunflower brand of sago flour at NTUC supermarket, leaving me to settle for tapioca flour for the most part.

Cheeselets

While almost all the other cookies are sweet, cheeselets provide a savoury alternative.
They are baked in thin strips so that the cheesy taste does not become too overwhelming.
My mother used a special serrated cutter or fluted pastry wheel that produced zig-zag
edges along the strips. You could simply settle for a knife to cut them into straight strips.

makes 30 to 40 sticks

165 g or 6 ounces butter
1 egg
220 g or 8 ounces cheddar cheese,
   grated
280 g or 10 ounces flour
½ teaspoon baking powder

1. Mix butter and egg by hand. Add flour, baking powder
and cheese. Knead into a dough. Chill in the refrigerator
for a few hours. Thaw for 10 to 20 minutes before using.

2. Preheat oven to 150 degrees C or 300 degrees F.

3. Line a tray with parchment paper.

4. Dust some flour on a table surface and a rolling pin.
Roll the dough flat into a thickness of 0.75 cm or ⅓ inch.
Use a sharp knife, or a zigzag cutter, to cut out thin strips,
each about 0.75 cm or ⅓ inch thick. Cut each strip into
3.5 cm or 1½ inches long.

5. Place the cookies on the baking tray. Bake in the oven
for 25 minutes or less until crisp.

Sugee Biscuits
Semolina Biscuits

This is an adaptation of the large round *sugee* biscuits I often saw in the Indian corner shops that sold candies and newspapers. They contain *ghee* which can be found in Indian grocery shops and is essentially clarified butter. *Sugee* is another term for semolina and it provides a wonderful texture to the biscuits, making them creamy and nutty at the same time. My mother was partial to the QBB brand.

makes 40 to 50 biscuits

230 g or 8 counces *ghee*, preferably QBB brand

230 g or 8 ounces castor sugar

450 g or 1 pound plain flour

1 teaspoon vanilla essence

30 g or 1 ounce semolina (*sugee*)

egg wash
2 to 3 eggs, beaten

1. Melt the *ghee*. (You can speed up the melting process with a microwave. Interrupt at 1 minute intervals to stir the *ghee*, stop when the *ghee* has melted completely.) Let it cool to room temperature, a process which takes about 30 minutes.

2. Beat the *ghee*, castor sugar and vanilla essence together.

3. Fold in the flour and the semolina a bit at a time until the mixture achieves a dough consistency.

4. Chill the dough in the refrigerator for at least 2 hours. Thaw for 10 to 20 minutes before using.

5. Preheat oven to 150 degrees C or 300 degrees F.

6. Line a tray with parchment paper.

7. Pinch and divide the dough into balls, each about 2.5 cm or 1 inch in diameter. Press each ball down slightly on the baking tray.

8. Brush the biscuits with egg wash.

9. Bake in the oven for 25 to 35 minutes until the biscuits turn a very light brown. Let them cool completely before storing in an airtight container.

Cats' Tongues

makes 30 to 40 biscuits
260 g or 9 ounces flour
250 g or 8 ounces butter
140 g or 5 ounces castor sugar

½ teaspoon vanilla essence
60 g or 2 ounces egg whites

1. Preheat oven to 120 degrees C or 250 degrees F.

2. Grease baking tray with soft butter or line with parchment paper.

3. Sift flour and set aside.

4. Cream butter, sugar and vanilla essence and set aside.

5. Beat egg whites until stiff. Fold into the creamed butter. Then fold in the sifted flour in three portions, taking care to fold completely before adding in the next amount of flour.

6. Spoon mixture into a decorating bag fitted with a nozzle. Pipe each biscuit about 3.75 to 5 cm (1 ½ to 2 inches) long, space them about 2 cm or 1 inch from one other.

7. Bake for 20 to 25 minutes until light brown.

8. Remove the tray from the oven and cool completely on a wire rack. Store the biscuits immediately in airtight containers to prevent curling.

(Image on Page 103 on the right, together with the round *sugee* biscuits on the left.)

Sagun
Crunchy Ground Rice and Roasted Grated Coconut

Sagun is a peculiar treat. It looks like bottled sand from the reclaimed beach, except that it is sugary sweet and also contains grated coconut. The one key ingredient used in the past to retain its crunchiness was *kapor* (slaked lime powder), the same ingredient added to pickled *achar* (page 61).

The children I knew often found it amusing to be able to eat 'sand', especially since we lived in Katong and were close to the beach. To serve it, we would pour some *sagun* into a bowl and use a teaspoon to scoop some to crunch in our mouths.

makes about 3.6 kg or 6 pounds
900 g or 2 pounds grated coconut
1.8 kg or 4 pounds rice flour
   (*tepong beras*)

9 egg yolks
2 tablespoons salt
900 g or 2 pounds sugar

1. Mix the grated coconut and rice flour together.

2. Combine the egg yolks and salt. Beat together. Add to the coconut and *tepong beras* mixture, a bit at a time.

3. Fry the combined mixture in a dry pan or wok over a slow heat, stirring continually until it becomes golden brown.

4. Grind the mixture until it is fine. Let it cool. Then add sugar according to taste. Store in airtight containers.

Dominos

Aunty Paddy insists on Van Houten cocoa powder, which seems appropriate considering that Van Houten was the first company to produce prepared cocoa. The dough is similar to that for daisies (page 108), except that cocoa is added for flavour and contrast in making the checkered appearance of the dominos.

makes 40 to 50 cookies

250 g or 9 ounces butter
230 g or 8 ounces ground sugar
2 egg yolks
1 egg white

1 teaspoon vanilla essence
500 g or 1 pound 2 ounces flour
8 tablespoons cocoa powder,
    Van Houten brand

1. Mix butter, sugar, egg yolks, egg whites and vanilla by hand.

2. Add the flour and knead.

3. Remove two-thirds of the dough and knead in the cocoa powder.

4. Chill the two batches of dough in the refrigerator for a few hours. Thaw for 10 to 20 minutes before using.

5. Preheat oven to 150 to 180 degrees C or 300 to 350 degrees F.

6. Line a tray with parchment paper.

7. Dust some flour on a table surface and a rolling pin. Roll the first batch of dough (plain) flat into a thickness of 0.75 cm or $^1/_3$ inches. Cut into 4 long strips, each about 1 cm or $^1/_2$ inch thick.

8. Clean the table surface and rolling pin. Dust some flour once again. Roll the second batch of dough (cocoa) flat into a thickness of 0.75 cm or $^1/_3$ inches. Cut into 5 long strips, each about 1 cm or $^1/_2$ inch thick.

9. To assemble and produce checkered cookies, the base layer should start with a base white strip in between two cocoa strips. The second layer should alternate such that a cocoa strip is now between two base white strips. The top layer should be a base white strip in between two cocoa strips again.

10. Make sure that the strips are bound tightly together to form a large squared strip comprised of the nine strips. Wrap and chill for at least an hour.

11. Remove from the refrigerator. Use a sharp knife to slice through the strip, about 1 cm or $^1/_2$ inch thick. To prevent the dough from sticking to the knife blade, dip the knife in a glass of cold water after each slicing.

12. Place the cookies on the baking tray. Bake in the oven for 20 minutes or less until crisp.

Daisies

This recipe is similar to that for the basic dough for dominos (page 107). Egg white is added to ensure that the cookies are less brittle and do not break. The dough texture also has to be firmer to prevent broken flowers. The importance lies in mastering the nozzle to achieve the flowered appearance of each cookie. You need the patience and skill to make these pretty flowers. I, like my mother, can sometimes border on severe impatience.

makes 30 to 40 cookies

230 g or 8 ounces butter
230 g or 8 ounces sugar
1 egg yolk
Egg white from half an egg

340 g or 12 ounces flour
1 teaspoon vanilla essence
Maraschino cherries, about 8

1. Mix butter, sugar, egg yolks and egg white by hand.

2. Add the flour and knead.

3. Chill the dough in the refrigerator for a few hours. Thaw for 10 to 20 minutes before using. However, ensure that the dough texture is firmer than usual so that it can be manipulated for the flower design.

4. Preheat oven to 150 to 180 degrees C or 300 to 350 degrees F.

5. Line a tray with parchment paper.

6. Using an icing bag and nozzle, fill the bag up to two-thirds with the dough. Bring the nozzle close to the lined baking tray. Use your writing hand to steady the icing bag and nozzle; use the other hand to squeeze the bag gently. Squeeze out a flower, turning slightly clockwise and anti-clockwise to form jagged petals. Jerk and twist off.

7. Pit the cherries and dice into fine pieces. Dot each center of the cookies with a fine bit of cherry.

8. Place the cookies on the baking tray. Bake in the oven for 20 minutes or less until crisp.

Kueh Koya
Moulded Ground Mung Bean Cookies

I am adding this recipe for posterity. These cookies are the perfect embodiment of most things Nonya—a beautiful creation often only made with skill and patience and with the luxury of time of a bygone era. These days, it is hard to find someone who can make *kueh koya*—the best ones are made in Malacca. My best friend's mother, a Malaccan Nonya, gets her relatives to send them over for Chinese New Year. Her supply tastes just like the ones I remember from my childhood. Everything else I have had does not compare. Even in my mother's generation, not many women could accomplish making *kueh koya* perfectly. It involved sun-drying and grinding *kachang hijau* (green mung beans), packing them compactly into the intricate wooden moulds, baking them in the sun and praying that the weather would be dry, not humid. One also had to be careful when one *ketok* (knocks) the *kueh* out of the mould so that they would not crumble.

makes 40 to 50 cookies servings

450 g or 1 pound dried mung beans, skinned

3¾ cups castor sugar

¾ cups water

1. Sort through the dried beans to remove impurities.

2. Preheat an oven to 95 degrees C or 200 degrees F. Spread the beans on a tray in a single layer and bake in the oven for 1 to 1½ hours, until fragrant and dry.

3. Grind the beans to a fine powder. Divide the powder into three portions. Use one portion at a time. The reason being that the mixture should not dry out too quickly before you knock the *kueh* out of the mould. When you have moulded the first batch, you can then repeat the process with the remaining two portions.

4. Stir one portion with 1¼ cup of the castor sugar and blend well. Then add a teaspoon of water and press down with the back of a wooden spoon. Make sure that the sugar does not form lumps. The mixture should begin to resemble fine breadcrumbs. Press down hard with the wooden spoon, alternating with a teaspoon of water each time. Keep doing this until the mixture looks like a damp flour mixture.

5. Scoop enough of the mixture to fill one cavity of a *kueh koya* mould and press down hard to ensure that the cavity is packed. Do not press down too hard because the *kueh* will end up being overpacked and hence, hard. At the same time, it should not be too loose since the whole *kueh* will not hold together and will crumble. Scrape off any excess with a knife or spatula, until mixture is level with each cavity. While you are doing this, cover the mixing bowl with a damp cloth so the mixture does not dry out.

6. When you have moulded the *kueh*, tilt the mould gently at an angle onto a baking tray to knock them out. This may take a few tries before they come out perfectly whole.

7. Place the baking tray in an oven at 95 degrees C or 200 degrees F for 6 hours or overnight. The *kueh* need to be dried out and are done if they feel light and the centre is not damp.

8. Cool and then store in an airtight container.

NOTE: If the cookies turn soft, pop them back into the oven to dry out before serving.

Kueh Bolu

Mini Moulded Sponge Cakes

This is the Nonya version of the French *madeleine*. Delicate and flowery in look and taste, it is sponge-like and requires its own special mould. The old antique moulds are traditionally made of brass and used over a hot charcoal stove. It had several cavities in one large mould to bake several *kueh* at any one time. My mother, amazingly enough, knew when to remove a baked *kueh bolu* in time so as not to burn it. She often set aside part of the batter and added cocoa powder for colour contrast. Using a satay stick, she would dip into the cocoa batter and then dribble it over each *kueh bolu* to create a flower pattern. Charcoal was and is still considered the best way to make *kueh bolu*. I cannot remember my mother using any other method.

Of course, this will be too challenging for most of us who live in apartments. Therefore, I have adapted the baking of *kueh bolu* in a conventional oven as an alternative method.

makes 40 to 50 mini cakes

15 eggs, separated into egg
    whites and yolks
340 g or 12 ounces sugar
1 teaspoon vanilla or rose essence
675 g or 1½ pounds flour
1 teaspoon baking powder

1. Preheat oven to 220 degrees C or 425 degrees F.

2. Beat the egg whites with half the amount of sugar with an egg-beater until light and fluffy. Then add the remaining sugar, a little at a time, followed by the egg yolks, a few at a time; and finally the vanilla or rose essence. Combine the flour and baking powder. Fold in the flour mixture, a little at a time. *At this point, if the batter is too thin, you can thicken it with a flour and egg mixture.

3. Brush the *kueh bolu* mould with melted butter. Fill three quarters of each cavity with batter. Bake in the oven for 8 minutes.

4. Insert a skewer or *satay* stick into the middle of each *kueh bolu* to test if it is done. It is cooked if the stick comes out clean. Use a butter knife and gently scrape the *kueh bolu* out of the cavity from the sides.

5. Repeat the baking with the remaining batter.

6. If you intend to use a charcoal stove, prepare the stove beforehand. Place the mould over the stove and fill three quarters of each cavity with batter. Cook for about 2 to 3 minutes before using a stick to check it if is cooked.

* To thicken the batter, you can add 3 tablespoons of flour mixed with 2 eggs, beaten.

Kueh Lapis Spekkoek
Dutch-Indonesian Layered Spice Cake

My mother baked several of these and gave them away to her friends for Chinese New Year. The perception is that baking *spekkoek* is a laborious task because one would have to stand by the oven and spread a new layer of batter every few minutes or so. It does not actually take as much time if you have prepped the oven temperature properly.

To judge if a *spekkoek* is of refined quality, one looks at the thinness of each layer. My mother would use a *satay* stick to prick any air bubbles found in each layer. She also had a wooden stamp to press down the baked layer before adding batter to make the next layer.

The important thing is to make your own spice powder. It makes a world of difference.

In the past, *spekkoek* was baked over charcoal. Beginning in the 1960s, my mother only used one special oven to make her *spekkoek*. It was a Baby Belling and could double up as a grill and an oven. For my mother, the oven's appeal was that it could set the temperature lower at the bottom of the oven, higher at the top. This ensured that the cake would not burn so easily. If you do not have a Baby Belling, you can bake *spekkoek* in most modern-day ovens since these would also include a grilling feature.

makes 8 to 12 servings

450 g or 1 pound plain flour

1 teaspoon baking powder

1 teaspoon mixed spice powder (*bumbu kueh*) [See next column]

2 teaspoons ground nutmeg (*buah pala*)

12 egg whites

510 g or 1 pound 2 ounces sugar

30 egg yolks

740 g or 1 pound 10 ounces butter, softened

2 tablespoons condensed milk

90 g or 3 ounces ground almond (optional)

1 teaspoon vanilla essence

2 tablespoons brandy

mixed spice powder (*bumbu kueh*)

5 cm or 2 inches cassia bark (*kayu manis*)* or substitute with cinnamon stick, or 1 teaspoon ground cinnamon

15 to 20 cardamom pods

1 star anise

6 cloves (*bunga chingkay*)

* *Kayu manis* is often assumed to be cinnamon. It is actually cassia bark which is of a lower quality and tastes slightly different. You can distinguish between the two in that cassia is rolled from both sides toward the centre.

grinding the spice powder

1. Rinse and dry the ingredients. Place them on a pan over low heat for about 20 minutes to toast until fragrant.

2. Grind the ingredients, preferably in a clean coffee grinder, until the spices form a fine powder. Sieve through a fine mesh to filter out any small lumps. Store in an airtight container.

baking the cake

1. Preheat the oven using the grill mode at moderate heat (160 degrees C or 325 degrees F). Brush a rectangular cake tin about 22.5 cm by 27.5 cm (9 inches by 11 inches) with some butter. Line the base with parchment paper.

2. Combine the plain flour, baking powder, mixed spice powder and ground nutmeg. Sift and set aside.

3. Using a clean bowl, whisk the egg whites, adding half the sugar a little at a time. Beat until fluffy and set aside.

4. Similarly, beat the egg yolks in another bowl, adding the remaining half of the sugar, a little at a time.

5. Cream butter and condensed milk until fluffy. Fold in the beaten egg yolks. Then fold in the stiff egg white. Fold in the sifted flour mixture and optional ground almond. Finally, add the vanilla essence and brandy.

6. To build cake layers, begin by spreading a ladle of cake mixture on the bottom of the cake tray and grill this in the oven for 2 minutes. Pull out the tray from the oven. With a spatula, preferably a square or broad one, press down the baked layer flat.

7. Spread another ladle of the cake mixture and repeat the grilling process until you achieve at least 10 thin layers for the *spekkoek*.

8. Cover the cake surface with tin foil and switch to bake mode at 180 degrees C or 350 degrees F. Bake for about 5 minutes.

9. Remove the cake from the oven and let it cool. Place a wire rack over the top of the tin and invert to extract the cake out of the tin. Peel off the paper lining from the base of the cake. The cake is sliced and best served a few days later when the spice flavours have developed. Meanwhile, store the cake in an airtight container.

Kueh Bijan
Little Purses of Sesame Seeds

These little purses contain *bijan* or sesame seeds. The edges are twisted and turned in the same way as Indian curry puffs. It is also more convenient to purchase the bifold plastic mould for this treat. Bordering on savoury and sweet, they are delicious.

makes 40 to 50 purses

pastry
150 g or 5½ ounces butter

1 egg

300 g or 10½ ounces flour

½ teaspoon vanilla essence

30 ml or 1 fluid ounce water

filling
90 g or 3 ounces sesame seeds (*bijan*)

90 g or 3 ounces ground peanuts
(fried, then ground)

90 g or 3 ounces castor sugar

eggwash
2 to 3 eggs, beaten

1. For the pastry, mix the butter, egg and vanilla essence by hand. Add the flour and knead. Pour water a bit at a time as you knead, enough to make the dough pliable. Wrap and chill in a refrigerator for a few hours. Thaw for 10 to 20 minutes before using.

2. Preheat oven to 150 to 180 degrees C or 300 to 350 degrees F.

3. Line a tray with parchment paper.

4. Combine the ingredients for the filling in a bowl.

5. Dust a table surface and a rolling pin with some flour. Roll the dough flat into a thickness of 0.5 cm or ¼ inch. Use a circular cookie cutter to cut out rounds of pastry. Place a teaspoon of filling in the middle of each round, dab some water along the edges and fold along the diameter into a semi-circle. Twist and curl the edges. Brush with eggwash.

6. Place on the baking tray.

7. Bake in the oven for 20 minutes until light brown. Let the biscuits cool completely before storing in an airtight container.

Fruit Cake

Fruit cake reveals the Anglophile tendencies of the Peranakans. It was customary for many families to serve it during Chinese New Year. It is perhaps one of those quintessential British legacies shared by Britain's many colonies. I have a friend from Kerala, India, who swears that her mother soaks her candied fruit in brandy for many weeks. My mother would have agreed. The English soaked their fruits to preserve them on the long sea voyages to their territories. In the Caribbean, the fruit is soaked in rum for their version of fruit cake, which they call black cake.

My mother would only accept top-quality brandy for her fruit cake. That meant stashing away all those expensive bottles of Hennessy VSOP which my father would get from his business clients at Christmas-time. The VSOP was only used for her baking and nothing else!

Like the Caribbean black cake, my mother's fruit cake involved the use of a bittersweet caramel which I now know as 'browning'. At first, I could not fathom why her recipe required me to 'burn' brown sugar. The burnt sugar provided the dark brown colour and gave a special essence to the fruit cake.

My friend's parents used to make fruit cake and were always puzzled as to why their candied fruits would sink to the bottom of the cake. My mother's tip was that she coated these little raisins and sultanas in flour so that they would distribute evenly throughout the cake. She also made these cakes early enough before Chinese New Year, to give it time to get more moist and luscious. Ageing the fruit cake brought out the flavour. The cake could be kept for a year, maintained regularly by a sprinkling of brandy to keep the cake 'spiked'.

My mother also used this recipe for her daughters' wedding cakes. It would be a home-made affair of baking the cake, frosted with delicious royal icing layered over marzipan (no less!), cut into individual rectangular slices, wrapped in tin foil to prevent oil seepage before going into pretty silver boxes.

Making fruit cake is a labour of love involving neat chopping of candied fruit and days of preparation. I hope that you make this cake for those you love and in turn, those who receive it will eat it with tremendous joy and appreciate your effort.

makes 6 to 10 servings

230 g or 8 ounces candied
    blackcurrants

230 g or 8 ounces sultanas

230 g or 8 ounces raisins

110 g or 4 ounces candied lemon peel

110 g or 4 ounces glazed cherries
    (a mix of red and green cherries
    adds more colour)

4 tablespoons brandy

1 tablespoon treacle or molasses

60 g or 2 ounces almond, thinly
    slivered

200 g or 7 ounces brown sugar

2 tablespoons water

4 tablespoons evaporated milk

280 g or 10 ounces all-purpose flour

1 teaspoon ground cinnamon

1 teaspoon ground mace

1 teaspoon ground cloves

1 teaspoon ground nutmeg

1 teaspoon salt

230 g or 8 ounces (2 sticks)
    butter, softened

5 eggs

1 teaspoon vanilla extract

to be done the night before

1. Slice or dice blackcurrants, sultanas, raisins and lemon peel into small pieces, about 0.5 cm or ¼ inch.

2. Cut the cherries into eighths.

3. Avoid chopping the fruits haphazardly; otherwise they turn to a sticky mush. If your knife gets sticky, rinse it.

4. Pour in the brandy and toss the candied fruit around. Stir in the treacle or molasses and almond slivers. Leave overnight.

the day you bake

1. Prepare the caramel mixture. Boil 3 tablespoons of the brown sugar with 2 tablespoons of water. Bring down to a simmer until the sugar mixture caramelises to a dark brown tone and the sugar dissolves. Avoid burning it black. Remove from the heat and cool completely. Stir in the evaporated milk, stir and blend. Be careful not to curdle the milk. Set aside.

2. Combine the flour, ground spices (cinnamon, mace, cloves and nutmeg) and salt. Sift the mixture together. Scoop out half of the flour mixture and transfer to a second bowl. In this second bowl, stir in all the chopped fruit and almond slivers and toss to coat evenly.

3. Grease a cake tin about 17.5cm wide by 24cm long or 7 inches by 9 ½ inches. Line with parchment paper. Set aside.

4. Preset oven to 180 degrees C or 350 degrees F.

5. Cream the butter using an electric eggbeater. Pour in the remaining sugar, a bit at a time. Then add one egg at a time, ensuring that each egg is fully creamed before adding the next. Add the vanilla extract and caramel mixture. Continue to beat until the mixture is light. Brown sugar has a higher composition of water than plain white sugar, so be careful not to beat until too watery.

6. Fold in some of the remaining flour, alternate with the fruit mixture, in three to four additions, turn and fold until the cake mixture is well-blended.

7. Pour cake mixture into the greased tin. Bake in the oven for 45 minutes. Lower the heat to 150 degrees C or 300 degrees F and continue to bake for another 1 to 1 ½ hours, depending on the thickness of the cake. The cake is done when it is firm, and when a knife inserted into the middle comes out clean.

8. When the cake is done, leave it in the tin overnight, wrapped tightly in tin foil or stored in an airtight container. The cake is best eaten at least three days after it has been baked. To keep it moist, you can drizzle some brandy on the cake every few weeks and wrap it back up again.

NOTE: Some fruit cake recipes call for baking powder. Some do not. My mother's recipes omitted this. To make sure that she did not make a mistake, I tested her recipe with ½ teaspoon baking powder. While fruit cake without baking powder may look more compact, fruit cake with baking powder seems dryer, tastes a bit more astringent and has a duller shine to the fruit because baking powder acts as a chemical agent.

Sugee Cake
Semolina Cake

There was one particular cake shop in Katong synonymous with *sugee* cake—Cona's Confectionery. The older generation would speak wonderful things about its *sugee* cake and its appearance in many Eurasian weddings where a *sugee* wedding cake was *de rigueur*.

My mother learnt to make *sugee* cake from various friends but ultimately, her recipe was an adaptation of what she considered the best parts of each recipe. A few versions of my mother's recipe included mixed spice powder (*bumbu kueh*, page 114). I have chosen to include it in this recipe, even if most conventional recipes do not, because I recall a distinct spicy kick in her *sugee* cake and suspect that it was attributed to the nutmeg.

makes 6 to 10 servings

230 g or 8 ounces (2 sticks)
    butter, softened
2 tablespoons condensed milk
230 g or 8 ounces semolina
3 tablespoons plain flour
1 teaspoon baking powder
¼ teaspoon mixed spice powder
    (*bumbu kueh*) *
13 egg yolks

230 g or 8 ounces sugar
1 teaspoon vanilla essence
3 egg whites
60 g or 2 ounces almonds, skinned and
    finely chopped
4 tablespoons brandy

* Refer to *kueh lapis spekkoek* (page 114)
for the mixed spice powder recipe.

1. Whisk butter, condensed milk and semolina until white for about 10 minutes. Set aside overnight. Make sure the mixture does not get too soft or greasy.

2. Combine plain flour, baking powder, mixed spice powder and sift. Set aside.

3. When about to bake, preheat oven at 180 degrees C or 350 degrees F. Butter a round cake tin about 22.5 cm or 9 inches in diameter with some butter. Line the base with parchment paper.

4. In a clean bowl, beat the egg yolks, pour in the sugar a bit at a time, followed by the vanilla essence. Beat until the mixture is thick.

5. In another bowl, beat egg whites until light and fluffy.

6. Fold the beaten egg yolks into the semolina mixture, a bit at a time to ensure the batter does not get lumpy. Turn and fold in the flour mixture, followed by the ground almond. Finally, fold in the beaten egg whites. Turn and fold until the cake mixture is well combined.

7. Pour the cake mixture into the greased tin. Bake in the oven for 45 to 60 minutes until the cake surface is golden brown and a stick comes out clean when inserted into it. Cover the top lightly with tin foil if the surface begins to darken too much.

8. Let the cake cool. Place a wire rack over the top of the cake tin and turn it over to get the cake out. Remove the paper lining at the base of the cake.

9. Drizzle the brandy over the cake. The cake will taste better after a day or two. Keep in an airtight container.

Sunday Family Gatherings

*The family was reunited
once again and my mother
made it a tradition
for us all to gather on Sundays.*

My two sisters, Beng and Maggie, returned from London in the late 1970s after having spent several years there. The family was reunited once again and my mother made it a tradition for us all to gather on Sundays for lunch. She spent the morning cooking one of the many one-meal dishes in her repertoire and included a sweet Nonya dessert to conclude it.

While the pounding sounds from the mortar and pestle began in the kitchen, the cool morning breeze would blow through the house and gently stir the curtains. My father would rest on the sofa, read the newspapers and follow "The Road to Wembley" which would be blaring on the television. My sisters often arrived by noontime, dogs in tow. The family would tuck into lunch, sit around to catch up, and even exchange clothes. One sister might have unwittingly bought clothes she no longer fancied or preferred to barter for

A picnic at Changi beach.

Lining up for a traditional hawker treat at Changi beach.

The front patio of our Yarrow Garden house.

a handbag another sister had bought and which she now envied. To this day, we continue to have our 'jumble sale' as we exchange our clothes and accessories with one another. My sister Molly keeps a mental history log to track each item.

In those days, the brothers-in-law and my father played mahjong in the afternoon. Then, everyone would pause for tea and enjoy my mother's special Nonya dessert such as *kueh bongkong* (page 288)—strangely, a favourite among the three of us who are incidentally left-handed—*pulot hitam* (page 296) or *bubor cha cha* (page 301).

In the afternoon, some of us also frequently took a short drive to the beach. We would go for a walk and have some fresh coconut juice. By evening time, we would all gather again for a second round of the same food we had at lunchtime. The food often tasted better this second time round, because the flavours had matured. As the dishes were eaten for two meals, it meant that my mother had to cook in large quantities, as she soon got accustomed to doing so.

My mother preferred to cook what we liked best—*laksa* (page 125), *mee siam* (page 133) or *mee rebus* (page 134). Nonya *laksa* was my all-time favourite. It tasted even better with teaspoonfuls full of my mother's fresh chilli paste, made specially to complement the gravy. *Mee rebus* was Molly's favourite and she often requested for it around her birthday in March.

At other times, my mother would also cook some Malay dishes, including *gado gado* (page 138). "Mummy's *gado gado* is more Indonesian, just like this one," my father once proudly reminisced when we ate in an Indonesian restaurant in New York. In that, he meant that hers included cucumbers and iceberg lettuce, as opposed to the more traditional Malay *gado gado* which relied on boiled cut cabbage, long beans and bean sprouts.

We sometimes also had *nasi lemak* (page 127). Ours was a table spread laden with prawn *sambal* (page 131), sliced cucumber and delicious *otak otak* (page 130) grilled in banana leaves.

This Sunday ritual fed us well, but more importantly, provided a reason for the family to come together on a regular basis. With grandchildren in tow, Sundays meant going to *mama*'s house and it signified very clearly that my mother was the matriarch who held her family together through her lovingly prepared food.

These days, the grandchildren have grown up and prefer spending time on their sports or getting involved in church. Nonetheless, my sisters make it a point to catch up every so often with a family group dinner at one of the seafood restaurants. Sometimes, they still congregate on a Sunday afternoon to carry on their 'jumble sale'. And yet another legacy lives on—they would still sometimes pause for tea and Nonya *kueh* in the afternoon, the way they were taught to by our mother.

Laksa

Rice Noodles in Spicy Coconut Gravy, with Prawns (Shrimps) and Fish Cake

This dish took me under two hours to make. Before this, I had procrastinated making *laksa*, always assuming that it was a painstakingly long process. How wrong I was!

My mother sometimes prepared the spice paste for the gravy ahead of time. In fact, cooking the gravy a day ahead makes it even tastier when you serve. She also believed in blanching the noodles only just before serving, so that the noodles would not become soggy or *kembang*, as she would say.

makes 8 servings

spice paste
60 g or 2 ounces dried chillies, stemmed and deseeded

110 g or 4 ounces candlenuts, diced

300 g or 10½ ounces galangal (*lengkuas*), skinned and cut into strips

250 g or 9 oz lemon grass (*seray*), upper stalks and outer layers removed, sliced thinly

60 g or 2 ounces turmeric (*kunyit*), skinned and cut into strips

1 tablespoon coriander seeds (*ketumbar*), crushed

90 g or 3 ounces *belachan*, cut into small cubes

340 g or 12 ounces shallots, peeled and diced

other ingredients
230 g or 8 ounces dried shrimps

700 g or 1½ pounds medium-size prawns (shrimps), leave shells on

3½ cups coconut milk

15 cups water

½ cup oil

60 g or 2 ounces dried chilli

1 teaspoon *belachan*

1 tablespoon sugar or less, to taste

3 tablespoon salt or less, to taste

1.5 kg or 3 pounds 5 ounces rice noodles

450 g or 1 pound bean sprouts, roots plucked

garnish(can be prepared ahead of time)
20 red chillies, stemmed and deseeded, sliced and ground into a fine paste

1 cucumber, skinned, deseeded and sliced into fine 2.5 cm or 1 inch strips

230 g or 8 ounces fish cake, shallow-fried, sliced into 2.5 cm or 1 inch pieces

1 cup *laksa* leaves (*daun kesom*), optional, sliced finely

1. Soak dried chillies in hot water for 10 minutes. Drain and slice.

2. Grind in sequence candlenuts, galangal, lemon grass, turmeric, coriander seeds, dried chilli, *belachan* and shallots into a paste. To do this, place the first ingredient in a blender, pulse grind, remove the lid, use a spatula to press down the paste, then add the next ingredient and repeat the process. Add water if necessary to form a fine paste. Reserve for Step 5. This can be done ahead of time—freeze the spice paste and thaw it before cooking.

3. Soak the dried shrimps in water for 10 minutes. Drain and dry, then grind until fine.

4. Boil the prawns in 6 cups of water for 20 minutes. Remove and reserve the stock for the gravy. Shell and devein prawns, set aside as garnish.

5. Heat a Dutch oven, then add oil. When the oil is ready for frying, add the dried chillies and *belachan* (this gives the dish a flavourful kick). Stir-fry for 10 minutes to flavour the oil. Discard dried chillies and *belachan*. Lower to medium heat, then add spice paste and ground dried shrimps. Fry till mixture is fragrant and slightly crispy.

6. Add half the coconut milk and 5 cups of water to the paste, stir and bring to a boil for twenty minutes. Then add the prawn stock. Continue to boil, stirring occasionally for 10 minutes. Taste and dilute by adding more liquid if necessary. Add sugar or salt to taste.

7. Thicken with remaining coconut milk and 4 cups of water. Add sugar and salt according to taste. Stirring now and then, simmer uncovered until a layer of red oil surfaces. Turn off heat.

8. When ready to serve, boil some water in a stockpot. Blanch rice noodles and bean sprouts. For each individual serving bowl equivalent to a pasta or soup bowl, place a handful of sprouts at the bottom of the bowl. Top the sprouts with rice noodles. Pour the gravy over the noodles. Using a perforated ladle to press against the noodles, drain the gravy back into the pot. This first pouring of gravy is to 'bathe' and flavour the noodles.

11. Pour the gravy a second time into the bowl of noodles.

12. Garnish with a teaspoon each of cucumber strips, fish cake, fresh chilli paste, a few prawns and a sprinkling of *laksa* leaves. Serve.

Nasi Lemak

Pandan-flavoured Coconut Rice served with Crispy Anchovies and Omelette

It was an old Baba custom to serve *nasi lemak* on the 12th day of a Baba wedding. The elaborate wedding is rarely experienced now. My mother often told me the stories of such a day's events. It would start with the bride's family providing the groom's mother with a section of the bedsheet used on the wedding night. Lime juice was used to test the evidence of the bride's virtue... or lack thereof. If all went well, a roasted suckling pig on a tray took pride of place at a street procession to the bride's family home, for all to see! Then, the wedding would end with a sumptuous meal of *nasi lemak*.

We had our *nasi lemak* on many Sundays. My mother served her *pandan*-flavoured coconut rice with crispy anchovies (*ikan bilis*) (page 128), fried omelette (page 128), cucumber slices, prawn (shrimp) *sambal* (page 133) and best of all, *otak otak* (page 130). Just eating the fragrant coconut rice is so refreshing, and it tastes even more delicious when paired with the numerous side dishes.

If possible, I try not to use jasmine rice. The fragrance of the rice somewhat undermines the full essence that stems from the pandan leaves and the coconut milk. The combined amount of liquid added to the rice should level one pinky finger segment above the layer of rice. In ascribing the term '*lemak*' to a dish, you are referring to the lusciousness derived from the coconut milk. Hence, if you prefer to make the rice more *lemak*, use a higher ratio of coconut milk to water. The coconut cream is often added at the very end because it curdles when exposed to too much heat. If you are using canned coconut milk, you can set aside the creamy layer at the top and add it after the rice is cooked.

makes 8 to 12 servings

2 cups long grain rice

1 cup coconut milk

1 to 1½ cups water

1 ½ teaspoons salt

1 tablespoon lemon juice (optional)

6 *pandan* leaves

½ cup coconut cream

crispy anchovies (*ikan bilis*)
450 g or 1 pound *ikan bilis*
(dried anchovies)

½ to 1 cup peanuts (optional)

Salt to taste

Sugar to taste

fried omelette
6 eggs

Salt to taste

White pepper to taste

1 onion, peeled and sliced thinly (optional)

3 red chillies, sliced thinly (optional)

cucumber slices
For the cucumber slices, skin
2 cucumbers and then slice them
0.5 cm or ¼ inch thick. You may
scoop out the seeds if you prefer.

1.   Rinse the rice about 3 times until the water runs clear. Drain well.

2.   If using a rice cooker, place the rice in the rice cooker pot and add the coconut milk, water, salt and lemon juice. Tie 3 *pandan* leaves into a knot and add to the pot. Cook rice according to the instructions for the rice cooker. When the rice is cooked, stir in the coconut cream and cover for about 5 minutes until the cream is fully absorbed. Remove the *pandan* leaves before dishing out the rice.

3.   If you are not using a rice cooker, add the rice, coconut milk, water, salt and *pandan* leaves to a medium saucepan and bring to a boil. Then lower the heat and simmer, covered. The rice should cook in about 20 minutes but make sure you keep watching the pot to prevent the rice from scorching. You may add more water and fluff the rice to prevent the rice from sticking to the bottom of the pot. When the rice is cooked, add the coconut cream and cover again for about 5 minutes until the cream is fully absorbed. Remove the *pandan* leaves before serving.

4.   As an optional extra step, you could place the cooked rice on a shallow tray that fits into a steamer pot. Steam the rice, along with the remaining *pandan* leaves tied into a knot, for 5 to 10 minutes. Then serve. I find this extra step adds a richer flavour and texture to the rice.

5.   My mother's *nasi lemak* is served with crispy anchovies, fried omelette, cucumber slices, prawn (shrimp) *sambal* and *otak otak* (recipes follow below and overleaf).

crispy anchovies (*ikan bilis*)

1.   The better dried anchovies are sold in local provision shops in Asia or in the medicinal shops in Chinatowns abroad. I prefer mine about medium in size with more body than head.

2.   Rinse the anchovies in water and pat dry with paper towels. Shallow-fry in a wok of hot oil, along with the peanuts if you are adding them. Remove with a strainer and transfer to a plate lined with paper towels to draw the excess oil out. Add sugar and salt to taste.

fried omelette

1.   Beat 6 eggs in a bowl and add a pinch of salt and white pepper. You can also add sliced onions and/or fresh red chillies.

2.   Heat a frying pan and add a coating of oil. When the oil glistens, add enough egg to form a thin omelette. When bubbles appear, press them down with a spatula and fry until the omelette lifts off easily from the pan. Be careful not to burn. To cook the underside, slide the omelette over to a plate, then flip the plate over and release the omelette into the pan for a brief moment. Transfer to a plate to cool before cutting up into eighths.

Otak Otak

Spicy Fish Paste Grilled in Banana Leaves

Unlike the skinny sticks of *otak otak* commonly available today, this Nonya recipe below produces *otak otak* that are plump with fish meat and hence, very delicious.

When I have to use frozen banana leaves instead of fresh ones, I buy double the amount required. Frozen leaves, in my experience, tend to tear easily even after I thaw and scald them gently. It never hurts to have spare leaves lying around. Make sure to blend the paste to a fine texture. *Otak otak* is supposed to be smooth.

makes 12 large portions

230 g or 8 ounces fresh banana leaves or 450 g or 1 pound frozen banana leaves

20 sharp toothpicks (alternatively, use metal staples)

800 g or 1¾ pound Spanish mackerel (*ikan tenggiri*) fillet, or a mix of mackerel and red snapper

spice paste
1½ cups coconut milk
1 egg
1 tablespoon sugar
½ teaspoon salt

1 tablespoon cornflour

2 teaspoons coriander seeds (*ketumbar*)

170 g or 6 ounces galangal (*lengkuas*), skinned and julienned

85 g or 3 ounces lemon grass (*seray*) upper stalks and outer layers removed, sliced thinly

30 g or 1 ounce turmeric (*kunyit*), skinned and julienned

30 g or 1 ounce *belachan*

15 dried red chillies, soaked in hot water

5 red chillies

110 g or 4 ounces shallots, peeled diced

1. Pour boiling water over banana leaves to soften them. Wipe leaves dry. With a pair of scissors, trim the veins along edges of the leaves. Cut half of the leaves into 25 cm or 10 inches square. Cut the remaining leaves into small 8-cm or 3-inch squares.

2. Clean fish and remove any bones. Cut into small pieces. Mince or blend fish into a paste.

3. Combine the coconut milk, egg, sugar, salt and cornflour in a bowl. Stir to remove any lumps. Set aside.

4. Pound or grind the coriander seeds and sieve to retain the fine powder.

5. Add and pound the rest of the spice paste ingredients in the order of sequence given. Add the bowl of coconut milk and egg mixture. Blend the ingredients well into a fine mixture. Do this in batches if necessary.

6. Add the spice paste to the fish paste and well mix together.

7. To wrap *otak otak*, use a larger square piece of banana leaf, as the base. Place a smaller banana leaf in the middle of the large leaf and spread with 4 tablespoons of fish paste. Then cover the paste with another small banana leaf. Fold two opposite ends of the large base leaf over to close the parcel. Then fold over the two short ends and fasten with toothpicks or staple to seal the edges. Repeat with remaining ingredients.

8. Grill or broil *otak otak* for approximately 15 minutes. Turn parcels over occasionally to cook all sides.

Prawn (Shrimp) Sambal

My mother, like many Nonyas of her generation, used food nomenclature to create nicknames and describe people or things. For a classmate of mine who was often giggly and flirtatious, my mother had this to say: "*Meglitik macham udang kenar chelor*", which translated means "prawn (shrimp) jumping around after getting scalded". Ouch.

makes 4 to 8 servings

450 g or 1 pound small prawns (shrimps)

4 tablespoons tamarind (*assam*), soaked in 1½ cups hot water

15 g or ½ ounce dried chillies, soaked in hot water

1 teaspoon *belachan*, diced

300 g or 10½ ounces shallots, peeled and diced

2 tablespoons oil

1 teaspoon salt

1 tablespoon sugar

1. Shell the prawns and set aside.

2. Strain the tamarind juice and discard the seeds and fibre.

3. Remove the dried chillies from bowl of water.

4. Blend or pound the dried chillies, *belachan* and shallots in this order.

5. Pre-heat a wok or frying pan over high heat. Add oil and when it is glistening, lower heat. Fry pounded ingredients until red oil bubbles through.

6. Add salt and sugar. Pour in the tamarind juice. Finally add the shelled prawns and stir until they are just cooked. Do not overcook the prawns.

Mee Siam

Spicy Fried Vermicelli with Prawn (Shrimp) and Egg Garnish

Family friends often called my mother, urging her to teach them how to prepare her lovely version of *mee siam*. It was a family favourite and appeared regularly at children's birthday parties as tea-time fare for the adults.

makes 8 servings

spice paste
170 g or 6 ounces dried shrimps, soaked in hot water for 10 minutes and pat dry

60 g or 2 ounces dried chillies, stemmed and deseeded, soaked in hot water

60 g or 2 ounces *belachan* cut into small cubes

230 g or 8 ounces shallots, peeled and diced

other ingredients
500 g or 1½ pounds dried vermicelli (*bee hoon*)

¾ cup oil for frying

350 g or 2 pounds bean sprouts (*taugeh*), roots plucked

2 cups water

1 tablespoon salt

2 tablespoons sugar

150 g or 5¼ ounces fermented soy bean paste (*taucheo*)

100 g or 3 ounces tamarind (*assam*), soaked in 2½ cups of hot water

4 cups thin coconut milk (add 5 cups water to a 425 ml or 14 oz tin of coconut milk and measure from there)

2 big red onions, peeled and sliced

2 to 6 tablespoon sugar, or more if gravy is salty

garnish (can be prepared ahead of time)
4 pieces firm bean curd (*taukua*), seared brown on all sides and cut into 1-cm or ½-inch cubes

450 g or 1 pound medium prawns (shrimps), boiled, shelled and sliced into halves

12 calamansi limes (*limau kesturi*), cut into halves

10 hard-boiled eggs, peeled and sliced or quartered

1 bunch garlic chives (*ku chai*), chopped into short lengths

1. In a blender, add dried shrimps, dried chillies, *belachan* and shallots in that order. Process to a fine paste. This can be prepared ahead of time and frozen. Thaw before cooking.

2. Soak vermicelli in hot water for 1 hour to soften. Then drain the vermicelli. Line a baking sheet with parchment paper. This will be used to hold the noodles later.

3. Heat oil in a wok over high heat. When oil glistens, lower heat and pour in the spice paste. Stir-fry till fragrant and red oil bubbles through. Scoop out some oil and about ½ cup spice paste to reserve for the gravy.

4. Add water, salt and sugar to remaining spice paste and let it boil. Add bean sprouts and stir for a minute. Set aside bean sprouts. Add vermicelli to the wok. Stir with tongs and let the vermicelli soak in the spice paste. Return the bean sprouts to the wok to mix through.

5. Lower the heat to medium, stir continuously. Be careful not to let vermicelli stick to the bottom of the wok. Cook till vermicelli is soft and slightly moist. Transfer to the tray lined with parchment paper. Let cool before serving.

6. In a pot, add the reserved spice paste and oil, along with the fermented bean paste. Strain the tamarind juice and pour into the pot. Add the coconut milk slowly and let boil. Then add the sliced red onion. Turn down heat to simmer. Add sugar to taste. If gravy is salty, add more water and sugar and stir.

7. To serve, dish out vermicelli and top with bean curd cubes and sliced prawns. Spoon gravy over. Squeeze lime juice over the dish, arrange sliced eggs on top and sprinkle with chopped chives. Add a dab of prawn *sambal* (page 131) to kick up the spiciness.

Mee Rebus

Yellow Noodles in a Spicy-Sweet Gravy with Garnish

As a child, Friday night was movie night for me. I continue this tradition with my children today. Back then, my mother would turn the air conditioner on and the lights out in her bedroom. We would cuddle on her bed or a mattress on the floor. Our 13-inch black-and-white TV would be tuned in to Malaysia's RTM to catch a classic feature such as a 1950s film by Malaysia's movie and TV legend, P. Ramlee, who was incidentally our neighbour at Yarrow Gardens. In the film, the characters would often sit by a roadside hut slurping *mee rebus*—or at least that's what I imagined the dish to be. *Mee rebus* was a staple in school tuckshops during my school days and the dish is still a favourite of my sister Molly, who often requested my mother to make it for her birthday.

makes 8 servings

spice paste
1 teaspoon ground coriander (*ketumbar*)
5 cm or 2 inch galangal (*lengkuas*), skinned and julienned
2.5 cm or 1 inch turmeric (*kunyit*), skinned and julienned
1 clove garlic, peeled
8 shallots, peeled and diced finely
½ teaspoon *belachan*
6 dried chillies, soaked in hot water

other ingredients
4 tablespoons oil
2 tablespoons curry powder, made into a paste with some water
3 tablespoons fermented soy bean paste (*taucheo*), pounded finely
6 cups water
2 tablespoons plain flour, made into a slurry with some water
½ teaspoon salt
3 potatoes, peeled and quartered; or 3 tomatoes, quartered (optional)*

600 g or 1 pound 5 ounces yellow noodles
300 g or 11 ounces bean sprouts, roots plucked

garnish
300 g or 11 ounces prawns (shrimps), boiled and shelled
1 piece firm bean curd (*taukua*), seared brown on all sides, cut into small cubes
3 hard-boiled eggs, peeled and sliced
6 shallots, peeled, sliced finely and fried until crispy and brown
3 green chillies, sliced
1 bunch garlic chives (*ku chai*), chopped finely
4 calamansi limes (*limau kesturi*), halved

* Boiled and simmered potatoes are sometimes added to thicken the gravy. My mother sometimes even substituted potatoes for tomatoes, to give the *mee rebus* added flavour.

1. Pound or blend the ground coriander, galangal, turmeric, garlic, shallots, *belachan*, dried chillies in the order given. Pound the mixture into a fine paste.

2. Heat oil in a wok or Dutch oven till it glistens. Lower heat and stir in spice paste, followed by curry paste, then fermented soy bean paste. Be careful not to scorch the mixture. When fragrant, add water and bring to a boil.

Add potatoes or tomatoes, if used. Add the flour slurry and stir to avoid lumps forming. Turn down heat and simmer until gravy thickens, about 15 minutes. Season with salt.

3. Blanch noodles and bean sprouts. Portion noodles and sprouts into serving bowls and spoon gravy over. Top with a bit of each garnish and serve.

Hokkien Mee Soup
Yellow Noodles in Soup with Prawn (Shrimp) Garnish

Back in the early 1980s, even as a large family, we would gather at our favourite *makan* (eating) spots from time to time. One was at the Hong Lim HDB Complex near Chinatown which was coincidentally named after our ancestor. But the more important reason was that the hawker centre there had a concentration of very good Hokkien *mee* soup stalls.

As the family got bigger and it became harder to seat everyone, my mother began to include this noodle soup in her Sunday repertoire. Unfortunately, her recipe for this was incomplete when I did my research and I had to approximate as much as I could, at the same time acknowledging that it would never mirror the secret recipe that the hawkers used. I incorporated sensible things that a home cook would do to improve the flavour of a soup stock, by brewing sufficiently long and by enhancing the taste through the contribution of the various ingredients.

What I most remember of all those meals at the Hong Lim hawker centre was the large prawns (shrimps) that enhanced the dish. And to me, it seemed like the larger the prawns, the better the dish tasted.

makes 6 to 8 servings

soup stock

300 g or 10½ ounces pork ribs

450 g or 1 pound large prawns (shrimps)

50 g or 1½ ounces pork fat, cut into 0.5 cm or ¼ inch cubes

10 shallots, peeled and sliced thinly crosswise

3 cloves garlic, peeled and minced

1½ tablespoons sugar

300 g or 10½ ounces belly pork

½ teaspoon salt

1 teaspoon dark soy sauce

1½ tablespoons light soy sauce

noodles and garnish

400 g water convolvulus (*kang kong*), lower stems removed and leafy part cut into 3 cm or 1½ inches lengths

300 g or 10½ ounces bean sprouts, heads and tails plucked

200 g or 7 ounces rice vermicelli (*bee hoon*)

450 g or 1 pound yellow noodles

4 red chillies, sliced finely

3 tablespoons light soy sauce

soup stock

1. Rinse pork ribs in cold water, then dab dry with paper towels.

2. Boil a pot of water. Blanch the prawns until cooked, a few at a time using a wire strainer. Remove the prawns and let them cool. Then peel and devein the prawns. Reserve the shells. Set aside.

3. Place a large stockpot over medium heat. Add the pork fat and let it fry until golden brown and crispy. During this process, the fat will release oil. Remove the crispy pork fat cubes and transfer these to a plate lined with paper towels.

4. Reserve the oil in the stockpot. Add some more frying oil if needed. Add the sliced shallots and fry until light brown and crispy. Remove the crispy shallots.

5. Finally, add the minced garlic, sugar, prawn shells and pork ribs to the stockpot. Brown all sides of the pork bones, then cover with just enough cold water. Bring the water to a boil, then cover and simmer for 2 hours until you obtain a tasty stock. Skim occasionally to remove any froth and gristle.

6. Remove the ribs and using a strainer, remove and discard the prawn shells. Turn up the heat, add the pork belly into the pot and boil until it is well-cooked. Remove the pork belly and let it cool. Turn off the heat. Slice the pork into thin pieces for garnish.

7. If possible, strain once again with a fine sieve to clarify the stock. Season the stock with salt and dark and light soy sauces.

noodles and garnish

1. Bring a large pot of water to a rolling boil. Next to it, prepare a large pot of cold water. Do the next steps only when you are about to serve.

2. Prepare, in a large wire strainer, and in the order given, some water convolvulus, bean sprouts, a small handful of rice vermicelli and twice the amount of yellow noodles. Scald these in the pot of boiling water for 1 to 2 minutes. Remove and soak in the pot of cold water. Tilt the strainer handle over and transfer the cooked ingredients into a soup bowl.

3. Ladle enough warm soup stock to cover the noodles. Garnish with 2 or 3 large prawns, sliced pork belly, crispy pork cubes and fried shallots. Place some light soy sauce in a small sauce dish with some sliced red chillies on the side. Serve immediately.

Gado Gado
Salad with Peanut Sauce Dressing

A few years ago, my father and I went to an Indonesian restaurant and ordered *gado gado*. He told me that my mother's *gado gado* was rather similar to the Indonesian version, as it included cucumbers and fresh lettuce. Our family also prefers to have *ikan tamban* crackers or prawn crackers with our *gado gado*.

makes 4 to 6 servings

peanut sauce

45 g or 1½ ounce dried chillies, soaked hot water for ½ hour

55 g or 2 ounces tamarind (*assam*), soaked in 2 cups hot water

70 g or 2½ ounces shallots, peeled and diced

30 g or 1 ounce garlic, peeled

1½ teaspoons *belachan*

¾ cup oil

60 g or 2 ounces white sugar

30 g or 1 ounce *gula melaka*

40 g or 1½ ounce brown sugar

10 g or 1 ounce salt

2 tablespoons rice wine vinegar

¼ cup coconut milk

340 g or 12 ounces ground peanut

salad

½ head lettuce, leaves cut into 2.5 cm or 1 inch squares

500 g or 1 pound 2 ounces red bliss potatoes

½ head cabbage, leaves cut into 2.5 cm or 1 inch squares

150 g or 5½ ounces long beans, trimmed and cut into 5 cm or 2 inch pieces

150 g or 5½ ounces bean sprouts, heads and tails plucked

3 pieces firm soy bean curd (*taukua*)

2 pieces fermented soy bean cakes (*tempeh*) (optional)

1 cucumber, seeds removed and cut into bite-size pieces

4 hard-boiled eggs, peeled and quartered

300 g or 11 ounces compressed rice cakes (*lontong*), diced into 2.5 cm or 1 inch cubes (optional) *

Prawn crackers (*keropok*)

* The compressed rice cake can be prepared by cooking the rice using a rice cooker. When the rice is fully cooked and still hot, compress it into a loaf tin, invert and slice into 2.5-cm or 1-inch cubes.

peanut sauce

1. Drain soaked chillies and set aside. Strain the tamarind juice and discard the seeds and fibre.

2. Combine the chillies, shallots, garlic and *belachan* and pound or grind to a fine paste. Heat a wok with some oil over low heat and fry the spice paste until fragrant.

3. Add 1½ cups of the tamarind juice, followed by white sugar, *gula melaka*, brown sugar and salt. Stir till the sugars and salt dissolve. Add rice wine vinegar and bring to a boil. Lower heat and simmer. Stir in coconut milk and ground peanuts, continue to simmer till it reaches desired consistency. If gravy is too thick, add more tamarind juice to thin out. Set aside.

salad

1. Place potatoes in a pot of cold water and bring to boil. After 20 minutes or so, when a knife can be inserted easily into a potato, remove and shock potatoes in a pot of ice cold water. Drain and leave to cool. Skin potatoes and quarter.

2. Bring another pot of salted water to a boil. Using a strainer, blanch the cabbage, long beans and bean sprouts a portion at a time. Shock the blanched vegetables in a pot of ice cold water to stop the cooking process. Drain in a colander, then leave on a large tray to cool.

3. Add some oil to a hot frying pan. Shallow-fry the firm bean curd until it turns light golden brown. Rest it on a plate lined with paper towels. Repeat to fry the fermented soy bean cakes. Rest these also on another plate lined with paper towels. When cool, slice the firm bean curd and fermented soy bean cakes into 2.5-cm or 1-inch squares. Set aside.

4. To serve, arrange a bit of each vegetable, firm bean curd, fermented soy bean cakes, egg and rice cakes on serving plates. Dress with some of the peanut sauce. On the side, add a few prawn crackers.

5. Let each guest toss his or her own *gado gado* just before eating.

Life of the Party

*My mother loved to throw parties.
There were the expected weddings and
children's birthday parties.*

A buffet party at Yarrow Gardens.

The buffet table was set up in the driveway.

No place held as esteemed a place for her as the Spring Court restaurant, when it was still situated along Upper East Coast Road. My sisters and I teased her that she had a secret share in the business. Later, I learnt why Spring Court held a special place in her heart. The original location was in the old Great World Amusement Park where my parents met for the first time. Romantic notions aside, the Chinese restaurant also maintained the traditional banquet dishes we were accustomed to, less modernised and interfered with by ambitious chefs.

For parties, my mother usually co-ordinated all the tasks. She had a tiny red book that contained the names and addresses of old family friends and guests. Even today, we refer to the book when we have to send out invitations.

My paternal grandmother blowing out candles
for her 64th birthday.

Angela greeting Father Christmas
at Loyang where our family used to
celebrate the holidays.

A joget with eepoh Seck Choo,
a distant grandaunt.

A tok panjang to celebrate my paternal
grandmother's birthday.

In the later years, planning for parties reinvigorated my mother and was a healthy distraction; they injected life into her as much as she did to them. As time went on, there seemed fewer parties to plan for. She began to focus on her declining health instead. I tried to motivate her. During our last lucid phone call before her final and sudden hospitalisation, I urged her to start planning my father's 75th birthday party. She let out a calm laugh, almost like a brief sigh, which seemed to signal she was no longer as energetic and interested in organising parties.

Even when parties were held in a Chinese restaurant, my mother would also go the extra mile to prepare and bring the customary red eggs (page 190) and *yew peng* (page 191) for a baby's first month celebration, or *kueh ku* (page 188)

for birthdays. She did just that for her 70th birthday. She made *ang ku kueh* (or red *kueh ku*) and packed 10 in each clear plastic box for each guest. More recently, on my father's 80th birthday, my sister Nancy tried to repeat the same feat. We had to scout for the best *ang ku kueh* in town.

Other parties were often hosted at home and my mother went into high gear for a few days to cook the buffet spread. The guest list remained the same for decades, a testament to the enduring friendships my parents kept.

My childhood birthday parties were delightful. The beverage company my father worked for lent us the playground set in addition to child-sized tables and chairs. The company also delivered crates of soft drinks and the children loved the orange soda or 7-Up. My father could also cater a wide selection of *dimsum* from the Stadium restaurant that he managed. To complement the children's selection, my mother served up cream puffs, chicken drumsticks and meatbuns called bun *susi* or *pang susi* (page 168). The adults had their own buffet prepared by my mother. This would surely include *mee siam* (page 131), ever a crowd-pleaser.

When each of my sisters turned 21, it was customary to have the key-shaped cake. Most times, it was pre-ordered from a reliable Katong bakery. However, I believe my mother made one or two of those cakes by using tracing paper to draw out a key template for the sponge cake. To cater to the preferences of the young adults, she contributed more Western dishes. Plenty of prawn fritters, chicken drumsticks, sweet and sour pork, and a dish now forgotten to us—a large tender slab of beefsteak rolled and tied, cushioning a line of hard boiled eggs in the centre.

Smaller gatherings would see us having a sit-down popiah (page 33) party around the dining table. We would even compete to see who could eat the most popiah. Leftover filling was recycled the next day into fried *popiah* (page 153), or *pai ti* (page 149), crispy cups that held the filling.

When our family friends reunited once again at my father's 80th birthday, we all reminisced about those gatherings, the incredibly delicious spread, the laughter, and the good times.

Nancy helping me cut my birthday cake.

A tok panjang on my sister Nancy's wedding day.

My mother (left) and one of her best friends, Aunty Brown—a regular guest at our parties.

A few of the same grandaunts, many decades later. My mother's stepsister, Eng, is on the extreme right.

My parent's 50th wedding anniversary, one of the happiest celebrations in my mother's life.

Popiah

Spring Rolls of Shreds of Bamboo Shoots, Jicama, Pork and Prawns (Shrimps)

There are a couple of tips to make delicious *popiah*. It is always better to make the filling the day before to allow the flavour to flourish by the time you serve the meal. In the olden days and right up to my childhood in the 1980s, the filling was cooked over a slow charcoal fire. My mother would set up a makeshift charcoal stove and have her huge military-sized pot ready to cook her *popiah*. Alas, we no longer use charcoal. Nevertheless, a slow simmering fire is still best.

My father also recalls that in our family, we used more *bangkuang* than bamboo shoots, the opposite of many other *popiah* recipes. This is because *bangkuang* provides a sweeter flavour and crunchier texture to the filling.

As for the garnishing, my mother made egg omelette which she would then cut into strips. When we ran out of omelette strips, we would replenish with hard-boiled eggs.

My mother often wrapped *popiah* for her guests to take home. To ensure that they stayed intact and not break up, she wrapped a sheet of typing paper or a clear plastic sheet around each *popiah* roll to protect it.

Once again, the Nonya cook's *popiah* skills were based on the fineness of her *bangkuang* and bamboo shoot strips. They had to be *alus* (fine), not *kasar* (coarse). Unless you have a fastidious father like mine, or wish to impress a future Nonya mother-in-law, you might as well forget about cutting and slicing the *bangkuang* and bamboo shoot strips so finely because the time and effort may frustrate you and kill your joy over having future *popiah* parties. It's okay to cheat if you have to, by using an excellent food processor or Japanese mandolin to do the slicing work for you. It will cut down your prep work by more than half.

There was always individual preference as to what was spread first on the *popiah* skin—chilli paste, garlic, the dark sweet sauce or the lettuce. Everyone had a strong conviction. I'll tell you mine on page 148.

makes 20 servings

filling

600 g or 1¼ pounds pork (legmeat or belly pork, depending on preference)

600 g or 1¼ pounds small-to medium-sized prawns (shrimps), shells and heads intact

1 large tin bamboo shoots (in chunks), dry weight of 500g or 1 pound 1 ounce

2.5 kg or 5½ pounds jicama (*bangkuang*)

About ½ cup oil for frying

4 square pieces of firm soy bean curd (*taukua*)

300 g or 12 ounces garlic, peeled and pounded into a paste

6 tablespoons fermented soy bean paste (*taucheo*), finely pounded if necessary

5 tablespoons dark soy sauce

1 to 1½ tablespoons salt, adjust according to taste

2 tablespoons sugar

filling

1. Rinse and pat dry the pork. Place in a pot filled with sufficient cold water to cover. Boil for about 15 minutes until pork is half-cooked. Skim off any froth or gristle from stock. Remove the pork and set the stock aside.

2. Shell and devein the prawns Reserve the shells and set aside. Heat 2 tablespoons of oil in a pot. Fry shells until they turn orange and fragrant. Add the pork stock and bring to a boil. Lower heat and simmer for as long as an hour. Sieve the stock and discard the shells. At this point, you should have at least 5 cups of stock. For a richer taste, I prefer to grind my shells along with the stock in the food processor, then boil and simmer the entire stock before straining.

3. Rinse bamboo shoots and place in a small pot with enough cold water to cover them. Add some salt. Bring to a boil for about 20 minutes. Drain and leave aside to cool before slicing.

4. Peel and quarter the jicama. Slice into fine strips of about 4 cm or 1½ inches long and less than 0.25 cm or ⅛ inches thin. Slice bamboo shoots and pork into fine strips of the same dimensions as the jicama.

5. Heat ¼ cup of oil in a frying pan. Sear the firm bean curd briefly on all sides until golden brown. Remove and slice thinly into the same dimensions as jicama strips. Set aside.

6. Heat remaining oil in a large wok or pot. When the oil glistens, fry the minced garlic paste until golden brown. Stir in the fermented soy bean paste and fry until it is fragrant. Add the prawn and pork strips.

7. Add the bamboo shoots and jicama strips, followed by half of the pork and prawn stock. Bring the pot to a boil; stir in the soy sauce, sugar and a tablespoon of salt. Bring down the heat and simmer for about an hour.

8. Add the *taukua*. Simmer for another 30 minutes, adding the remaining pork and prawn stock, as well as salt if needed. If you run out of stock and the gravy looks dry, you may add water. Adjust the amount of salt and sugar according to taste.

9. Stir the filling occasionally to prevent any of it from sticking to the bottom of the pot.

10. Leave the filling aside to cool thoroughly before refrigerating. Be careful not to let the filling go rancid, especially in a hot climate.

11. The filling should be out of the refrigerator at least 2 hours before serving, and warmed up over a medium heat 30 minutes beforehand. I leave the filling to simmer over low heat throughout the meal.

garnish

2 kg or 4 pounds *popiah* skin, plain skin
   or egg skin or combination of both

450 g or 1 pound Chinese lettuce,
   about 2 heads

900 g or 2 pounds cucumber

450 g or 1 pound red chillies

450 g or 1 pound garlic

450 g or 1 pound bean sprouts,
   heads and roots plucked

5 Chinese sausages (*lapcheong*),
   steamed and sliced

450 g or 1 pound small- to medium- sized
   prawns (shrimps), shelled and deveined
   (the shells could go towards preparing
   the stock for the filling)

1.5 kg or 3 pounds 5½ ounces fresh crab
   or 500g or 1 pound frozen crab meat
   (only if it is the chunky authentic meat)

4 eggs

1 bottle sweet flour sauce

1 bunch coriander (cilantro) leaves,
   stems removed

450 g or 1 pound peanuts, roasted and ground

garnish

1.   Seal and refrigerate *popiah* skin or store in an air-tight container. If refrigerated, bring it out about 15 to 30 minutes before serving and cover with a damp cloth.

2.   Remove the heads from the lettuce. Tear the leaves into halves, along the length of the stem. Break the stem or remove altogether. Rinse three times in a large pot of cold water to remove dirt. Pat dry.

3.   Skin the cucumber. Slice into pieces, each about 4 cm or 1½ inches long. Discard the core of seeds. Julienne into thin matchstick strips, using a mandolin if you have one.

4.   Remove the stems from the chillies, and remove the seeds if you prefer. Pound or grind into a fine red paste. Store in a container prior to serving. This can be done a few days beforehand.

5.   Peel the garlic. Pound into a fine paste. Store in an airtight container prior to serving. This can be done a few days beforehand. You may fry a third of the pounded garlic until a crispy light brown. Use it as a garnish to add to a *popiah*.

6.   Prepare a steamer. Use the boiling water to blanch the bean sprouts in an instant. Shock the bean sprouts in cold water and drain. Set aside.

7.   Steam the Chinese sausages for about 5 minutes. Slice thinly.

8.   Place the prawns in the steamer and let them cook until they are bright red. Leave aside to cool before halving each prawn along its length.

9.   Rinse and pat dry the crab. Steam the crab until the shell turns a bright red. Let it cool before cracking the shell open to dig out the crab meat flakes. If you are using frozen crabmeat, thaw it in the refrigerator overnight and drain any excess liquid.

10. With the eggs, you may prepare hard-boiled ones if you run out of time. Remove the shell and slice each egg into eight segments. Otherwise, break the eggs into a bowl, season with some salt and pepper. Heat a thin layer of oil in a small omelette pan. Scoop some of the egg mixture onto the pan to fry an omelette. Repeat until you use up the eggs. Let it cool completely. Then roll up each omelette tightly and slice into very fine strips.

table layout

1. Arrange a set of small bowls and platters to contain the various garnishes. Each set of this should serve at least 4 guests. Hence, if you are seating at long table with at least 8 guests, you should place a bowl at each of the two ends of the table.

2. One large platter of *popiah* skin would suffice and could be passed around the table. My mother had a special round Tupperware container just for her *popiah* skin. It was essential to cover it at all times, either in a container or under a damp cloth so that the skin would not dry out. (Note: If they happen to dry out, you can sprinkle water over it and microwave for a minute or steam for less than 5 minutes to make it supple once again.)

3. The filling should be presented in large bowls (similar to pasta or salad bowls).

4. Excess gravy has a tendency to drench and disintegrate a wrapped *popiah*. To prevent that, I place a colander inside the serving bowl so that it holds the filling while it drains excess gravy away. (Note: Traditionally, a smaller rice bowl was inverted and placed in the middle of the serving bowl before the filling was piled in. The empty space under the inverted bowl served as a catchment area for excess gravy.)

5. I tend to arrange my small platters of garnish around the bowl, in the order of which it would be used to wrap a *popiah*. Each platter has its own teaspoon. There would be a platter of the lettuce leaves, followed by the small bowl of black sweet flour sauce, dish of garlic paste and dish of chilli paste. Next comes the filling. After that, the Chinese sausage, prawns, crabmeat, omelette strips, cucumber strips, bean sprouts, coriander leaves and finally, the ground peanuts.

wrap and roll

1. Often, *popiah* ends up getting eaten with the hands. I also leave a lot of paper napkins around to wipe the plate dry before wrapping *popiah*. It was traditional for Baba families like mine to use our British Sheffield knives to slice *popiah*.

2. To wrap a *popiah*, line the plate with one *popiah* skin. Then tear half of another skin, preferably the tougher white skin and place it on top of the lower half of the first skin. This top layer serves as extra protection to prevent any tearing if the *popiah* gets too wet.

3. Spread a layer of the sweet sauce in a line, across the lower third of the skin, then add garlic and chilli paste. Adjust the amounts according to taste.

4. Next, lay the lettuce to over the spread of condiments. This is followed by 2 tablespoons of filling arranged nicely to form a 'cylinder' over the lettuce leaf. I would then garnish with the Chinese sausage, prawns, crabmeat, omelette strips, cucumber strips, bean sprouts and coriander leaves, plus a generous sprinkling of ground peanuts.

5. To create the *popiah*, lift the lowest half of the skin (closest to you) and fold over the filling away from you. Then fold the left and right sides over the filling. Roll upwards, away from you until the *popiah* becomes a tight roll packed with the filling. You may eat the *popiah* as one big roll starting from one end. Alternatively, you may cut the popiah into thick slices of 3 cm or 1½ inches using a knife.

Pai Ti

Crispy Cups with Popiah Filling

Each delicate little crispy shell holds the same *popiah* filling. Laced with chilli *chuka* sauce (page 160) and topped with coriander leaves. Never had I realised how much I took these *pai ti* shells for granted, until I tried frying them. These days in Singapore, it is easy to buy a plastic canister of such cups—quite costly I might add. Yet the true satisfaction is in making them yourself.

The first time I made these shells, I used a brass mould purchased a while back at the old CK Tang. After attempting 10 brown and black shells which then floated in overheated black oil, and setting off my fire alarm, my arm began to ache from the weightiness of the mould.

I then asked Aunty Paddy for her little secret. It turned out that her moulds were passed down two generations and had been in use for more than 50 years. To begin with, they were hollow resembling tiny muffin cups and were made of aluminum, a metal lighter than brass or some alloy. Aunty Paddy also used two special brands of flour. She and my mother also added *kapor* (slaked lime powder) to the batter to increase the crisp and crunch.

As a result of my research, I went hunting once again for a lighter mould. While Aunty Paddy's hollow, aluminum ones are priceless antiques that no longer exist, it is good news that the contemporary moulds are much lighter in weight than the brass ones I had bought a decade back. It is best to season the mould with cooking oil for a week prior to the first use. This enables the *pai ti* shells to come off more easily.

Here, I am also including the filling and garnish recipes. While you can still refer to the *popiah* filling recipe (page 146), this one in particular is for a smaller portion.

serves 10 to 12

450 g or 1 pound plain flour (preferably Sunflower or Orchid Brand)
¼ teaspoon slaked lime powder (*kapor*)
Pinch of salt
1 egg, beaten
3¾ cups water, approximately

1. Combine the flour, slaked lime powder and salt. Create a hole in the middle and add the egg. Pour in the water, a little at a time and mix to a smooth batter.

2. Heat a deep pan of oil until 180 to 190 degrees C or 350 to 375 degrees F. Dip the dry *pai ti* mould in the pan to get it equally hot. To begin frying, dip the mould in the batter, returning it back into the oil. Fry the batter until crispy.

3. Use the pointed tip of a paring knife to separate the shell from the mould. Let it float in the oil for a little while longer until crispy.

4. Strain the shell out of the pan and transfer to a platter lined with absorbent paper. Repeat the process until the batter is used up.

pai ti filling

1.2 kg to 1.8 kg or 2¾ to 4 pounds
  bamboo shoots

1.8 kg jicama (*bangkuang*)

4 tablespoons oil

4 pieces firm soy bean curd (*taukua*)

350 g or 12 ounces pork (boiled)

110 g or 4 ounces garlic, peeled and
  minced

350 g or 12 ounces prawn (shrimp),
  shelled, deveined and chopped

1 tablespoon dark soy sauce sauce
  (for colour)

Salt to taste

Sugar to taste

garnish

3 eggs, fried into thin omelettes and
  cut into fine strips

110 g or 4 ounces garlic (pounded
  and fried until golden brown)

1 bunch of coriander leaves (cilantro),
  stems removed

1 small tin of crab flakes or 2 crabs,
  steamed and flaked

1. Julienne the bamboo shoots and jicama separately into thin strips.

2. Heat 2 tablespoons of oil in a frying pan. Sear the soy bean cakes until light golden brown. Transfer to a plate.

3. Boil the pork in a pot of water and retain the stock for later use.

4. Slice the soy bean cakes and the streaky pork into thin strips the size of matchsticks.

5. Boil the bamboo shoots until cooked. Strain under cold running water and set aside.

6. Heat 2 tablespoons of oil in a wok. Fry the jicama until half cooked. Remove and drain oil. In the same wok, fry the minced garlic until golden brown, then add the prawns. Add the sliced pork, bamboo shoots, jicama and bean curd; followed by the pork stock. Pour the stock a little at a time to avoid adding too much liquid which will make the filling soggy.

7. Drizzle dark soy sauce, just enough to produce a brown colour to the filling. Add salt and sugar to taste.

8. Simmer on a low fire until liquid is absorbed, adding a little more stock if needed. Let cool.

9. When ready to serve, fill the crispy *pai ti* shells with the cooked mixture. Garnish with egg strips, coriander leaves, fried garlic and crab meat. Serve with chilli *chuka* sauce (page 160).

Popiah Goreng
Fried *Popiah*

Given my mother's tendency to always make more food than our guests could eat, we never failed to have extra filling the next day after a *popiah* party. By then, however, the fresh *popiah* skin from Joo Chiat Road would not be so fresh after all. So my mother would *bungkus* (wrap) the remaining filling into smaller popiahs and deep fry them. They were especially delicious with *chilli chuka* sauce (page 160) and were a teatime treat. My mother also made these specifically for the children's parties which often took place in the late afternoon. The *popiah* should ideally be smaller and shorter than the fresh ones so that when you deep-fry them, they will not break up in the hot oil. The aim is to get a great crunchy coat out of the *popiah* skin. If you take too long to fry the filling on the inside, you might also end up burning the outer skin. For *popiah* goreng, I actually prefer to use the frozen *popiah* skin from a brand like Tee Yih Jia. It is thicker and less porous, making it suitable for deep-frying.

makes 20 servings

Use the same ingredients and cooking method for *popiah* filling (page 146); or the prepared leftover

additional ingredients
3 tablespoons cornflour
3 tablespoons water

12 cups peanut oil *
Chilli *chuka* sauce (page 160)
Sweet flour sauce

* Peanut oil (Asian brand) imparts a nice flavour. It also has a high smoke point and is especially suitable for deep-frying.

1. Combine the cornflour and water to form a slurry or paste.

2. Wrap the *popiah* the same way you would for a fresh one, except make it smaller. Spread the slurry along the edges of the popiah skin and seal the edges securely.

3. Repeat to make several *popiah*. Arrange them on a platter and set aside.

4. Heat a Dutch oven or wok and add enough oil to fill up halfway. When the oil reaches 180 to 190 degrees C or 350 to 375 degrees F, add a few *popiah* to fry. Let them fry for about 5 minutes before turning them over. Try not to turn them too frequently. When they turn golden brown and crispy, transfer to a plate lined with absorbent paper.

5. It is best to serve them hot, along with chilli *chuka* (page 160) and the sweet, dark flour sauce.

Paper-wrapped Fried Chicken

My mother made this for every reunion dinner on the eve of Chinese New Year. They were also popular at the buffet parties. Individual chicken parts were sealed in a parchment paper envelope and fried in a big wok of hot oil. While most recipes would recommend discarding the paper envelopes before serving, my mother left them intact. The family members would then play a guessing game of which chicken part we got when we opened our envelope.

Because deep-frying paper-wrapped chicken can get pretty stressful when I have a lot of other dishes to manage in my small kitchen, I have experimented with a different method which I first encountered in a *dimsum* restaurant in San Francisco's Chinatown. I substitute the paper envelopes with aluminum tin foil and wrap each chicken part on a square sheet, edges folded tightly to seal in the juices. I place all the packets on a baking sheet and broil them for about half an hour. They taste just as good and come out less greasy.

makes 12 servings

- 1 kg or 2¼ pounds chicken, cut into pieces (alternatively, chicken wings or thighs)
- 5 cm or 2 inches ginger knob, skinned and julienned
- 6 sprigs spring onions, chopped into 3.75 cm or 1½ inch strips
- 2 teaspoons salt
- 2 teaspoons sugar
- ½ teaspoon white pepper
- 1 tablespoon *Shaoxing* wine
- 2 teaspoons light soy sauce
- 2 teaspoons sesame oil
- 2 teaspoons oyster sauce

for deep-frying
- 4 to 6 cups oil, preferably peanut oil *

* Peanut oil (of an Asian brand) imparts a nice flavour. It also has a high smoke point and is especially suitable for deep-frying.

1. Season the chicken with all the ingredients above. Refrigerate for at least 2 hours.

2. About half an hour before frying or broiling, leave the chicken out of the refrigerator.

3. Wrap each piece of chicken in parchment paper envelope (seal by stapling or with a slurry or paste made from cornflour and some water).

4. Heat half a wok of oil. When oil is glistening, at about 180 to 220 degrees C or 355 to 425 degrees F, add a few envelopes, Fry for about 10 to 15 minutes until the chicken is fully cooked. Set aside and drain excess oil. Continue frying the remaining envelopes.

alternate method—broiling

1. Preheat a broiler oven on high (at least 200 degrees C or 400 degrees F).

2. Wrap each piece of chicken using a square piece of aluminum foil large enough to fold over the chicken piece on all sides. Wrap edges tightly.

3. Place the wrapped chicken on a baking tray.

4. Place the tray in the middle rack of the oven and broil for 30 to 45 minutes until the chicken is fully cooked. (To test, unwrap a packet to check on the pinkness of the chicken).

5. You may serve the chicken pieces on a platter garnished with sliced tomatoes and cucumbers. You may also choose to leave them intact in their wrapping if you wish.

Chicken Drumsticks

These drumsticks are an all-time family favourite. Nowadays, I describe them as chicken lollipops. My mother took the time to fashion the chicken drumettes (the meaty first joint of the wing, also called wingsticks) into 'meaty balls on bone sticks', hence looking very much like drum mallets ... or lollipops in the eyes of my daughter Lizzie.

makes 12 servings

1.2 kg or 2¾ pounds chicken wings (or drumettes only if you want to fashion them)

1 egg white, optional

2 tablespoons cornflour

2 teaspoons sugar

2 teaspoons salt

1 teaspoon white pepper powder

2 tablespoons oyster sauce

2 tablespoons light soy sauce

2 teaspoons sesame oil

2 teaspoons Chinese rice wine

Plain flour for dredging

4 to 6 cups of oil, preferably peanut oil *

* Peanut oil (Asian brand) imparts a nice flavour. It also has a high smoke point and is especially suitable for deep-frying.

1.   Clean the chicken drumettes.

2.   To fashion the drumettes into lollipops, use a paring knife and slice around the narrow tip of each drumette to detach the skin from the bone. Scrape the skin and meat towards the broader tip of the drumette. Invert the skin and meat so that they go over the broad tip.

3.   Season the chicken with the cornflour, sugar, salt, white pepper, oyster sauce, light soy sauce, sesame oil, Chinese rice wine and egg white. Leave aside for at least an hour.

4.   When ready to fry, heat a wok or deep frying pan. Add sufficient oil to cover a layer of drumettes.

5.   Dredge the drumettes in flour. When the oil is shimmering, add a few drumettes. Do not overcrowd or the drumettes will steam, not fry. Turn the drumettes occasionally with a pair of tongs. Fry them until they are half-cooked. Just before serving, fry the drumettes again in hot oil until they turn golden brown. Rest them on parchment paper before serving.

TIPS: For convenience, I fry the drumettes once until they turn golden brown. I let the drumettes rest on a layer of parchment paper. I then warm up the drumettes in a 200 degrees C or 400 degree F oven prior to serving, for added crispiness.

You could just use chicken wings instead and hence forego the shaping of each drumette.

The chicken is best seasoned at least 2 hours beforehand.

Sweet and Sour Pork

The sauce ingredients listed below bear testament to a colonial heritage. I believe this recipe was adapted by a Hainanese chef. These chefs—largely working behind the stoves of private colonial clubs, homes of British civil servants and kitchens of army barracks—pioneered the art of marrying British food products like HP Sauce with Chinese ingredients.

You can also substitute the 300 g or 10½ ounces of pork with the same amount of fish fillet or 600 g or 1 pound 5½ ounces of large prawns. In this instance, leave the sodium bicarbonate and water out of the marinade.

makes 12 servings

300 g or 10½ ounces pork (shoulder)
¼ teaspoon sodium bicarbonate
1 teaspoon salt
½ teaspoon sugar
1 tablespoon water
1 egg yolk
½ tablespoon cornflour
6 cups oil for frying, preferably peanut oil*
Cornflour for dredging

sauce
10 tablespoons water
1½ teaspoons salt
1 teaspoon sesame oil
4 tablespoons sugar
4 tablespoons tomato ketchup
1 tablespoon Lea & Perrins Worcestershire sauce
1 tablespoon A1 Steak Sauce or HP Sauce
1½ to 2 tablespoons vinegar
½ tablespoon chilli sauce, preferably Lingham's

slurry
1½ tablespoon cornflour
2 tablespoons water

garnish
1 large onion, skinned and cut into wedges
3 stalks spring onions (scallions), discard white portion, cut into 2.5 cm or 1 inch pieces
1 red chilli, seeded and cut into shreds
1 cucumber, skinned and cored, sliced finely
1 tomato, cut into wedges

* Peanut oil (Asian brand) imparts a nice flavour. It also has a high smoke point and is especially suitable for deep-frying.

1. Cut the pork into 2.5 cm or 1 inch cubes and marinate in the sodium bicarbonate, salt, sugar, water and egg yolk. Sprinkle the ½ tablespoon of cornflour and mix well to coat. Leave aside for at least 15 minutes.

2. Prepare the sauce by combining all the sauce ingredients. Prepare the slurry separately and set aside.

3. Heat a deep Dutch oven or wok and add the oil. Dredge the marinated pork in the cornflour and deep-fry until lightly golden and crispy, turning once over halfway through. Remove and transfer to a tray lined with absorbent paper.

4. Fry the pork a second time for crispiness. Transfer to a serving dish.

5. Remove the oil, leaving only 2 tablespoons of it. Stir-fry the onion wedges. Pour in the sauce, bring to a boil and then lower heat to simmer. Add the slurry a bit at a time to thicken sauce. Pour the sauce over the fried pork and garnish with spring onions, red chilli, cucumber and tomato. Serve immediately.

Chilli Chuka

Tangy Chilli-Vinegar Sauce

In our household, chilli *chuka* was more essential than ketchup (in our case, Maggi tomato sauce) or Lingham's chilli sauce. It ranked high among our condiments, along with *sambal belachan* (page 75). Best of all, it was home-made and cooked in a large pot, then siphoned using a plastic funnel and bottled into recycled Ribena or Maggi sauce glass bottles. The sauce truly enhances the taste of chicken drumsticks (page 157), *ngo hiang* (page 73), *popiah goreng* (page 153), and *pai ti* (page 149).

While shopping in a farmers' market in Chiang Mai, I was taught how to gauge the dried chillies before buying. You could press your hand down on the batch of dried chillies and 'feel' the heat. Be careful about how much dried chillies you add in. Start with a little of the paste first because the spiciness of the dried chillies varies with each batch.

It is also important to note that the smaller the chilli, the hotter it will taste. Hence, deseed the chillies or cut back on the quantity if you end up using small red chillies, particularly the fresh ones.

makes about 3¹/₂ cups

15 g or ½ ounce to 30 g or 1 ounce
    dried chillies, soaked in hot water
230 g or 8 ounces red chillies
90 g or 3 ounces garlic
300 ml or 1¼ cups rice vinegar
1 teaspoon salt
1 cup sugar
2 cups water

1. Separately, blend the dried chillies and fresh chillies into semi-fine pastes and set aside.

2. Blend the garlic. Mix in half of the dried chilli paste and half of the fresh chilli paste. Add more if you wish to increase the hot taste. Dilute the paste with vinegar. Add salt and sugar, adjusting the amount according to preferred taste. Boil until the sugar dissolves. Add water slowly to achieve a thin consistency. Make sure that the sauce does not become too thin, and adjust amount of water accordingly. Leave to cool completely before you bottle the sauce.

NOTE: If the sauce is far too spicy, you could add more sugar and subsequently, dilute with more water to tone down the heat.

Satay

Skewers of Grilled Spicy Marinated Meat, with Peanut Gravy

This recipe applies to beef, mutton or chicken. It came from my mother's Indonesian friend and differs from the Nonya version.

When many of us think of *satay*, we recall the days of Satay Club by the Esplanade. Our family sometimes met up at the Satay Club for a *satay* treat and I remember then, the hawker charged us according to the number of dirty sticks left on the table.

makes 4 to 8 servings

450 g or 1 pound fillet of beef, mutton or chicken breast

½ tablespoon salt

½ teaspoon sodium bicarbonate

1 tablespoon ground coriander (*ketumbar*)

1 teaspoon cumin (*jintan puteh*)

½ teaspoon fennel (*jintan manis*)

1 inch galangal (*lengkuas*), skinned and julienned finely

½ inch turmeric (*kunyit*), skinned and julienned finely

1 stalk lemon grass (*seray*), use bottom third, chopped finely (reserve the top parts of stalks)

2½ candlenuts (*buah keras*), chopped coarsely

11 shallots, peeled and cubed

5 cloves garlic, peeled

60 g or 2 ounces *gula melaka*

1½ tablespoons sugar

60 satay sticks

peanut gravy

300 g or 10½ ounces peanuts, roasted and ground

Pinch of salt

2 cups water

2 tomatoes, quartered

2 slices galangal (*lengkuas*), skinned and julienned finely

1 stalk lemon grass (*seray*), use bottom third, chopped finely

10 dried red chillies, soaked in hot water for 20 minutes

5 shallots, peeled and quartered

1 clove garlic, peeled and minced

15 g or ½ ounce *belachan*

½ cup peanut oil

Salt to taste

Sugar to taste

1. Slice the fillet of meat into 1 cm or ½ inch pieces. Season with salt and sodium bicarbonate.

2. Prepare paste to marinate meat. Blend or pound the remaining ingredients (except for *gula melaka* and sugar) in the order stated.

3. Marinate the meat with the blended paste, along with the *gula melaka* and sugar. Leave aside overnight or at least 2 hours in a refrigerator. Meanwhile, prepare the peanut gravy.

4. Remove the marinated meat from the refrigerator and begin to skewer the meat on the *satay* sticks.

5. According to the original recipe, the amount of beef should produce 50 sticks, the mutton about 50 sticks and the chicken, 30 sticks.

6. Each stick should have about 5 cm or 2 inches of meat, grouped tightly together starting at the top end of the stick. Make sure that each small piece of meat is poked twice through the stick so that it does not fall off during grilling.

7. When ready, grill the *satay* over red hot charcoal, turning over now and then so that the meat grills evenly. Dip the top parts of the lemon grass stalks in oil and brush the satay before turning them over on the grill.

8. Satay is best served with rice *ketupat* (compressed rice cakes), cut chunks of fresh cucumber and quartered white onions, alongside the gravy.

gravy

1. Combine the ground peanuts, some salt and water in a saucepan. Bring to a boil.

2. Add the tomatoes and use a spatula or wooden spoon to crush the tomatoes. Turn off heat and set aside.

3. Pound or grind the galangal, lemon grass, red chilli, shallots, garlic and *belachan* in the order given.

4. Heat a saucepan and add the oil. Stir in the spice paste and fry until fragrant.

5. Stir the peanut mixture, a little at a time, stirring to form a thick gravy consistency. Bring to a boil and then to a simmer. Season with salt and sugar if necessary.

Nonya Pork Satay

I suppose this is a classic example of the Babas adopting a dish and infusing their own preference. They liked the concept of *satay* but wanted to use pork. Also, instead of serving fresh onions and cucumbers to go with the satay and gravy, the Nonyas liked to accompany it with pineapple. In my opinion, the *satay* gravy is the key, more so than the seasoning for the meat. The peanuts serve as a thickener and should be roasted to bring out the flavour.

We sometimes had this with our buffet spread. We also included it in our many barbecue gatherings, along with the *otak otak*, prawns and chicken wings, as well as marinated thin slices of steak.

makes 6 to 10 servings

600 g or 1¼ pounds pork fillet

½ teaspoon ground cinnamon

½ inch piece of turmeric

1 stalk lemon grass (seray), upper
    stalks and outer layers removed,
    sliced thinly

½ teaspoon white pepper

1 teaspoon sugar

½ teaspoon salt

60 satay sticks

gravy

115 g or 4 ounces tamarind (assam),
    soaked in 2 cups hot water

300 g or 10½ ounces peanuts,
    toasted and ground

2 slices galangal (lengkuas) skinned
    and sliced finely

2 stalks lemon grass (seray), upper
    stalks and outer layers removed,
    sliced thinly

60 g or 2 ounces candlenuts
    (buah keras), chopped coarsely

5 dried chillies, soaked in hot water
    for 20 minutes

3 red chillies, sliced finely

300 g shallots, peeled and quartered

15 g or ½ ounce belachan

½ cup peanut oil

Sugar to taste

Salt to taste

½ fresh pineapple, skinned and
    eyes removed, grated

1.   Slice the pork into 1 cm or ½ inch pieces.

2.   Blend or pound the cinnamon, lemon grass and white
pepper into a fine paste.

3.   Marinate the pork with the paste. Season with sugar
and salt. Leave aside overnight or at least 2 hours
in a refrigerator. Meanwhile, prepare the gravy.

4.   Remove the marinated pork from the refrigerator and
begin to skewer the meat on the satay sticks. Each stick
should have about 5 cm or 2 inches of meat, grouped tightly
together starting at the top end of the stick. Make sure that
each small piece of meat is poked twice through the stick
so that it does not fall off during grilling.

5.   When ready, grill the satay over red hot charcoal,
turning over often so that the meat grills evenly.

6.   Satay is best served with ketupat (compressed rice
cakes), cut chunks of fresh cucumber and quartered white
onions, alongside the gravy.

gravy

1.   Heat a wok and add peanut oil. When the oil is
glistening, fry the peanuts. Remove with a slotted spoon
and transfer to a bowl lined with absorbent paper. Let
peanuts cool completely before grinding to a fine powder.

2.   Strain the tamarind juice and discard the seeds
and fibre.

3.   Combine the ground peanuts, some salt and tamarind
water in a saucepan. Bring to a boil. Remove from heat and
set aside.

4.   Pound or grind the galangal, lemon grass, candlenuts,
dried chillies, 2 red chillies, shallots and belachan in the
order stated.

5.   Heat oil in a large saucepan. Stir in the pounded
ingredients and fry until fragrant.

6.   Add the peanut mixture, a little at a time, stirring to
form a thick gravy. Bring to a boil and then to a simmer.
Season with salt and sugar.

7.   Stir in the grated pineapple and the 1 red chilli
into the gravy and serve alongside the satay.

Curry Puffs

Pastry Puffs with Diced Chicken Curry, Potatoes and Eggs

My mother served this as a tea-time treat, with hot Lipton's tea. I can feel the warmth from the frying just writing about this. She was very quick with her hands when crimping the edges along the half-moon puffs. Nowadays, you can buy a plastic mould to do the trick. You may use the same recipe for chicken curry to make the filling or recycle leftovers. If so, remove the eggs and potatoes and dice them finely, individually. Debone the chicken meat and dice finely too. Then recombine in sufficient leftover gravy to make a moist filling. For the fastest way to delicious puffs, use frozen puff pastry and leftover chicken curry filling.

makes 20 servings

filling
230 g or 8 ounces minced beef or pork
2 tablespoons curry powder (page 44)
2 tablespoons lard or cooking oil
1 clove garlic, peeled and minced
2 shallots, peeled and pounded
1 big onion, peeled and finely diced
½ tablespoon ground chilli
1 teaspoon salt
½ teaspoon white pepper
1 teaspoon sugar (optional)

pastry
280 g or 10 ounces plain flour
15 g or 1 tablespoon butter
180 g or 6½ ounces margarine
    or shortening*
1 egg, beaten
½ teaspoon salt
90 ml or 3 fluid ounces water

* The original recipe suggested suet which
can be hard to find and too rich in cholesterol.

filling

1. Marinate the minced meat with the curry powder and set aside for at least half an hour.

2. Heat oil in a saucepan. When oil is glistening, fry the garlic and shallots until fragrant, not burnt. Add the diced onion, followed by the marinated minced meat.

3. Add the ground chilli, salt and white pepper, adjust according to taste. Sprinkle some sugar if desired.

4. Transfer to a bowl and leave to cool.

pastry and puffs

1. With your fingertips only, rub the butter into the flour until you form fine crumbs. Then rub in the margarine. Make a well in the centre and add the egg and salt. Knead to form a pastry dough, pouring water a bit at a time to moisten it. Make sure not to add too much water, as it will make the dough too sticky.

2. Form the dough into a ball and cover tightly with cling wrap. Chill in the refrigerator for at least an hour. Thaw for at least half an hour before baking. This will soften the dough and make it easier to form the puffs.

3. Pull a door knob size of dough and flatten it into a disc. Scoop 2 to 3 teaspoons of filling into the middle of the disc. Dab some water along the edges. Fold over along the middle to form a semi-circle puff. Twist along the edges to crimp and seal.

4. Alternatively, place the flat disc of dough into the hollow of a plastic crimper. Spoon the filling into the hollow, dab some water along the edges and fold the crimper over to form the puff.

5. Heat a deep fryer and add enough oil to fill half of the pot. When the oil reaches a temperature of 180 degrees C or 350 degrees F, drop in a few puffs at a time to fry. Do not turn the puffs around for the first five minutes and not too frequently thereafter. Otherwise, you may break the puffs. When they float up to the surface, remove with a strainer and transfer to a plate lined with absorbent paper to remove the excess grease. Best served when piping hot.

Pang Susi
Meat Buns

Little meat buns; these were always present at our birthday parties and children loved them. Variations of them exist in the bread-and-bun stores throughout Singapore, as sweetly glazed bread dough enclosing meat filling. My father has since become a habitual consumer of these as a result of my mother's *pang susi*. In his old age, we told him to cut back on them. One day, my sister Maggie and I offered him a lift home from Parkway Parade Mall. He seemed coy about something. Out of curiosity, I looked into his shoulder bag and found a trove of meat buns. The old man had smuggled the lot of them for his daily tea-time treat.

makes 20 servings

yeast mix
45 g or 1½ ounces dry yeast powder

1 teaspoon sugar

1 tablespoon flour

¾ cup warm water

dough
110 g or 4 ounces butter

5 egg yolks

110 g or 4 ounces sugar

½ teaspoon salt

1¼ cup warm milk

680 g or 1½ pounds plain flour

2 small sweet potatoes, boiled
and mashed

filling
1 cup oil

3 tablespoons finely sliced shallots

8 shallots, sliced finely

1 tablespoon minced garlic

680 g or 1½ pounds minced meat
(pork or beef)

280 g or 10 ounces potatoes, diced
into fine cubes and parboiled

2 teaspoons white pepper

1½ teaspoons salt

3 tablespoons sugar

2 tablespoons dark soy sauce

¼ teaspoon ground nutmeg

4 tablespoons water

slurry
2 tablespoons cornflour

3 tablespoons water

egg wash
2 eggs, beaten

pastry

1. Combine the dry yeast powder, sugar and salt in a bowl. Add warm water and stir. Allow to stand for 10 minutes until the volume increases.

2. Beat butter, egg yolks, sugar and salt together in a mixing bowl with an electric beater. Add milk, a little at a time. Stir in a cup of flour until it is fully absorbed into the dough mixture. Add activated yeast solution and mashed potato followed by the rest of the flour, a little at a time. Continue to beat until the dough leaves the sides of the mixing bowl. Cover the bowl with a moist cloth and leave the dough to rise until it has doubled in size.

filling and forming

1. Heat oil in a wok. When the oil is glistening, fry the shallots until they are brown and crispy. Remove with a strainer and transfer to a plate lined with absorbent paper. Pour away most of the oil, leaving enough to fry the minced garlic until golden brown. Add the minced meat and stir-fry

for 5 minutes. Then add the potatoes and fry for another 5 minutes. Meanwhile, combine and stir the remaining ingredients in a separate bowl. Pour the mixture into the wok of meat and potatoes.

2. Make the slurry and stir in, a bit at a time, to thicken. You may adjust the amount of slurry according to the desired thickness of the gravy. Stir in the crispy shallots. Leave the cooked filling to cool completely.

3. Return to the dough. Pull a bit of the dough to form a flat disk about half the size of a palm. Scoop a tablespoon or two of the meat filling onto the centre of the disc, fold and fashion into a round bun. Repeat. Place the buns on a tray and leave aside for 30 minutes.

4. Preheat the oven to 180 degrees C or 350 degrees F. Bake the buns for 20 minutes until they turn golden brown.

5. Glaze with egg wash when the buns are still piping hot to give a shine.

Kueh Kledek

Deep-fried Sweet Potato Balls stuffed with *Kueh Chang* filling

My mother, for a brief period, sold these to a shop in Orchard Road. There was even a family tale that a very prominent Baba politician used to send his chauffeur over to buy them occasionally. Our family chomped them and sometimes complained about how *jeluak* (surfeited) we were, by the sight of sweet preserved melon being chopped into small cubes and the oil and pungency of the deep frying. My mother then rarely made them. After her passing, we yearned for *kueh kledek*, especially since these were hard to find. This is one of the most missed items. It also took a while for me to find the recipe amidst her trove.

makes 25 dumplings

pastry
900 g or 2 pounds sweet potato, steamed
    and mashed with 1 tablespoon sugar
140 g or 5 ounces glutinous rice flour
105 g or 3¾ ounces rice flour
½ to 1 cup water, enough to form
    a firm dough

filling
450 g or 1 pound lean pork
60 g or 2 ounces pork fat
5 tablespoons lard or oil
8 dried mushrooms (soaked in
    hot water until soft)

3 tablespoons garlic, peeled and
    pounded finely
10 shallots, peeled and pounded finely
½ to 1 teaspoon salt
100 g or 3½ ounces sugar
1 tablespoons white pepper powder
4 tablespoons toasted coriander seeds,
    pounded till fine and sieved
2 tablespoons dark soy sauce
100 g or 3½ ounces candied melon
    (*tang kueh*), diced
5 to 8 cups oil for deep frying

pastry

1. Skin sweet potatoes and dice them. Steam till soft. Add sugar to the sweet potatoes and mash until smooth.

2. Sieve the two types of flour and add to the mashed sweet potato. Add water, a little at a time until you have a firm dough. Set aside.

filling and forming

1. Bring water to the boil and add the pork and pork fat. When water boils again, remove pork fat but leave the pork to boil for another 30 minutes. Remove the pork and set aside the stock. Cool the pork fat and pork under cold running water. Pat dry.

2. Remove the softened dried mushrooms from the pot of water. Dice the pork, pork fat and dried mushrooms into fine cubes. Set aside separately.

3. Heat oil in a wok. Fry garlic and shallots till fragrant, not burnt. Add diced pork and mushrooms.

4. Add salt, sugar, white pepper, coriander seeds and dark soy sauce. Add about ¾ cups of pork stock, candied melon and pork fat. Bring to a boil, then lower to a simmer till sauce is thick. Leave aside to cool.

5. When the mixture is completely cooled, use a teaspoon to scoop the mixture and fashion into round balls.

6. Pinch half a handful of sweet potato dough and form a flat disk. Hold a portion of pork mixture in the middle and roll into a ball. Repeat to make several balls.

7. Heat oil in a wok or fryer. The oil should be 180 degrees C or 350 degrees F and should not be too hot, or the balls will burst open. Deep-fry the balls until golden brown, a few at a time (do not overcrowd the wok). Strain. Transfer to a plate lined with absorbent paper before serving.

Cream Puffs

My mother always made cream puffs for my birthday parties. My mother's cream puffs were dainty and the custard was creamy. Yet, today, I still appreciate the somewhat inferior, localised version of large, flat and almost soggy cream puffs with hardened yellow custard, almost of a jello consistency. The best of these could be found at the landmark Red House Bakery along East Coast Road and now at nearby Chin Mee Chin Confectionery.

Since Singapore did not use fresh milk cream heavily in the old days, especially since it would get stale very quickly in the tropical heat, my mother's filling was derived from evaporated milk. My mother's recipe also called for baking powder which in most traditional choux pastry recipes, is not required.

Also, little did the children know that the custard filling also had brandy! Yum yum!

makes 20 servings

choux pastry
½ cup water
30 g or 1 ounce butter, cut into
    small cubes
90 g or 3 ounces plain flour
¼ teaspoon baking powder (optional)
1 teaspoon vanilla essence
3 small eggs

custard filling
¾ cup evaporated milk
¾ cup water
30 g or 1 ounce butter
60 g or 2 ounces flour
45 g or 1½ ounces sugar
½ teaspoon vanilla essence
1 egg, lightly beaten
½ tablespoon brandy

choux pastry

1.   Preheat oven to 200 to 230 degrees C or 400 to 450 degrees F.

2.   Add water to a saucepan and bring to a boil. Drop in the cubes of butter and stir until the butter melts. Add the flour and baking powder, a little at a time, and stir gently until the paste leaves the sides of the saucepan. Leave to cool for approximately 5 to 10 minutes.

3.   Add the vanilla essence, followed by the eggs, one at a time, stirring continuously to ensure that each egg is fully absorbed.

4.   Drop a teaspoon of the pastry dough onto a tray lined with parchment paper. Repeat. Bake in the oven for 25 to 30 minutes until the pastry is light brown. Remove tray from the oven and cool completely.

custard filling

1.   Combine the milk and water in a saucepan and bring to a gentle boil. Quickly lower the heat and bring the mixture to a simmer, being careful not to have the milk boil over. Add the butter, flour and sugar and stir until the sugar dissolves and the mixture is smooth. Add vanilla essence, egg and brandy. Remove saucepan from heat and let mixture cool or refrigerate to chill.

2.   Use a paring knife or scissors, make a slit in each puff. Scoop custard filling into a piping bag (or a plastic bag with a corner snipped to make a 1 cm or ½ inch hole). To avoid making the cream puffs soggy, fill each puff with some custard just before serving

Almond Jelly with Lychees in Syrup

I am old-fashioned and still prefer to use the raffia-like *agar* strips. Also, make sure to get a good quality almond extract. Try it first, otherwise your jelly may end up tasting very chemical.

makes 12 servings

30 g or 1 ounce *agar* strips, cut into 2.5 cm or 1 inch pieces *

10 cups water

1½ teaspoons gelatine powder, dissolved in 1 cup water

600 g or 1 pound 5 ounces sugar

1½ cups evaporated milk

1 tablespoon almond extract

2 cans lychees (you may substitute with fruit cocktail if you prefer)

* Can be substituted with a similar amount of *agar* powder

1. Soak the *agar* strips in a bowl of water for 5 minutes.

2. Fill a large pot with 10 cups water and bring to a boil.

3. Drain the *agar* strips using a strainer and add to the boiling water. Stir occasionally to dissolve the strips.

4. Add the gelatine powder solution and sugar. Continue to stir to dissolve any remaining lumps.

5. When the jelly begins to thicken, turn off the heat. Pour the mixture through a strainer, to obtain a more concentrated and clear jelly. Press down on the strainer to extract as much flavour and gelatine as possible. Allow to cool. Then add the evaporated milk and almond extract and stir well.

6. Pour the jelly mixture into two large bowls. Cool for about half an hour at room temperature. Then chill them in a refrigerator for 4 hours or overnight until the jelly sets. Chill the 2 cans of lychees or fruit cocktail as well.

7. When ready to serve, spoon the almond jelly into smaller dessert bowls and top each bowl with a few lychees. Drizzle with some of the lychee syrup for added flavour.

Bijik Selaseh

Ice-Cold Rose Syrup with Jelly Basil Seeds

Our neighbour Aunty Paddy always welcomed us with this refreshing drink when we visited her. It simply takes minutes to make. *Bijik selaseh* (basil seeds) can be found in Indian grocery stores. The Indian community make a drink using these tiny seeds which they call *takmaria*. They look like sesame when you first purchase them, but take on a gelatinous coating after soaking in water for fifteen minutes. It is velvety soft on the outside and crunchy on the inside. We called them 'tadpoles' or 'frogs' eggs'. Don't let the appearance scare you. The seeds, according to Aunty Paddy, help alleviate haemorrhoids.

makes 8 servings

2 tablespoons dry basil seeds
(*bijik selaseh*)

**1 cup rose syrup (try to use
TG Kiat or F&N brands)**

**6 to 8 cups drinking water
or soda water**

1. Place the dry basil seeds in a bowl and soak in water for 15 minutes.

2. Skim off dry husks from the surface.

3. For each glass, add 6 teaspoons of the soaked *bijik selaseh*. Also add 6 teaspoons of rose syrup and fill the rest of the glass with cold water. You may add more rose syrup if you prefer a sweeter concoction.

4. Chill the drink in the refrigerator before you serve.

A Very Festive Family

The Baba families celebrated the same festivals as the Chinese. There was the Dragon Boat Festival in the spring (typically in May).

While these Chinese rice dumplings were wrapped in dry lotus leaves, filled with meat and had a salty tinge to it, the Nonyas created their own version. Theirs were wrapped in a large variant of *pandan* leaves instead to impart a fragrant flavour, some of the rice was dyed in blue using the local *bunga telang* flower, and the pork filling was sweetened with preserved melon. The Nonyas adapted the Chinese dumplings to suit their own palate by infusing the filling with ground coriander.

My mother took orders from friends and made her famous Nonya dumplings, called *kueh chang* (as opposed to the traditional Chinese ones which are referred to as *bak chang*).

This *kueh chang*, so synonymous with the Peranakans, traces its history to ancient China during the time of the Warring States. Qu Yuan, an honest and beloved government official in the Kingdom of Chu, was wrongfully accused of corruption by backstabbing peers. Humiliated, he took his own life and drowned himself in the river. The local villagers went out in boats to search for him, beating drums and gongs during the search. They also threw rice dumplings into the river to distract the fish so that they would not eat his body; hence, the tradition of the Dragon Boat festival and eating rice dumplings during this time.

My mother's rice was steamed to make it stickier and easier to shape into pyramids. The pork was also pre-boiled to make it firmer to dice. Each dumpling was wrapped with the special *pandan* leaf—mainly available in May—tied tightly with raffia string. They each looked like a fat soprano spilling out of her seams. Her dumplings also cost twice as much and good reason why. My mother's ratio of meat to the blue and white sticky rice was twice as much as others. She spent a week making these, but spent at least an extra week preparing. Ah Seng the grocer would haul in a literal forest of broad *pandan* leaves, several times thicker, sturdier and taller than the leaves used for *kueh*. They rested in the red plastic buckets in the outdoor kitchen. My mother would cut and blister her fingers as she used a paring knife to scrape down the thorns on the underside vein of each leaf.

She set up a charcoal stove to boil her *kueh chang*; they hung in groups of 10 from a bamboo pole, identical to those used to sun-dry laundry.

There was also a peculiar Chinese festival that took place for a day in December. It was called *Tang Chek* (Winter Solstice Festival). It apparently predicted the weather for the upcoming Chinese New Year. My mother told me that if *Tang Chek* day was hot, it meant that the first day of Chinese New Year would be rainy, and vice versa. To our knowledge, Chinese New Year was always hot! To celebrate *Tang Chek*, my mother made a dessert that consisted of red and white glutinous balls in a clear sweet soup—*kueh ee* (page 196).

We also celebrated birthdays and the birth of babies in a special way. Birthdays meant that we had to have noodles as they symbolised long life, denoting a sweet and long life.

Newborn babies were welcome into the family with boiled eggs dyed in red, and a sticky rice dish. The rice dish, *yew peng* (page 191), was savoury and topped with Chinese sausages, fried shallots and dried mushrooms. These special treats were served on the day which marked the first month of a baby's life. Particularly if the newborn was a grandson, or the first grandchild, the celebration became more lavish with a Chinese banquet for relatives, and frosted cakes from the bakery delivered to the homes of the guests; along with the red eggs (page 190) and *yew peng*.

Nonya Kueh Chang

Glutinous Rice and Pork Dumplings wrapped in Pandan Leaf

Around May of each year, my mother took orders for her famous *kueh chang*. They were known for being twice the size of the average *kueh chang* sold elsewhere. An indelible image of my mother would be of her standing forever beside the dining table as she sliced the hard *tang kueh* (candied melon), mushrooms, pork and lard into fine cubes. The kitchen would then be turned into a grease pit with tall pots boiling away atop charcoal stoves. The *kueh chang* were tied into bunches of 10 dumplings each. As they emerged from the scalding pot, they were propped up with a metal pole to drip dry, their oily droplets falling to old newspaper sheets lining the floor. One could feel the atmosphere soaked in oil, fragranced with *pandan*, permeating with humid heat from the hot pots. This was my mother's workshop for 15 hours a day for an entire week or two. Yet she never complained because she thoroughly enjoyed skilfully wrapping each dumpling. This annual project kept her routinely occupied.

Be assured that this is a scene of a mini factory where my mother would almost single-handedly churn out a thousand of these dumplings to sell to friends who persuaded her to make them. The recipe that follows is on a smaller scale.

makes 6 to 10 servings

filling

20 g or ½ ounce Chinese mushrooms, soaked in hot water for 30 minutes

230 g or 8 ounces candied melon (*tang kueh*)

600 g or 1 pound 5 ounces lean pork

70 g or 2½ ounces streaky pork (*samchan bak*)

70 g or 2½ ounces pork skin (boil with pork stock until tender)

½ cup pork stock

20 g or ½ ounce garlic, peeled

70 g or 2½ ounces shallots or small red onions, peeled

2 tablespoons dark soy sauce

1 teaspoon salt

115 g or 4 ounces sugar

½ tablespoon white pepper

15g or ½ ounce ground coriander (*ketumbar*), toasted until fragrant

Lard for frying (or substitute with oil)

rice

1 kg or 2 pounds 3 ounces glutinous rice

5 to 6 drops of blue food colouring or ½ cup dried clitoria (*bunga telang*) soaked in ½ cup water

¾ cup water

¾ cup oil (or lard)

¼ tablespoon ground white pepper

½ tablespoon salt

wrapping materials

20 to 30 large *pandan* leaves (can be ordered when the festival draws near) or dried bamboo leaves

1 roll raffia string, cut into strips of about 40 cm or 16 inches long

filling (can be made a day ahead)

1. The night before, soak the Chinese mushrooms in hot water.

2. Remove the Chinese mushrooms from the water and squeeze dry. Discard the hard stems. Slice the mushrooms into fine cubes, about sides of 0.5cm or ¼ inch.

3. Similarly, slice the candied melon into cubes of the same size.

4. Bring a pot of salted water to a boil. Turn heat down to medium. Cook lean pork and streaky pork in the boiling water for about 30 to 40 minutes until tender. Boil the pork skin in pork stock until tender. Drain the meats individually and set aside to cool. Chop each of these into small fine cubes, sides of about 0.5 cm or ¼ inch.

5. Pound the garlic and cut the shallots into thin slices.

6. Heat a wok and add some oil. Fry the garlic till light brown and remove from pan, then fry the sliced onions until light brown.

7. Mix together the pork cubes and candied melon with the dark soy sauce.

8. Heat one tablespoon of lard, fry the mushrooms for 3 to 5 minutes and add pork mixture. Cook for 5 minutes. Add salt, sugar, white pepper, ground coriander, fried garlic and shallots. Add pork stock and cook over moderate heat for 10 to 15 minutes. Remove from heat and allow to cool in basin. Drain off excess oil.

rice

1. Scan the rice and pick out broken or transparent grains and small pebbles. You can do this days before at a more leisurely pace.

2. The night before, rinse the rice three times until the water runs clear. Separate a third of the rice and soak it in a pot of water with the blue food colouring added to the water. Soak the remaining rice in another pot with enough water to cover the rice. Leave overnight.

3. The next day, drain the rice grains from both pots. Prepare a large steamer pot with a tray about 3 cm or 1 inch deep. Spread enough rice (both blue and plain rice grains) to fill three-quarters of the tray and steam over high heat for an hour until the rice is transparent and soft. You may have to cook the rice in batches depending on the size of your steamer.

4. Meanwhile, combine salt and white pepper with the ¾ cup of water.

5. Remove the cooked rice and use it to make the dumplings while the rice is still warm. Sprinkle rice with the water mixture of salt and white pepper. Pour the lard and mix evenly. Cover with a damp cloth to keep warm as cold rice will not bind well and may harden.

filling and wrapping

1. Trim both ends of each leaf to neaten the edges. If using bamboo leaves, prepare a pot of boiling water. Dip the leaves in the water briefly, then wipe them clean and dry.

2. Take two leaves laid over each other, smooth side facing you. Use one leaf if it is a big one. Fold over each end to form a cone, using the broader end as the top layer overlapping the smaller end. Both ends should face in the same direction as you form an inverted cone. Place half a handful of plain glutinous rice into the cupped leaf, along with a large pinch of blue rice. Press down to pack tightly, forming a little depression in the middle. Fill the hollow with the meat filling—be generous—and top with more glutinous rice. Make sure to pack the rice and filling tightly. Do not fill right to the top, leave some allowance.

3. Fold both remaining ends of the leaf towards you and fold over the rice to form an inverted pyamid. Fold the leaf down to wrap around the dumpling, which should be moulded at this point into a pyramid shape. Trim off excess leaf.

4. Use a raffia string to tie tightly around the middle of each dumpling, going around at least twice. Knot tightly to secure the dumpling. Leave some string free, at least 30 cm or 12 inches long.

5. For every 10 dumplings, tie the free ends of the strings together to form a bundle.

6. To boil *kueh chang*, add 1 tablespoon of salt to a large pot of boiling water. Submerge the bundle of dumplings in boiling water and boil for 2½ hours. Hang them up to drip dry. The dumplings are often eaten the next day and can be refrigerated. Steam once again before eating.

Kaolak Chang

Savoury Glutinous Rice Dumplings with Chestnuts and Pork

This is my favourite. The Nonya *kueh chang* is special because of its blue rice and sweet yet savoury taste, but my mother's *kaolak chang* felt substantial with its filling of chestnuts, pork, dried shrimps and Chinese mushrooms. The variance in texture also titillates the tastebuds.

makes 6 to 10 servings

filling

70 g or 2½ ounces Chinese mushrooms, soaked in hot water for 30 minutes

600 g or 1 pound 5 ounces pork leg fillet

70 g or 2½ ounces dried shrimps, soaked in hot water for 30 minutes

45 g or 1½ ounces garlic, peeled and pounded

150 g or 5 ounces shallots or small red onions peeled and sliced finely

2 tablespoons dark soy sauce

1 tablespoon salt

3 tablespoons sugar

1 teaspoon five-spice powder

230 g or 8 ounces chestnuts (*kaolak*), shelled and chopped roughly

rice

600 g or 1 pund 5 ounces glutinous rice

½ cup peanut oil

30 g or 1 ounce garlic, peeled and minced

40 g or 1½ ounces shallots, peeled and sliced finely

4 tablespoons dark soy sauce

1 tablespoon light soy sauce

1 teaspoon five-spice powder

½ teaspoon salt

1 teaspoon sugar

wrapping materials

50 pieces dried bamboo leaves

1 roll raffia string, cut into strips of about 40 cm or 16 inches long

filling (can be made a day ahead)

1. Drain the Chinese mushrooms and squeeze dry. Discard the hard stems. Slice the mushrooms thinly, about 0.5 cm or ¼ inch in width.

2. Bring a pot of salted water to a boil. Turn heat down to medium. Cook the pork in the boiling water for 30 to 40 minutes until tender. Drain and cool the pork. Chop the pork into cubes of about sides 1 cm or ½ inch.

3. Drain and pat dry the dried shrimps.

4. Heat oil in a wok. Fry garlic till light brown and remove from wok, then fry the sliced onions until light brown.

5. In the same wok, fry the mushrooms for 3 to 5 minutes and add the pork and dried shrimps. Cook for 5 minutes. Add dark soy sauce, salt, sugar, five-spice powder and chestnuts. Cook on medium heat for 10 to 15 minutes. Remove from heat and allow to cool in basin. Drain off excess oil.

rice

1.   Scan the rice and pick out broken grains and small pebbles. You can do this days before at a more leisurely pace.

2.   The night before, rinse the glutinous rice three times until the water runs clear. Soak the rice in a pot with enough water to cover the rice. Leave overnight.

3.   Next day, drain the rice grains.

4.   Heat peanut oil in a wok and fry the minced garlic and shallots until light golden brown. Transfer to a plate lined with absorbent paper. In the same wok, add rice and season with the dark and light soy sauce, five-spice powder, salt and sugar. Add in fried garlic and shallots. Transfer to a platter, spread and let this cool.

filling and wrapping

1.   Prepare a pot of boiling water. Dip the bamboo leaves in the water briefly, then wipe them clean and dry.

2.   Take two leaves laid over each other, smooth side facing you. Use one leaf if it is a big one. Fold over each end to form a cone, using one end as the top layer overlapping the other end. Both ends should face in the same direction as you form an inverted cone. Place half a handful of the cooked glutinous rice into the cupped leaf. Press down to pack tightly, forming a little depression in the middle. Fill the hollow with the filling and top with more glutinous rice. Make sure to pack the rice and filling tightly. Do not fill right to the top, leave some allowance.

3.   Fold both remaining ends of the leaf towards you and fold over the rice to form an inverted pyamid. Fold the leaf down to wrap around the dumpling, which should be moulded at this point into a pyramid shape. Trim off excess leaf.

4.   Use a raffia string to tie tightly around the middle of each dumpling, going around at least twice. Knot tightly to secure the dumpling. Leave some string free, at least 30 cm or 12 inches long.

5.   For every 10 dumplings, tie the free ends of the strings together to form a bundle.

6.   To cook the *kaolak chang*, prepare a large pot of boiling water. Lower to a simmer and drop the *kaolak chang* into the pot and boil for 2 to 3 hours. Turn off the heat and soak the dumplings in the pot for a further 30 minutes. Hang them up to drip dry.

Kueh Chang Abu
Glutinous Rice Dumplings served with Sweet Sauce

After my mother had made all her Nonya *kueh chang*, she also took the time to make two other types of dumplings. This was considered the sweet one of the three types of *kueh chang* and acted like a dessert whereas the others were almost like the main course. It is described as *kueh chang abu* in reference to the alkaline water which Nonyas called *ayer abu*.

In most recipes, you will not find the dark sweet sauce that complemented my mother's *kueh chang abu*. She simply melted *gula melaka* into a syrup.

makes 6 to 10 servings

600 g or 1 pound 5 ounces glutinous rice
1 tablespoon alkaline water
1 tablespoon oil
70 g or 2½ ounces cylinder of *gula melaka*

wrapping materials
50 pieces dried bamboo leaves
1 roll raffia string, cut into strips each
    about 40 cm or 16 inches long

rice

1.   Scan the rice and pick out broken or transparent grains and small stones. You can do this days before at a more leisurely pace.

2.   The night before, rinse the glutinous rice three times until the water runs clear. Soak the rice in a pot with enough water to cover the rice. Leave overnight.

3.   Next day, drain the rice. Mix with alkaline solution and oil and set aside for 30 minutes.

filling and wrapping

1.   Prepare a pot of boiling water. Dip the bamboo leaves in the water briefly, then wipe them clean and dry.

2.   Take two leaves laid over each other, smooth side facing you. Use one leaf if it is a big one. Fold over each end to form a cone. Fold over and press down to form a hollow.

3.   Place a handful of plain glutinous rice into the cupped leaf. Pack the rice tightly almost to the top and leave some allowance.

4.   Fold the remaining ends of the leaves over the rice. Fold the leaves down to wrap around the dumpling, which should be moulded at this point into a pyramid shape. Trim off excess leaves.

5.   Use a raffia string to tie tightly around the middle of each dumpling at least twice.

6.   For every 10 dumplings, tie the free ends of the strings together to form a bundle.

7.   To cook the *kueh chang abu*, prepare a large pot of boiling water. Lower to a simmer and drop the *kueh chang abu* into the pot and boil for 5 hours. Turn off the heat and soak the *kueh chang* in the pot for a further 30 minutes. Hang them up to drip dry.

8.   To prepare the syrup, scrape the *gula melaka* and transfer to a small saucepan. Over low heat, let the *gula melaka* melt into a syrup. To avoid scorching, you may add a little water while melting the *gula melaka*. Serve alongside the *kueh chang abu*.

Kueh Ku

Glutinous Rice Flour Cakes filled with Mung Bean Paste

These usually come in red to symbolise good luck. In fact, they can be found in five colours— red, black, blue, green and white—but I have only seen the first two. The recipe below makes the red and black versions. Sweet potato is used here to give a softer texture to the dough, as glutinous rice flour is used in place of the traditional milled rice (which would have produced a sufficiently supple dough by itself). The red *kueh* were traditionally given to relatives to celebrate a baby's first month, along with red eggs, and were most often moulded into a tortoise shape, the tortoise being a symbol of longevity. When my mother celebrated her 70th birthday, she made her own *kueh ku* and lovingly packed them into plastic boxes to give away to her dear guests. Black ones were made for the Hungry Ghost festival, *Cheng Beng* (Ancestors' Day) festival or for death anniversaries.

I still have my mother's old wooden moulds. A good mould would have an inside pattern carved deep and clear so that the shape and intricate design would come out beautifully.

makes 6 to 10 servings

filling
1.2 kg or 2½ pounds mung beans, without skin

8 *pandan* leaves, tied into a knot

1.4 kg or 3 pounds sugar

1 cup water

black essence
90 g or 3 ounces mugwort leaves (*daun ramay*)

1 cup water

½ cup coconut milk

340 g or 12 ounces white sugar

110 g or 4 ounces *gula melaka*, scraped

dough
280 g or 10 ounces sweet potato, peeled and cubed

2¼ cups coconut milk

170 g or 6 ounces sugar

90 g or 3 ounces glutinous rice flour

¼ cup hot water

450 g or 1 pound glutinous rice flour

5 drops red food colouring or ½ teaspoon red food colouring powder

1 teaspoon *pandan* essence

moulding materials
½ cup coconut oil or vegetable oil.

8 to 10 banana leaves, scalded and then cut into squares each side 10 cm or 4 inches.

filling

1. Scan mung bean grains and pick out tiny pebbles. Soak the mung beans in water and leave overnight.

2. Drain beans and steam with the *pandan* leaves. Discard the *pandan* leaves and mash the beans while still hot. Using a ricer or stick blender would refine the mashed beans.

3. Combine water and sugar in a wok or Dutch oven. Bring to boil over low heat until the sugar dissolves. Add the mashed beans and stir continuously for about 30 minutes until the paste is thick and sticky.

4. Let the paste cool. Then pinch and divide the paste into balls, each about 3 cm or 1¼ inches, arranged on a platter.

black essence

1. Boil the mugwort leaves in a cup of water till leaves are thick and soft. Boil till liquid is concentrated to 2 tablespoons' worth. Strain the liquid and set aside. Then pound the leaves till very fine.

2. Combine the pounded leaves, concentrated liquid, coconut milk, sugar and *gula melaka* in a saucepan. Bring to boil over low heat until the mixture is thick and pasty.

dough

1. Boil sweet potatoes until tender. Mash while still hot.

2. Meanwhile, bring the coconut milk and sugar to a boil.

3. Combine glutinous rice flour and water in a bowl. Make a well in the centre. Slowly pour in the coconut milk mixture in the middle. Stir to form a fine dough. Blend in the mashed sweet potatoes. Divide the dough into two portions.

4. For the first portion, add the red food colouring and a teaspoon of *pandan* essence. This is for the red dough.

5. For the second portion, add the black essence prepared earlier. This is for the black dough.*

6. Place the dough in their individual bowls and cover each bowl with a damp cloth.

moulding

1. Divide the dough into round balls, each about 4 cm or 1½ inches in diameter.

2. Brush the inside of the wooden mould with oil.

3. Flatten one ball of dough into a disc using both palms. Place a ball of bean paste in the middle of the disc, overlap the edges and roll back into a ball, covering the mashed bean paste. Place the ball in the middle of the wooden mould and press down firmly with your palm such that the ball fills up the entire cavity of the mould and the base flattens out. Place a banana leaf over the flat base. Gently tap the *kueh* out of the mould by knocking the top with a teaspoon or tapping the mould against the table surface. Arrange the *kueh* on a tray.

4. Prepare a steamer. Steam the *kueh* gently over low heat for 10 minutes. Do not turn the heat too high, otherwise the dough will lose its shape and its design. Tie or wrap a damp cloth under the lid of the steamer to prevent condensed water from dripping onto the *kueh*.

5. Transfer to a rack and lightly brush the top of the *kueh* with some oil. When cooled, trim the excess banana leaf. To keep the *kueh* moist, cover with a large banana leaf brushed with oil.

*NOTE: You can skip the black pastry dough and substitute an extra 5 drops of red food colouring and 1 teaspoon of pandan essence instead.

Red Eggs

20 eggs
1 teaspoon salt
5 tablespoons red food colouring

1 cup hot water for making red dye
2 teaspoons white vinegar

1. Fill a pot with enough cold water to cover the eggs and add salt. Bring to a rolling boil. Add the eggs and boil for 15 minutes. Scoop each egg out gently and transfer to a colander. Let the eggs cool completely.

2. Prepare red dye. Combine red food colouring, hot water and vinegar. Mix well.

3. Dip one egg into the red dye. Roll the egg around with chopsticks or your fingertips to coat evenly. Gently remove the egg with a pair of tongs or a wire scoop. Transfer to a plate lined with absorbent paper or back to the cardboard egg tray to prevent smudging.

4. Check the shade of red on the first egg to see if it is too dark or too light. If too light, add more colouring. If too dark, add an equal amount of hot water and white vinegar to dilute the colouring mixture.

5. Let the eggs dry completely before distributing to friends and relatives.

Yew Peng
Mixed Savoury Glutinous Rice

Yew peng was given out to friends and relatives when we had a new baby in the family. My mother's was so delicious because she added a lot of toppings to the base of glutinous rice and garnished it with lots of coriander leaves (cilantro).

makes 6 to 10 servings

450 g or 1 pound glutinous rice

1½ teaspoons light soy sauce

1½ teaspoons dark soy sauce

Salt to taste

200 g or 7 ounces streaky pork (*samchan bak*)

20 g or ¾ ounce Chinese mushrooms, soaked in hot water for at least 30 minutes

40 g or 1½ ounces dried shrimps, soaked in hot water for at least 30 minutes

1 teaspoon oil

30 g or 1 ounce shallots, peeled and sliced finely

30 g or 1 ounce Chinese sausage, sliced

1 bunch coriander leaves (cilantro), chopped

1. Scan the rice and pick out broken grains and small pebbles. You can do this days before at a more leisurely pace.

2. The night before, rinse the glutinous rice three times until the water runs clear. Soak the rice in a pot with enough water to cover the rice. Leave overnight.

3. On the next day, drain the rice grains and put them in a steamer. When the rice is cooked, transfer it to a large tray, toss and spread out the cooked rice to cool.

2. Combine light and dark soy sauce and salt in a bowl.

3. Slice the streaky pork finely into thin strips. Strain the Chinese mushrooms, remove the stems and slice finely. Strain the dried shrimps. Add pork, mushrooms and dried shrimps to the soy sauce mixture.

4. Heat oil in a large wok. When the oil is glistening, add the sliced shallots and fry until light brown and fragrant. Lower the heat and add the glutinous rice. Stir to coat well.

5. Lay out a round metal tray, about 30 cm or 12 inches in diameter. Brush the tray with oil. Line the base of the tray with the Chinese sausage, the pork, Chinese mushrooms and dried shrimp. Top up with glutinous rice. Drizzle remaining soy sauce mixture over. Press the rice down in the tray with the back of a spoon to make it compact.

6. Cook the tray of rice for 45 minutes in a steamer.

7. To serve, place a large serving platter over the tray and turn over. Garnish with the chopped coriander leaves.

Mooncakes

My mother loved mooncakes. I do too. I still prefer the traditional *lengyong* (lotus seed) paste with the preserved egg yolks, the more yolks the merrier.

My mother learnt to make mooncakes from the Chinese *dimsum* chef who worked in the Stadium restaurant that my father managed in the 1970s. She acquired a repertoire of *dimsum* skills. I recall that Ah Yew often came to our Yarrow Garden house in the evenings to demonstrate to my mother how to make mooncakes. Over time, my mother made such good mooncakes that as usual, her friends persuaded her to make and sell these to them.

As with a few other *dimsum* recipes, you will need alkaline solution and what we term as Hong Kong flour. This flour type is essentially supermilled and hence, more refined. Prepared lotus seed paste is available, especially around the Mooncake Festival season.

As with *kueh ku*, the wooden moulds that have a deeper and sharper carving would produce a more brilliant pattern on the mooncake.

makes 12 to 18 servings
18 salted eggs
325 g or 11½ ounces Hong Kong flour
325 g or 11½ ounces plain flour
450 g or 1 pound golden syrup

¾ tablespoon corn oil
1 tablespoon alkaline water
1.35 kg or 3 pounds lotus seed paste
1 egg, beaten (for egg wash)

1. Steam the eggs for 5 minutes over low heat. Peel the salted eggs and remove the egg white portion.

2. Sift the Hong Kong and plain flour into a large bowl. Make a well in the middle. Pour in the golden syrup, corn oil and alkaline solution. Knead gently into a dough. Set aside for half an hour.

3. Meanwhile, pinch the lotus seed paste into balls, each weighing about 70 g or 2½ ounces. Wrap a ball of lotus paste around each egg yolk. Arrange the balls on a tray.

4. Pinch and divide the pastry dough into balls each weighing about 70 g or 2½ ounces.

5. Flatten each dough into a disc and wrap around the ball of lotus paste.

6. Preheat the oven to 180 degrees C or 350 degrees F.

7. Dab the mooncake mould with some oil. Place a ball of dough containing lotus paste into the mould cavity. Use your palm to press down firmly such that the ball fills up the entire cavity of the mold and the base flattens out. With the tip of a paring knife, separate the mooncake from the sides of the mould. Gently tap the mooncake out of the mould by tapping the mould against the table surface. Arrange the mooncakes on a tray lined with parchment paper or brushed with oil.

8. Bake the mooncakes for 5 minutes initially. Remove the tray of mooncakes and brush the top of each mooncake with egg wash. Bake for another 5 minutes. Brush again with egg wash. Return to the oven and bake for another 15 to 20 minutes. At the end, brush the mooncakes with some golden syrup for colouring and gloss.

NOTE: Hide the folds by facing them upwards in the mould so that when you invert the mould, the folds are hidden at the base of the mooncake.

Mee Sua

Fine Rice Noodles in Soup with Meatballs

My mother observed our birthdays on both the Chinese and Western calenders. Our Chinese lunar birth dates and animal zodiac signs were recorded on square white pieces of cloth, inked in Chinese characters. My mother had the habit of slotting her jewellery, cash and such family documents behind her cupboards and under the paper slips lining her drawers. She rarely took those cloths out and we have never found them.

Each year, sometime close to our Western birthday, we would wake up to find her preparing birthday *mee sua*. "It's your Chinese birthday so you must eat this for long life," was her command. I gather that she must have referred to these white cloths to recall our lunar birth dates. The birthday breakfast consisted of rice vermicelli served in a sweet syrup with one hard-boiled or half-boiled egg. I never knew how to react because the noodles were very sweet indeed but I was always terribly flattered that my mother would go a long way to ensure I had a long (hence the noodles) and sweet (represented by the syrup) life.

The recipe below is not the sweet version. It is the usual *mee sua* that we ate more commonly for breakfast or when we did not feel too well. My children love it and it takes very little time to make.

makes 4 servings

230 g or 8 ounces minced pork
1 teaspoon light soy sauce
Dash of white pepper
2 tablespoons vegetable oil
2 cloves garlic, peeled and minced

2 cups Chinese chicken broth
   (e.g. Swanson brand) or 2 cups water
   with 1 cube chicken flavouring
   (e.g. Knorr brand)
2 bundles fine rice vermicelli (*mee sua*)
1 egg, optional
Salt to taste

1. Combine the minced pork, light soy sauce and white pepper. Fashion lightly into meatballs

2. Heat oil in a saucepan. When the oil is glistening, add the minced garlic and fry until light brown and fragrant. Pour in the chicken broth or the plain water with the cube of chicken flavouring. Bring to a gentle boil.

3. Drop meatballs into the saucepan. Add the rice vermicelli and cook until are soft. Add egg to to poach, if desired. Season with salt according to taste.

4. Serve immediately as rice vermicelli tends to absorb liquid very quickly.

Kueh Ee
Red and White Glutinous Rice Balls in Syrup

My mother used to celebrate *Tang Chek*, a Chinese festival during the Winter Solstice in December. The day also marked the onset of preparations for the upcoming Chinese New Year. My mother used to say that if the weather was particularly hot on *Tang Chek*, it would rain on the first day of Chinese New Year, and vice versa. These red and white rice balls were largely prepared to observe Taoist customs in connection with *Tang Chek*. The two colours symbolised the yin and yang elements and while commercial rice balls are often filled with lotus paste, the Nonya version were purely sticky glutinous rice. When she became a Christian, she stopped making these rice balls. My family no longer observes the significance of this day too. *Kueh ee* was also prepared for weddings and I remember it being served at one of my relative's weddings.

makes 4 servings

230 g or 8 ounces glutinous rice flour
1 cup water
½ teaspoon red food colouring
230 g or 8 ounces sugar
4 cups water
3 *pandan* leaves, tied into a knot

1. Place the glutinous rice flour in a bowl and make a well in the centre. Add the 1 cup of water, a little at a time, in the middle. Use your hands or a metal spoon to mix the flour and water together to form a dough. Stop adding the water as soon as you obtain a nice consistency, to avoid making the dough too sticky.

2. Divide the dough into two portions .Add the red food colouring to one and knead well. Shape the dough to form little round balls of equal size, each about the size of a marble, 1.5 cm or ¾ inch in diameter.

3. Meanwhile, bring the sugar, 4 cups of water and *pandan* leaves to a boil in a pot and until the sugar dissolves.

4. Bring another large pot of water to a boil and drop the glutinous balls into the pot to boil, a few at a time. When the balls rise to the surface, use a slotted spoon to skim them off and transfer to the pot of sugar syrup.

5. Discard the *pandan* leaves. Serve the dessert in individual bowls.

The Secrets of Arab Street

My father was a sales manager for Fraser and Neave (F&N), then bottlers of Coca-Cola and producers of the local Tiger beer. He was offered the desirable job at a young age because of his soccer skills.

Playing for the Fraser and Neave football team as a Centre Right. My father is in the front row, second from right.

My father was recruited to play for the company team against the various trading houses established by the British. At F&N, as it was usually called, he handled several accounts and forged close friendships with several of his restaurant clients, including a famous Indian-Muslim restaurant called Jubilee.

In exchange for my father's tips on upcoming company parties to cater for, the original owner of Jubilee offered to teach my mother how to cook his restaurant's signature dishes such as *nasi biryani* (page 201) and *ayam kormak* (page 79). My father would drop my mother off at the Arab Street location so that she could observe what they were doing at the back of the restaurant. Of course, after half a day of class in the backstreet kitchen, she would walk a block away to the row of jewellers and check out their latest creations. There, up the flight of creaky wooden stairs to an air-conditioned room, the shop assistant served her F&N Orange Crush in its glass bottle with a green straw. Later, she would shop for a few yards of fabric for dresses she wanted to make for herself, haggling with the Indian-Muslim salesman before he would snip the textile from a ream and fold the piece of cloth several times into a floppy square. Those were her activities during her Arab Street excursion, often with me in tow.

My mother also befriended a network of Arab and Indonesian ladies who were renowned for their cakes and Malay dishes such as *soto ayam* (page 212) and *lontong* (page 208). She sought to be mentored by them. The Indonesian ladies were experts at the *lapis spekkoek* (page 114) and my mother was always open to learning new tips on how to improve her baking skills. Cik Wan, Khatijah and Rabeah were the ones we recall the most, as their names are scribbled at the top right hand corner of my mother's recipes. Their baking classes took place in their kitchens on many lazy schoolday afternoons, an intimate homely affair in a tree-lined residential street with children playing outside on their bicycles or picking pebbles.

We attended the lavish wedding banquets thrown by a few of these Arab and Indonesian families. Many of them were actually related by marriage, back when these prominent Arab families were residing in Indonesia. The patriarch lived in Telok Kurau, not too far from where my parents and grandparents had once lived. These elaborate wedding affairs demonstrated the ladies' talent and dedication because the meals, pastries, costumes and crafts were all home-made. I recall as a child, attending these wedding celebrations in their extensive garden compound. The lawn would be filled with dining tables and an endless supply of food would be brought out on three-foot long trays. Main courses such as *biryani* rice and meat were served on beautiful platters and pickles were presented in dainty glass dishes.

Some of my most vivid memories of those receptions are of the thirty-feet long tables displaying countless novelty cakes and colourful fruit gateaux. The three-dimensional cakes included a telephone and a doll and there was also

My parents at a party to celebrate my father's retirement from Fraser and Neave.

often a particularly delicious and fragrant orange cake. It is amazing how childhood memories can stay with you forever. To this day, I am always trying out an orange cake recipe, complete with orange-flavoured frosting, in a bid to re-create that special cake I first tasted as a child in that long hall, on that particular table.

The womenfolk took days to prepare these feasts. And while the festivities were taking place outside on the lawn, literally hidden behind the glamour of an impressive banquet and a delectable spread of gloriously frosted cakes, I would peek in to see them in their bedrooms, groaning in pain, aching from the strain of having cooked for a week straight, as the elder ladies massaged them with nutmeg oil.

These are indeed scenes of days past. The patriarch soon died in the late 1970s and the house was sold. A developer came and carved the lawn into lots, building on each lot a five-storey behemoth overshadowing a tiny concrete garden. The family broke into their nuclear units and moved into apartments. Without the generous kitchen space afforded them in the old house, they were never able to re-create the scale of such a banquet ever again.

When the original owner of the Jubilee died, the restaurant was taken over by a son-in-law. Over the years, the restaurant changed hands several times and my father soon lost touch with them.

Nasi Biryani
Rice Cooked in Ghee, served with Chicken in Spicy Gravy

My friend Anita who hails from Kerala makes *biryani* using only her mother's recipe. An acquaintance who is descended from a Rajasthani maharajah boasted that his recipe was royal. While I used to associate *biryani* only with Arab Street previously, it is no longer so. With the realisation that *nasi biryani* was rooted in Mughal culinary history and hence the evolution of India itself, I could now understand how an Indian–Muslim restaurant owner prided his restaurant's success on this one special dish.

It is often thought that the South East Asian version uses coconut milk, curry leaves and green chillies. The recipe below actually uses evaporated milk and a meat curry powder which my mother sourced from the wet market. I never recalled her adding her own home-made curry powder which was a Nonya version. Using a ready-made powder differed from the recipes of my Indian friends who may have ground their own fresh spice paste at the same time as they prepared this dish. I am very particular about the brand of *ghee* I use. I find *ghee* to be one of the richest and most flavourful ingredients, so it is important to use a brand that imparts a palatable taste.

makes 6 to 10 servings

600 g or 1 pound 5 ounces basmati rice

Water to parboil rice

2 teaspoons salt

1 whole chicken, each cut into 8 to 10 pieces

1 cardamom pod (*buah pelaga*)

1 small piece cassia bark (*kayu manis*)

3 cloves (*bunga chingkay*)

½ teaspoon cumin (*jintan puteh*)

½ teaspoon chilli powder

30 g or 1 ounce ginger, skinned and julienned

45 g or 1½ ounces garlic, peeled

250 g or 9 ounces *ghee* (preferably QBB brand)

150 g or 5 ounces shallots, peeled and sliced finely

1 teaspoon *biryani* chicken spice powder (suggest Shaan brand), mixed with 1 tablespoon water into a slurry

2 tomatoes, quartered

2 tablespoons tomato purée

1 bunch mint leaves, stemmed and plucked

½ cup evaporated milk, divided into two

½ teaspoon yellow food colouring

½ tablespoon rose water (*ayer mawa*)

1 bunch coriander leaves (cilantro), stemmed and chopped finely

3 green chillies, stemmed and sliced lengthwise

Lime juice (optional)

1. Rinse the rice until the water runs clear, about three times. Soak the rice for 30 minutes in cold water after rinsing ensuring that the water level is well over well over 10 cm or 4 inches above the level of the rice. Add 1 teaspoon salt and parboil the rice until it is three-quarters cooked. Strain the parboiled rice in a colander and set aside.

2. Meanwhile, rinse the chicken and pat dry. Leave aside or refrigerate.

3. Grind the cardamom, cassia, cloves, cumin, chilli powder, ginger and garlic into a fine paste.

4. Heat a pan and add the *ghee*. Fry the sliced shallots till light golden brown and set aside on a plate lined with absorbent paper. To the same pan, add the ground paste. Add the *biryani* chicken spice slurry, followed by the tomatoes, tomato purée and mint leaves. Fry until the tomatoes are softened. Add half of the evaporated milk and fry till fragrant. Add the chicken and cook on all sides to seal juices, about 5 minutes. Add remaining salt to season the chicken.

5. Place half of the parboiled rice in a large pot and scoop the curry gravy over the rice. Arrange the chicken over the rice. Then cover the chicken with the other half portion of rice. Combine the remaining evaporated milk, a teaspoon of salt, yellow food colouring and rose water. Drizzle solution evenly over the rice. Cover with a tight fitting lid and return to cooker to cook over low heat for about 30 minutes, till the rice is well cooked.

6. Garnish with the fried shallots, coriander leaves and green chillies. Stir in the optional lime juice.

Nasi Minyak

Rice Cooked in *Ghee*, to accompany gravy dishes

Nasi minyak provides a tasteful pairing for the gravy of *kormaks* and *rendang*s. When serving *nasi minyak*, my mother would throw in her *achar* pickles as a side dish.

makes 6 to 10 servings

900 g or 2 pounds basmati rice

110 g or 4 ounces *ghee*
(preferably QBB brand)

70 g or 2½ ounces shallots,
peeled and sliced finely

70 g or 2½ ounces garlic,
peeled and minced

1 tablespoon minced ginger

3 cups water

¾ cup evaporated milk

½ tablespoon lime juice

1. To cook the rice, rinse the rice until the water runs clear, about three times.

2. Heat a large saucepan and add the *ghee*. Fry the shallots until light golden brown, then add in the minced garlic and ginger. Lower heat and fry until fragrant. Pour in the water and turn up the heat to bring to a boil. Add the rice.

3. When the rice is boiling, lower to a simmer and cover the pot until the rice is cooked. Then use a fork to fluff the rice, stirring in the evaporated milk and lime juice. Cover and let it steam in its own heat for about 10 minutes.

Ikan Masak Ceylon

Fish Cooked Ceylon Style

My mother often asked me to read this particular recipe to her, given by one of her Malay friends. The fish tasted good and that is why I always had it in mind to include it.

makes 4 to 6 servings

3 to 4 steaks of mackerel (*ikan tenggiri*), each 5 cm or 2 inch thick

2 tablespoons coriander powder

1 teaspoon cumin (*jintan puteh*)

1 teaspoon fennel (*jintan manis*)

2 teaspoons black pepper cloves

30 dried chillies, deseeded

6 cloves garlic, peeled

20 shallots, peeled and quartered

3 tablespoons oil

120 g or 4 ounces tamarind (*assam*) paste, soaked in 1½ cup hot water

Salt to taste

1 bunch coriander leaves (cilantro), stemmed

Green and red chillies, sliced lengthwise

1. Rinse the fish steaks and pat dry.

2. Grind the coriander, cumin, fennel, black pepper and dried chilli, garlic, ginger and shallots.

3. Heat a saucepan and add oil. When the oil is glistening, gently fry the spice paste. Add the fish steaks.

4. Strain the *assam* and add the juice to the saucepan. Bring to a boil, then lower to a simmer until the fish is cooked through, and the gravy thickens.

5. Transfer to a serving platter. Garnish with coriander leaves (cilantro) and sliced chillies.

Ayam Panggang

Spicy Grilled Chicken

When I tire of the usual roast chicken seasoned with rosemary, thyme, garlic and lemon juice, I resort to a spicy grilled version that gives me more zest than the common roast chicken usually does. It is good enough to eat with plain white rice, some cucumber and tomato slices. Also, because I cook indoors, this dish can be as easily broiled as it is grilled.

makes 4 to 6 servings

- **1 whole chicken, cut into 8 to 10 pieces**
- **2.5 cm or 1 inch galangal (*lengkuas*), skinned and julienned**
- **2.5 cm or 1 inch turmeric (*kunyit*), skinned and julienned**
- **2 stalks lemon grass (*seray*), upper stalks and outer layers removed, sliced thinly**
- **20 shallots, peeled and quartered**
- **2 heads garlic, peeled**
- **8 to 10 red chillies**
- **½ cup oil**
- **1¾ cups coconut milk, reserve coconut cream**
- **1 tablespoon tamarind (*assam*), soaked in ½ cup hot water**
- **Salt**
- **Sugar**

1. Rinse the chicken pieces and pat dry.

2. Grind the galangal, turmeric, lemon grass, shallots, garlic and red chillies into a fine spice paste.

3. Heat a Dutch oven and add the oil. When the oil is glistening, gently fry the spice paste over low heat until fragrant, being careful not to burn the spice paste. Add the chicken pieces. Pour in the coconut milk, reserving the top layer of coconut cream for use later. Turn up the heat and bring to a boil. Strain the tamarind liquid and pour into the pot. Lower heat to a simmer. Season with salt and sugar.

4. When the chicken is tender, transfer the pieces to a baking tray (if broiling) or to a heated grill. Reserve the gravy. Grill until the pieces are golden brown. Transfer chicken to a serving platter and pour the gravy over or serve on the side.

Ayam Rendang
Chicken in Spicy Coconut Gravy

My mother learnt to make this from the old Jubilee restaurant. It was one of the dishes taught to her at the back of their Arab Street restaurant back in the 1960s. Over the years, she adjusted the ingredient amounts to suit her own palate and to make up for the evolutionary change in the flavours of these ingredients.

makes 4 to 6 servings

- 12 to 15 pieces chicken, preferably thighs or drumsticks
- 1 teaspoon fennel (*jintan manis*)
- 1 teaspoon cumin (*jintan puteh*)
- 1½ tablespoons chilli powder
- ½ teaspoon ground turmeric powder
- 70 g or 2½ ounces ginger, skinned and julienned
- 15 g or ½ ounce garlic, peeled
- 2 tablespoons oil
- 150 g or 5 ounces shallots, peeled and sliced finely
- 1 cup coconut milk, reserve coconut cream
- 2 tomatoes, quartered
- 1 bunch mint leaves, stems removed
- 1 bunch coriander leaves (cilantro), stems removed

1. Rinse chicken pieces and pat dry.

2. Grind the fennel, cumin, chilli powder, ground turmeric powder, ginger and garlic.

3. Heat a Dutch oven and add oil. Fry the sliced shallots until light golden brown. Add the ground ingredients and fry over low heat until fragrant, being careful not to burn the spice paste. Add the chicken pieces. Pour in the coconut milk, reserving the top layer of coconut cream for use later. Turn up the heat and bring to boil. Toss in the quartered tomatoes. Lower heat to a simmer. Season with salt.

4. Transfer to a serving dish and garnish with the mint and coriander leaves.

Lontong
Rice Cubes with Assorted Vegetables in Spicy Coconut Gravy

As a child, I used to tag along with my mother on *Hari Raya* day and have at least three *lontong* lunches at the various homes of her Muslim friends. Because they all lived close to one another in Telok Kurau, we travelled from one house to another on a *bek chia* (trishaw).

From my interpretation, *lontong* actually refers to a meal in which the staple is the compressed rice, also called *lontong*. The major sidekick is *sayur lodeh* which is made up of vegetables simmered in a spicy coconut gravy. A generous topping of *serunding* made of grated coconut thickens the gravy. That said, *lontong*, being a dish of vegetables, is typically served with *opor ayam* (page 215), beef *rendang* (page 216) and *bergedil* (page 211).

makes 8 to 10 servings

sayur lodeh

3 tablespoons coriander (*ketumbar*)

5 cm or 2 inches galangal (*lengkuas*), skinned and julienned

2.5 cm or 1 inch turmeric (*kunyit*), skinned and finely sliced

60 g or 2 ounces dried shrimps, rinsed and pat dry, then ground

15 shallots, peeled and quartered

10 dried chillies, soaked in hot water for at least 20 minutes

30 g or 1 ounce *belachan*

2 tablespoons oil

1 cup coconut milk, reserve coconut cream

4 cups water

200 g or 7 ounces long beans, trimmed and cut into 4 cm or 1½ inch lengths

200 g or 7 ounces jicama (*bangkuang*), peeled and julienned, then blanched

200 g or 7 ounces cabbage, cut into 2.5 cm or 1 inch squares

300 g or 11 ounces prawns (shrimps), peeled and deveined

4 pieces fermented bean curd cakes (*tempeh*), blanched in salted water and shallow-fried to light brown

4 pieces firm bean curd (*taukua*), each halved and seared to light brown

Salt to taste

Sugartp taste

900 g or 2 pounds rice, cooked to make compressed rice cakes (*lontong*) *

* The compressed rice cake can be prepared by cooking the rice in a rice cooker. When the rice is fully cooked and still hot, compress it into a loaf tin, invert and slice into 2.5-cm or 1-inch cubes.

sambal

10 shallots, peeled and quartered

3 cloves garlic, peeled

15 dried chillies, soaked in hot water
for at least 20 minutes

30 g or 1 ounce *belachan*

Sugar to taste

Oil for frying

serunding

2 tablespoons ground coriander
(*ketumbar*)

1 teaspoon cumin (*jintan puteh*)

2 teaspoons fennel (*jintan manis*)

2.5 cm or 1 inch galangal (*lengkuas*),
skinned and julienned

2.5 cm or 1 inch ginger,
skinned and julienned

2 stalks lemon grass (*seray*),
upper stalks and outer layers
removed, sliced thinly

10 dried chillies, soaked in hot
water for 30 minutes

5 cloves garlic, peeled

2 onions, peeled and chopped coarsely

200 g or 7 ounces ground beef

2 cups grated coconut

Salt

Sugar

sayur lodeh

1.   Grind the spice paste adding the ingredients in the order as follows: coriander, galangal, turmeric, dried shrimp, shallots, dried chillies and *belachan*.

2.   Heat a Dutch oven and add the oil. Fry the spice paste over low heat until fragrant. Add the coconut milk, setting aside the top layer of coconut cream for later. Pour in 2 cups of the water and bring to a boil.

3.   Add the long beans, jicama and boil a little longer until the long beans and jicama are tender. Then add in the cabbage and prawns. Bring to a simmer, adding more water but making sure not to dilute the gravy too much. Finally, add the coconut cream, followed by the fermented soy bean cake and bean curd. Continue to simmer for another 15 minutes and season with salt and sugar according to taste.

sambal

1.   Grind the shallots, garlic, dried chillies and *belachan*. Add sugar if necessary, according to taste. Heat a small pan and add some oil. Fry the *sambal* over low heat until fragrant. Transfer to a small serving dish.

serunding

1.   Grind in sequence, the ground coriander, cumin, fennel, galangal, ginger, lemon grass, dried chillies, garlic and onions into a fine spice paste.

2.   Combine with the ground beef.

3.   Heat a wok and dry-fry the grated coconut until it turns golden brown. Add the beef and spice mixture. Stir-fry until combined completely. The *serunding* should be dry. Season with more salt or sugar if necessary, according to taste.

serving the *lontong*

1.   In a shallow soup bowl, place a few cubes of the compressed rice cake.

2.   Ladle the *sayur lodeh* over the compressed rice cakes, providing enough gravy to make it a soupy dish.

3.   Garnish by sprinkling the *serunding* over the dish and serve with the *sambal* on the side. This dish can also be served with *bergedil* (page 211) on the side.

Bergedil
Fried Potato Croquettes

These fried potato patties are truly delicious with *lontong* (page 208) and *soto ayam* (page 212). Sometimes, my mother even served them for dinner, to go with rice and other meat dishes. They can also be served as a snack, on their own. My kids love them.

makes 8 servings

330 g or 1½ pounds russet potatoes

300 g or 11 ounces ground beef

2 stalks spring onions (scallions), use green part only, sliced very finely

2 tablespoons coriander leaves (cilantro), stemmed, chopped finely

2 teaspoons finely sliced shallots, fried

½ teaspoon ground nutmeg (*buah pala*)

1 teaspoon freshly ground black pepper

1 teaspoon salt

2 eggs, separate yolks from the white

3 cups corn oil

1. Place potatoes in a large saucepan and cover with sufficient cold water. Bring to a boil. When the potatoes can be pierced through easily with a paring knife, drain the water and let the potatoes cool. Peel and mash the potatoes.

2. Combine the mashed potatoes, ground beef, spring onions, coriander leaves, fried shallots, nutmeg, black pepper and salt. Add one egg yolk first. Mix well. If the mixture is still dry, add the second egg yolk.

3. Form the mixture into patties using about 2 tablespoons mixture per patty.

4. Beat egg whites and set aside.

5. Heat a wok and add the corn oil. When the oil is glistening, dip each *bergedil* patty into the egg whites and slide into the wok to fry until light golden brown. Do not overcrowd the wok. Turn the patties over midway.

6. Remove each patty carefully with a slotted spoon and transfer to a platter lined with absorbent paper. These *bergedil* are best served immediately.

Soto Ayam
Chicken Shreds and Rice Cubes in Spicy Chicken Broth

Soto ayam is a sensational soup. It gives a warm spicy kick in the belly like a chicken soup on fire. I like to dunk a *bergedil* (page 211) in the soup to make it hearty.

makes 4 to 6 servings

soup
1 whole chicken, about 1.4 kg or 3 pounds
4 tablespoons coriander seeds
   (*ketumbar*)
1 tablespoon white pepper cloves
1 tablespoon cumin (*jintan puteh*)
10 candlenuts (*buah keras*)
2 bunches lemon grass (*seray*) use bottom
   third, smashed and sliced finely
2.5 cm or 1 inch galangal (*lengkuas*),
   skinned and julienned
2.5 cm or 1 inch turmeric (*kunyit*),
   skinned and julienned
5cm or 2 inches ginger,
   skinned and julienned
5 cloves garlic, peeled
20 shallots, peeled and quartered
2 tablespoons oil
Salt to taste
600 g or 1 pound 5 ounces rice, cooked
   to make compressed cakes (*lontong*)*
200 g or 7 ounces glass vermicelli
   (*tang hoon*), soaked or blanched till
   tender, then strained

200 g or 7 ounces bean sprouts, tails
   plucked, blanched and strained
1 bunch spring onions (scallions), green
   portion only, chopped finely
1 bunch coriander leaves (cilantro)
5 tablespoons fried finely sliced shallots
Calamansi limes (*limau kesturi*) (optional)

spice sachet (optional)
4 tablespoons coriander (*ketumbar*)
2 tablespoons white pepper cloves
3 teaspoons cumin (*jintan puteh*)

sambal
60 g or 2 ounces bird's eye chilli (*cili padi*)
Salt to taste
Sugar to taste
Vinegar to taste

* The compressed rice cakes can be prepared by cooking the rice in a rice cooker. When the rice is fully cooked and still hot, compress it into a loaf tin. Invert and slice into 2.5-cm or 1-inch cubes.

1. Rinse chicken and pat dry. Place in a large pot and cover with cold water. Bring to a boil until chicken is tender and well-cooked. Transfer the chicken to a platter and let cool. Meanwhile, reserve the stock. Shred the chicken meat.

2. Grind the coriander seeds, white pepper cloves, cumin, candlenuts, lemon grass, galangal, turmeric, ginger, garlic and shallots.

3. Heat a Dutch oven and add the oil. Fry the ground ingredients over low heat until fragrant, being careful not to burn the spice paste. Then add the chicken stock and bring to a boil. At this point, drop the optional spice sachet into the pot.

4. When the soup is sufficiently flavourful, remove the sachet, if used. Season with salt.

5. To make the *sambal*, grind the bird's eye chilli into a semi-fine paste. Season with salt, sugar and vinegar according to taste.

6. To serve the *soto ayam*, arrange a few cubes of compressed rice in each soup bowl, followed by glass vermicelli, bean sprouts, shredded chicken and *bergedil* (page 211). Add soup to cover the rice cubes and vermicelli, then garnish with spring onions, coriander leaves and fried shallots. Add a dollop of *sambal*. Squeeze some lime juice over the *soto ayam* before serving, if preferred.

Opor Ayam
Chicken in Mild Coconut Sauce

There are two methods of cooking this dish. My mother's original recipe called for the coconut cream to be heated before adding the spice paste. This is often how Thai curries are prepared. Another method is to fry the spice paste over low heat, and then add the thin coconut milk, followed by the coconut cream at the end, so that the cream does not curdle. Here I provide both methods so you can try the different styles for yourself.

makes 4 to 6 servings

1 whole chicken, about 1.4 kg or 3 pounds, cut up into 8 to 10 pieces

1 teaspoon white pepper

3 tablespoons ground coriander (*ketumbar*)

¼ tablespoon turmeric (*kunyit*) powder

2 candlenuts (*buah keras*)

2.5 cm or 1 inch galangal (*lengkuas*), skinned and julienned

1 stalk lemon grass (*seray*), upper stalks and outer layers removed, sliced thinly

8 shallots, peeled (quartered if using Method 1, finely sliced if using Method 2)

1 clove garlic, peeled

¼ cup peanut or corn oil (if using Method 2)

4 tomatoes, quartered

Salt to taste

8 cups coconut milk, reserve coconut cream

2 tablespoons grated coconut, dry-fried or toasted

5 green chillies, sliced lengthwise

Method 1

1. Rinse chicken pieces and pat dry.

2. Grind the white pepper, ground coriander, ground turmeric, candlenuts, galangal, lemon grass, shallots and garlic into a fine spice paste. Marinate the chicken with the spice paste and set aside for at least an hour.

3. Heat a Dutch oven and add the coconut cream. Warm up the coconut cream until a greasy film appears. Add the marinated chicken. Then add the coconut milk and bring to a boil. Add the tomatoes. Lower to a simmer until the sauce thickens. Season with salt according to taste. Add the grated coconut and green chillies and serve.

Method 2

1. Rinse chicken pieces and pat dry.

2. Grind the white pepper, ground coriander, ground turmeric, candlenuts, galangal, lemon grass and garlic into a fine spice paste.

3. Heat a Dutch oven and add the oil. Fry the sliced shallots until these turn light golden brown. Add the ground ingredients and fry over low heat until fragrant, being careful not to burn the spice paste. Add the chicken pieces. Pour in the coconut milk, reserving the top layer of coconut cream for use later. Turn up the heat and bring to a boil. Toss in the quartered tomatoes. Then lower to a simmer. Season with salt according to taste. Add the coconut cream, grated coconut and green chillies and serve.

Beef Rendang
Beef Cubes Simmered in Spicy Coconut Gravy

The secret to a desirable beef *rendang* is to ensure that the beef is simmered slowly until it is tender and the gravy is thick. I have incorporated the French technique of searing the beef on all sides to lock in the juice before braising.

makes 4 to 6 servings

680 g or 1½ pounds beef fillet, cut into 2.5 cm or 1 inch cubes

2.5 cm or 1 inch galangal (*lengkuas*), skinned and julienned

2.5cm or 1 inch ginger, skinned and julienned

2 stalks lemon grass (*seray*), upper stalks and outer layers removed, sliced thinly

10 shallots, peeled

4 cloves garlic, peeled

10 dried chillies, soaked in hot water

30 g or 1 ounce *belachan*

Vegetable oil for frying

1 cup coconut milk, reserve coconut cream

1 tablespoon tamarind (*assam*) pulp, soaked in ½ cup hot water

2 kaffir lime leaves (*daun limau purut*)

6 *salam* leaves (*daun salam*), omit if not available

Salt to taste

Sugar to taste

1 cup grated coconut, dry-fried or toasted

1. Rinse beef cubes and pat dry.

2. Grind the galangal, ginger, lemon grass, shallots, garlic, dried chillies and *belachan* into a fine spice paste.

3. Heat a large saucepan and add the oil. Fry the spice paste over low heat until fragrant, being careful not to burn the spice paste. Add the beef cubes and make sure to sear all sides. Pour in the coconut milk, reserving the top layer of coconut cream for use later. Strain the tamarind juice into the saucepan. Add the kaffir lime leaves and *salam* leaves. Turn up the heat and bring to a boil. Lower heat, cover and simmer for an hour. Then uncover and turn up to medium heat to thicken the gravy. When the gravy thickens and the beef is tender, at least after another hour, pour in the coconut cream and remove from heat. Season with salt and sugar according to taste. Add the toasted grated coconut and serve.

Our Daily Fare

We did not always eat elaborate meals.
While my mother cooked all these special
occasion meals, threw parties and made
cookies and kueh chang to sell, she left the
daily meals in the care of the maid.

Ah Seng the delivery grocer came daily and recommended his fresh picks from the market. Without fail each morning, my mother would sigh *"Ini hari masak apa?"* ("What should I cook today?"), somewhat at a loss about how best to feed her brood with a variety of dishes. Yet, she never truly veered far off from a repertoire that we grew up on, recipes she knew by heart but which upon later research, I realised had been adapted from the cookbooks of Ellice Handy, Tham Yui Kai or Huang Su Huei.

She could be adventurous. When Kentucky Fried Chicken (KFC) first arrived, one of its first outlets was in Siglap. I loved KFC, which I still do today. My mother retrieved some fried chicken recipes from her Malay friends and replicated the entire meal for us, right down to the coleslaw and mashed potatoes, side dishes being rather alien to us then.

She got her groceries in various ways. For the most part, Ah Seng, whom I think of as the original webvan grocer, delivered most of my mother's meats and vegetables. Yet, every so often, she might run out of a particular ingredient and would have the maid walk two blocks to Siglap Market to pick it up. Sometimes, the poor maid might have to walk to the market five times! My mother also used a provision shop in Frankel Estate. Such shops are a rare sight these days. The dimly lit shop was lined with walls of wooden shelves displaying condiments and canned food. There were also storage jars of rice, mung beans, salted eggs and other grains. Upon receiving a phone call, the shopkeeper would take down the various ordered items, place them in a brown shopping bag with skinny red and white strings. He would then have someone bicycle the items over to the housewife. There was a charge account and the bill would be settled on a regular basis.

My father was very much an old-school Baba who believed that daily dinner should consist of a soup, one vegetable, perhaps some pickles and *belachan*, and two other dishes consisting of meat or fish. These were served family style, with plain white rice as the staple. It was his habit to scoop soup and drizzle it over his plain rice. He was particularly observant about table manners. He forbade us from stacking plates while we ate, saying that it was taboo or else one would owe money to others. He also disliked children eating with their elbows resting on the table. My mother had her superstitions too. One should not settle a bill while still eating or be subject to someone else sweeping at her feet while she was still dining. It was all symbolic of money matters.

Early on, we all scooped from a large communal soup bowl. Over time, it seemed only healthier to have our individual soup bowls. Besides, we also placed a serving spoon for each dish. We ate with a mish mash of cutlery. Contrary to the impression that all Babas ate with their fingers, we used the fork and spoon, following the Anglo-Indian tradition. Nevertheless, we were never supposed to eat with our left hand. It was the hand used for cleaning ourselves. Quite a challenge considering that my father, sister and I are left-handed!

We used to eat a lot more deep-fried food then. The oil used to fry these foods was siphoned off into a metal storage can and recycled for the next frying. MSG was a staple. Vegetables were not always featured, a habit that was the hardest to break after years of thinking that vegetables were too cheap to serve.

Because my parents lived through and survived the war, they were always very careful to store plenty of rice in the house. On the morning of September 11, 2001, the first thing my father told me when we talked on the phone was "Quick, rush downstairs and stock up on rice and canned food."

The Babas had their idiosyncratic customs. Watery rice porridge was only served if someone was ill! So even if we craved and cooked porridge, someone might exclaim "*Siapa sakit?*" ("Who's sick?").

I will best remember my father for his fondness for breakfasts. A few of these memorable dishes included canned corn beef or sardines mashed with fresh cut red chillies and onions; or bread toast with a topping of fried minced pork. Mornings smelled of a strange concoction of his Brylcreem hair cream and whatever was for breakfast.

My father sometimes came home late in the evenings after a long day at the orchid nursery or a game of mahjong. He used to bring home chicken *murtabak* from Adam Road; or seafood *horfun* wrapped in the white *opau* leaves. He was sometimes full of surprises upon his return. Once, he came back with two kittens for me. Another, he boxed up a live turkey. The turkey messed up the bathroom at the back and my father expected my mother to find a way to slaughter it in time for Christmas.

My father passed on a talent to our sister Beng. Both have a knack for finding nooks and corners in Singapore selling delicious food. Many years ago, Beng held her son's seventh birthday party at a divey Telok Kurau corner coffee shop. One of the stalls there served chilli crab which Beng insisted was "out of this world". By the end of the night, my father ranted that Beng was "out of her mind" hosting his grandson's birthday party in what he considered a dingey place. A few years later, a famous New-York based French chef, Jean-Georges Vongerichten, told *The Wall Street Journal* that one of his favourite Asian places to eat at was this particular chilli crab stall. By the same token, my father used to take me to the back kitchen of a Malay house in Telok Kurau. They sold *lontong* for breakfast which only those in the know knew about. The owner of the house actually stood by the door to collect money. Taxi drivers and security guards came by to eat.

Later on, my father got interested in Indian *thosai* sold in Ceylon Road. When my husband first visited Singapore, he used to run by the beach and then meet up with my father who had his early morning swim with his retiree friends. From there, my father would bike to Ceylon Road while my husband would run alongside him. They would take a break and have their *thosai* breakfast.

My father also introduced Tracy to *murtabak* (a pan-fried bread, usually stuffed with minced meat) and the two of them swore by Zam Zam along Arab Road. It became a ritual to touch down at Changi Airport and then zoom off to Zam Zam every time we visited Singapore.

Our family had a passion for consuming delicious food, whether they were legally sold or not. In the afternoons, we would wait for the fat *pao* man who came on a tricycle cart, the front of which was a multi-tier steamer containing *siew mai, har kow* and *cha siew pao*. Molly also had a standing account with the Magnolia ice cream man who drove by at 3 pm daily in his lightweight three-wheel scooter van to deliver Magnolia chocolate milk, and *potong* ice cream sandwiched with light golden wafers. Maggie also mentioned the truck that came around on Fridays to sell fish and chips. Most memorable of all was the Malay *satay* man who came with a grill tucked at the back of his bicycle. One day, he stationed himself outside Aunty Paddy's house, fanning the beef and chicken satay for us, laughing and joking and surrounded by a crowd of us neighbours, all of us oblivious to the fact that the Ministry of Health inspectors had just closed in. They lifted the man's bike with all our satay still on the grill, and hopped back into the van. They drove off, never to be seen again.

The family often walked to the Siglap Hill area whenever there was a *pasar malam* (night market) that ringed around the St. Stephen's school field. There, we would stock up on bags of *keropok* (fish crackers) or grab a late night snack of *goreng pisang* (banana fritters).

Weekends, one of us often walked to the old Siglap market to shop for *chai tow kway, chwee kway, packet nasi lemak, putu mayam* or *mee pok*. I liked my *chai tow kway* especially black with the sweet sauce and egg-crispy around the edges. We would never forget to buy *tauhway chwee* (fresh soy milk) in rectangular packets suspended by thin red plastic strings.

Lunch was sometimes a trip to Katong to pick up *kon loh meen*, chicken rice or our family favourite, *o pau* (stuffed tofu cakes). Tay Buan Guan was the supermarket we grew up with and it was a treat for me as a child to go there. I could sit in the supermarket trolley, I got my first Easter chocolate bunny from there and had my first whiff of strawberries which we rarely bought because they were pricey. I always longed for those plump and fragrant strawberries and from young, associated them with what was best and fresh about living overseas.

My mother personally trained each new maid the rudiments of her cooking and then supervised them over a repertoire of our regular meals. They also assisted whenever she personally prepared the Sunday meals and party buffets. When they left our employ and returned to their native countries, they would in turn open their own restaurants. After my mother passed away, my sister in fact re-employed a former housekeeper simply because she knew how we ate and could replicate the dishes that my father was accustomed to.

As my parents got older, they spent their leisurely afternoons being served tea or Milo, along with some pastries. As with many old Baba families, my parents observed the English tradition of afternoon tea. I guess you could strip the old British colonial surroundings away from them, but never the Anglophilic habits instilled from young.

Ikan Nanas

Fish in Spicy Soup with Pineapple

Many recipes abound with a version that includes shrimp and titled *udang masak pedas nanas*. When I asked my father, he recalled that we often made ours with fish. He simply called it *ikan nanas*.

The pineapple imparts a sweet and sour tang to the thin gravy. We drizzled the gravy over the plain white rice and it made all the difference to the meal.

makes 6 to 8 servings

spice paste
1 cm or ½ inch galangal (*lengkuas*), skinned and julienned finely
1 cm or ½ inch turmeric (*kunyit*), skinned and sliced finely
5 candlenuts (*buah keras*)
3 fresh red chillies, stems removed
140 g or 5 ounces shallots, peeled and quartered
1 tablespoon *belachan*

main dish
600 g or 1¼ pounds *ikan parang* (dorab or wolf herring)* or *ikan kekek* (silver belly bream)
1 pineapple, sweet
110 g or 4 ounces tamarind (*assam*) pulp, soaked in hot water for 30 minutes
8 cups hot water
1 tablespoon oil
1 tablespoon salt
1 tablespoon sugar

* You may substitute with prawns (shrimps). Devein and trim the feelers.

spice paste

1. Pound or blend the ingredients in the order given until you achieve a fine paste.

main dish

1. Rinse and pat dry the fish.

2. Skin and core the pineapple. Remove the eyes. Slice into triangles, about 3 cm or 1½ inches.

3. Strain the tamarind and discard the pulp. Reserve the tamarind juice.

4. Heat a deep saucepan and add oil. Fry spice paste, lower the heat so as not to burn. Add half of the tamarind juice and bring to boil. Add the pineapple slices and lower the heat to a simmer.

5. After 10 minutes, add the fish and more of the tamarind juice to cover the fish. Simmer until the fish turns opaque and is cooked. Season with salt and sugar, adjusting the amount of sugar depending on the sweetness of the pineapple.

6. You can add more of the tamarind juice if you like your dish to be more soupy.

Squid Stuffed with Minced Pork in Soup

A few of my mother's friends made a business of cooking for families whose parents both worked. They simply cooked extra what they would serve their own family, and charged on a weekly basis. This home catering still exists despite the onslaught of maids, frozen prepared food and hawker centres. If I had been one of those modern working mothers in the 1970s, and had found it challenging to work and cook, I would surely have done the same because it just seems so much more wholesome than hawker food. Each evening, the mothers would drive over and pick up a tiffin full of home-cooked food. In addition, there would be a separate metal *tingkat* for soup. And it might surely have included this delicious soup of *sotong* stuffed with minced pork.

I rarely see this soup in any restaurant. I gather that this is truly one of those dishes you would only find at home.

makes 4 to 6 servings

450 g or 1 pound squid, whole

90 g or 3 ounces glass vermicelli (*tang hoon*), soaked in warm water

230 g or 8 ounces ground pork

½ teaspoon salt

¼ teaspoon white pepper

3 teaspoons light soy sauce

2 stalks spring onion (scallion), use green part only, sliced finely

1 tablespoon vegetable oil

2 cloves garlic, minced

6 cups water

1 teaspoon salt

1 teaspoon pepper

1 teaspoon light soy sauce

1 bunch coriander leaves (cilantro), chopped finely

1. Rinse the squid. Discard the head and tentacles and pull out the insides including the quill and ink sac. Strain in a colander or pat dry. Refrigerate for the time being.

2. Soak the glass vermicelli in a bowl of warm water.

3. Combine the ground pork, salt, white pepper, light soy sauce and spring onion. Set aside for at least 30 minutes. Stuff the pork mixture into the cavity of each squid, filling up to three-quarters of the squid and not more. (The squid will shrink after cooking).

4. Roll the remaining pork mixture into balls. Set aside on a plate and refrigerate.

5. Meanwhile, heat a large saucepan and add the oil. When the oil is warm, add the minced garlic. Fry until light brown and fragrant, then pour in the water. Bring to a boil.

6. Add in the stuffed squid and additional meatballs and let boil briefly, then lower to a simmer until the squid and meatballs float to the surface. Add the salt, pepper and light soy sauce according to taste.

7. Strain the glass vermicelli soaking in the bowl of warm water. Add to the soup when just about to serve— glass vermicelli has a tendency to soak up the soup and turn soggy. Garnish with coriander leaves and serve.

Chicken Macaroni Soup

My mother liked to serve this soup at her *popiah* parties. I do not know how this came about—perhaps to feed children who may not have acquired a taste for *popiah*. To spiff it up, she threw in coriander leaves (cilantro), fried shallots, lots of croutons and chunky, meaty shreds of chicken.

makes 6 servings

1 whole chicken, about 1.2 kg or 2½ pounds

10 cups cold water

1 teaspoon whole black peppercorns

1 teaspoon light soy sauce

½ teaspoon sesame oil

1 teaspoon salt

½ teaspoon white pepper

8 slices white bread

2 cups corn oil

140 g or 5 ounces shallots, peeled and sliced finely

½ bunch coriander leaves (cilantro), stems removed

macaroni

400 g or 1 pound uncooked macaroni pasta (also called elbow pasta)

20 cups cold water

1 teaspoon salt

1. Rinse the chicken and pat dry. Trim off excess skin, fat and the tail end. Place in a stockpot and fill with the cold water (adding more water to cover the chicken if necessary), along with the black peppercorns. Bring to a boil, partially covered, and then turn heat down to a simmer, covered, for another 30 minutes. Skim the surface of the stock to remove impurities.

2. Reserving the stock, scoop the cooked chicken into a colander and place it under cold running water to stop the cooking process. Let the chicken cool completely.

3. Remove the chicken skin and peel the meat off the bones, tearing the meat into shreds. Return the carcass to the stockpot and continue to simmer for another 30 minutes. Season the stock with the light soy sauce, sesame oil, salt and white pepper, adjusting according to taste. Clarify the stock by passing through a sieve.

4. Meanwhile, using a bread knife, trim the crusts off the white bread. Then, slice the bread into 1-cm or ½-inch cubes. Heat a wok or deep stir-fry pan on high and fill with the corn oil. When the oil is glistening, fry the bread cubes, a cup at a time. Turn over occasionally. When the cubes are light golden brown, use a slotted spoon to transfer them to a plate lined with absorbent paper.

5. After the bread cubes have been prepared, use the same oil to fry the shallots until these turn light golden brown. Remove to a separate plate lined with absorbent paper.

6. Fill a large pot with 20 cups of cold water and a teaspoon of salt. Bring to a rapid boil. Boil the macaroni pasta according to box instructions. Test the pasta when it reaches to ¾ of the cooking time specified on the box to check for *al dente* consistency. When the pasta is cooked to your preference, about 5 to 6 minutes in total, strain the pot of water and pour the cooked pasta into a colander. Run it under cold water to stop the cooking process.

7. To serve the macaroni, place some of the cooked macaroni pasta in a bowl, top with shreds of chicken. Ladle some soup stock over, garnish with croutons, fried shallots and coriander leaves.

NOTE: Remove the croutons and shallots while they are still light golden brown as they will darken further out of the pan.

Pork Meatballs and Tofu Soup

To counter spicy dishes in any given evening's menu, my mother would balance the meal with something gentler on the stomach. This meatball soup was a perfect accompaniment. It is also a good introduction to solid food for young children. Meat and tofu are nutritious ingredients for growing toddlers.

In the past, the soup stock would have been derived from boiling water and adding a stock cube. These days, I prefer to prepare or buy natural chicken stock which should not contain monosodium glutamate.

makes 4 to 6 servings

340 g or 12 ounces minced pork
2 teaspoons light soy sauce
1 teaspoon salt
2 teaspoons sugar
2 teaspoons cornflour
2 stalks spring onion (scallion), white part discarded, green chopped finely

1 tablespoon cooking oil
2 cloves garlic, minced
4 cups chicken stock, preferably an Asian derived stock
340 g or 12 ounces soft soy bean curd
1 teaspoon salt
½ teaspoon white pepper

1.   Combine the minced pork, light soy sauce, salt, sugar, cornstarch and 2 teaspoons of the chopped spring onion. Set aside to season for at least 15 minutes.

2.   Heat a large saucepan and add the oil. Fry the minced garlic until fragrant and light brown. Pour in the chicken stock, cover and bring to a boil.

3.   Fashion the pork mixture and form balls of equal size, about 2.5 cm or 1 inch in diameter. Drop them into the stock. Bring to a gentle boil. Then lower to a simmer.

4.   Cut the soft bean curd into 2.5-cm or 1-inch cubes. Drop them into the soup and continue to simmer until the pork balls rise to the surface. Season the soup with salt and white pepper to taste. Garnish with the remaining slices of spring onion.

Ayam Kombak

Chicken and Dried Mushrooms Simmered in Fermented Soy Bean Paste

My mother preferred to keep this for a few days and serve it for breakfast with French loaf bread (baguette). It was one of my father's favourite morning treats. The aroma evokes memories of him sitting at the kitchen table, freshly Brylcreemed and shaven, scooping up the *kombak* gravy with a pinch of bread. This dish can taste salty on its own and is best eaten with rice or bread. As with many similar Nonya gravy dishes, *ayam kombak* tastes even better the next day.

makes 6 servings

1.5 kg or 3¼ pounds chicken, cut into serving pieces

1 tablespoon dark soy sauce

1 tablespoon sugar

10 dried Chinese mushrooms, soaked in hot water for 30 minutes

2 tablespoons vegetable oil

3 cloves garlic, minced

230 g or 8 ounces fermented soy beans (*taucheo*), lightly mashed

2 cups water

Red or green chillies, optional

1. Rinse and pat dry the chicken pieces. Marinate with the black soy sauce and sugar. Set aside for at least an hour.

2. Remove the Chinese mushrooms from the hot water. Stem each mushroom.

3. Heat a Dutch oven or wok and add the oil. When the oil begins to glisten, add in the minced garlic and mashed soy bean paste. Stir fry for half a minute, then add in the chicken. Turn the chicken parts over to ensure that each is glazed on all sides.

4. Add the water and Chinese mushrooms and bring to a boil. Turn down the heat to simmer, covered, for at least 30 minutes until the chicken is tender. Serve with red or green chillies, if desired.

Udang Garam Assam

Prawns in Thin Spicy Tangy Tamarind Gravy

My mother left a recipe for *rempah garam assam* (or *garam assam* spice paste). I have also tried this dish using fish, particularly red snapper or sea bass.

makes 4 to 6 servings

spice paste

90 g or 3 ounces galangal (*lengkuas*), skinned and julienned finely

30 g or 1 ounce turmeric (*kunyit*), skinned and sliced finely

110 g or 4 ounces lemon grass (*seray*), upper stalks and outer layers removed, sliced thinly

45 g or 1½ ounces candlenuts

200 g or 7 ounces red chillies, stemmed

450 g or 1 pound shallots, peeled and quartered

90 g or 3 ounces *belachan*

main dish

450 g or 1 pound large prawns (shrimps) or Spanish mackerel (*ikan tenggiri*)

2 tablespoons tamarind (*assam*) pulp, soaked in 4 cups hot water for 30 minutes

1 tablespoon vegetable oil

1 teaspoon salt

1 tablespoon sugar

spice paste

1. Pound or blend the ingredients in the order given until you achieve a fine paste.

main dish

1. Rinse and pat dry the fish. Cut into 2.5-cm or 1-inch thick fillet. (If using prawns, devein the prawns. Leave heads on but trim off the sharp, pokey feelers.)

2. Strain the tamarind juice and discard the seeds and fibre. Reserve the tamarind juice.

3. Heat a saucepan and add oil. When the oil shimmers, add the spice paste. Lower the heat and fry until fragrant.

4. Pour in half of the tamarind juice. Bring to a boil. Then lower to a simmer.

5. Finally, add the fish or prawns and let it boil very briefly, lower the heat to a simmer until the gravy thickens. Add more tamarind juice if the gravy is too thick. Season with salt and sugar.

Ikan Gulai

Fish Simmered in Spicy Gravy with Ladies' Fingers and Brinjal (Eggplant)

I remember this hearty dish more for its soft brinjal than for its fish or thick gravy. I think it was the one way my mother could get me to try brinjal (eggplant), scraping the soft flesh and seeds off the skin and meshing it with my white rice. I personally prefer the dish with red snapper although traditionally stingray (*ikan pari*) fillet was used. Nowadays, an almost similar dish can be found in *kopitiams*, almost like a Chinese type of fish head curry.

makes 6 to 8 servings

spice paste
30 g or 1 ounce turmeric (*kunyit*), skinned and sliced finely
60 g or 2 ounces lemon grass (*seray*), upper stalks and outer layers removed, sliced thinly
5 candlenuts (*buah keras*)
600 g or 1¼ pound shallots, peeled and quartered
60 g or 2 ounces dried chillies, soaked in hot water to soften, then strained
5 tablespoons sugar
½ tablespoon salt

main dish
900 g or 2 pounds Spanish mackerel (*ikan tenggiri*) or yellow snapper
3 tablespoons tamarind (*assam*) pulp, soaked in hot water for 30 minutes
4 cups hot water
1 tablespoon oil
230 g or 8 ounces ladies' fingers (okra)
230 g or 8 ounces brinjal (eggplant), trimmed, halved and sliced lengthwise
4 stalks *laksa* leaves (optional), stemmed
1 teaspoons salt
2 tablespoons sugar

spice paste

1. Pound or blend the turmeric, lemon grass, candlenuts, shallots and dried chilli in the order given until you achieve a fine paste. Season with sugar and salt.

main dish

1. Rinse and pat dry the fish.

2. Strain the tamarind juice and discard the seeds and fibre. Reserve the tamarind juice.

3. Trim the ends of the ladies' fingers.

4. Trim the brinjal, half lengthwise and crosswise.

5. Heat a saucepan and add oil. When the oil shimmers, add the spice paste. Lower the heat and fry until fragrant.

6. Pour in the tamarind juice. Bring to a boil. Add the ladies' fingers and eggplant, lower to a simmer and cook until the vegetable softens, half cooked.

7. Then add the fish and *laksa* leaves let it boil very briefly, lower the heat to a simmer until the gravy thickens. Season with salt and sugar.

Ayam Tempra

When most people think of Nonya food, they think of all the usual suspects like ayam *buah keluak, laksa, mee siam* and *nonya chicken curry*. It was only a few years back that my sister Molly talked about how she missed having *ayam tempra* for dinner. Then only did I realise that it was indeed a low-key Nonya dish we ate often. 'Tempra' is a Malay word related to the Portuguese word *'tempero'* which means 'seasoning' or 'gravy' in English.

The sauce was garnished with fresh cut red chilli and sliced onions. The main component would be thin slices of pork or chicken, even chicken wings, shrimp or a whole fried fish but it also went well with *bubor* (porridge) because of its sauce, as an alternative to *tauk yu bak* (page 235).

makes 4 to 6 servings

230 g or 8 ounces chicken breast,
   sliced finely *
1 tablespoon dark soy sauce
1 tablespoon lime juice
30 g or 1 ounce *belachan*
1 teaspoon salt
2 teaspoons sugar
2 tablespoons vegetable oil
2 cloves garlic, minced
2.5 cm or 1 inch ginger, skinned
   and julienned

1 stalk lemon grass (*seray*),
   use bottom third, slice finely
2 red chillies, sliced
1 large yellow onion, peeled and sliced
3 kaffir lime leaves
   (*daun limau purut*)
2 cups water

* The chicken breast can be substituted with chicken wings or sliced pork fillet, a whole fried fish or prawns (shrimps) with shell on.

1. Season the chicken with the dark soy sauce, lime juice, *belachan*, salt and sugar. Set aside for at least half an hour.

2. Heat a saucepan and add the oil. When the oil is glistening, fry the minced garlic, ginger, lemon grass, red chillies and yellow onion slices until fragrant. Add the seasoned chicken, followed by the lime leaves. Fry for about 2 to 3 minutes on high heat. Pour in the water and let boil, then turn down to simmer for about 5 minutes.

Tauk Yu Bak
Pork Cubes Simmered in Dark Soya Sauce Gravy

In a typical Baba household, a sick person would typically be fed *bubor* (rice porridge) and *tauk yu bak*. This is a signature comfort dish. The fatty pork, crunchy *taupok* and hard-boiled eggs combine to give different textures; and the sauce adds flavour for the accompanying rice or porridge.

makes 6 to 8 servings

680 g or 1½ pounds belly pork,
 cut into 1-inch or 2.5-cm cubes
 with skin intact

2 tablespoons sugar

6 tablespoons dark soy sauce

2 tablespoons oil

4 cloves garlic, peeled and minced

2½ cups water

4 hard-boiled eggs

4 pieces deep fried bean curd (*taupok*),
 quartered

1. Rinse and pat dry the pork cubes. Season with the sugar and 2 tablespoons of the dark soy sauce. Leave to marinate for at least half an hour.

2. Heat a saucepan and add the oil. Fry the minced garlic, being careful not to burn. Add in the seasoned pork. Use tongs to turn the pork over several times to ensure an even glaze all around each piece of pork.

3. Add the water and remaining soy sauce. Bring to a boil, then lower heat and cover. Simmer covered, for at least an hour until the pork is tender, skimming the scum and excess oil off the gravy every once in a while.

4. Remove shells off the boiled eggs. Add the eggs and quartered bean curd puffs to the dish. Serve warm with rice or rice porridge.

Ayam Limau Purut
Chicken Simmered with Kaffir Lime Leaves

Ten years ago, kaffir lime leaves were relatively unknown in the United States. My mother grew the plant in our backyard. These days, the fragrant leaves have been deservingly applied to scented candles, dishwashing detergent and airspray. I have always loved the smell of these double rounded leaves and would pluck and tear them just so that I could inhale the refreshing scent. Naturally, cooking with these leaves imparts a wonderful aroma to this chicken dish—one of my favourites.

makes 6 servings

spice paste
150 g or 5 ounces galangal (*lengkuas*), skinned and julienned
150 g or 5 ounces lemon grass (*seray*), upper stalks and outer layers removed, sliced thinly
5 cloves garlic, peeled
300 g or 10½ ounces shallots, peeled and diced
60 g or 2 ounces red chilli powder

main dish
1 chicken, cut into serving pieces
2 tablespoons oil
1½ tablespoons tamarind (*assam*) pulp, soaked in hot water for 30 minutes
5 pieces kaffir lime leaves (*daun limau purut*), stemmed
1 cup coconut milk
Salt to taste
Sugar to taste

1. Rinse the chicken parts and pat dry.

2. Pound or blend the galangal, lemon grass, garlic, shallots, red chilli powder into a fine paste.

3. Heat a Dutch oven and add the oil. Fry the spice paste over low heat until fragrant. Add the chicken parts and toss to coat with the spice paste.

4. Strain the tamarind juice and discard the seeds and fibre. Pour tamarind juice into the pot, along with the coconut milk and kaffir leaves. Add salt and sugar to taste. Bring to a boil and then lower to a simmer. Cook until the gravy thickens and the chicken is tender.

Prawns Stir-fried in Soy Sauce

A tip my mother used to keep prawns (shrimps) 'fresh' in the refrigerator or freezer was to add sugar to a bag of prawns (shrimps) beforehand.
This soy sauce concoction can also be used with chicken wings or squid.

makes 6 servings

600 g or 1 pound 5 ounces large
    prawns (shrimps)
4 tablespoons light soy sauce
1 tablespoon oyster sauce
1 tablespoon sugar
1 tablespoon cornflour

2 tablespoons water
4 tablespoons vegetable oil
1 teaspoon salt

1. Rinse the prawns and pat dry. Marinate with the light soy sauce, oyster sauce and sugar for at least 15 minutes.

2. Add the water to the cornflour, a bit at a time, to form a slurry.

3. Heat a sauté pan and add the vegetable oil. When the oil is glistening, fry the prawns until fully cooked. Add some slurry to thicken the sauce. Season with salt according to taste. Transfer the prawns to a plate and serve.

Prawns Stir-fried in Chilli Paste

We used big prawns (shrimps) with their shells intact. Prawns (shrimps) were considered expensive so my mother sometimes rationed us to two or three. This chilli paste can also be applied to fried chicken wings.

makes 6 servings

600 g or 1¼ kg large prawns (shrimps)

5 dried chillies, soaked in hot water for at least 15 minutes

10 fresh red chillies, deseeded if preferred

½ teaspoon *belachan*

300 ml or 1¼ cups vegetable oil

2 large yellow onions, peeled and sliced

1 teaspoon sugar

1 to 2 tablespoons lime juice

¼ teaspoon salt

1. Rinse the prawns and pat dry.

2. Remove the stems from the dried and fresh chillies. Pound or blend the chillies, along with the *belachan*, until fine.

3. Heat a sauté pan and add half of the vegetable oil. When the oil is hot, fry the prawns until they turn bright fiery red. Using a slotted spoon or tongs, transfer the prawns to a plate.

4. Add the remaining oil and when it begins to glisten, fry the chilli paste over low heat until fragrant. Add the sliced onions and fry until the slices soften. Return the fried prawns to the pan; coat well with the chilli paste. Season with the sugar, lime juice and salt.

Sambal Stuffed Sotong
Squid Stuffed with Prawn (Shrimp) and Spice Paste

This makes the squid (calamari) look like stuffed sausages. However, make sure not to overstuff each one as the squid (calamari) will shrink when cooked.

makes 6 servings

230 g or 8 ounces medium-sized squid

stuffing

1 dried chilli, stem removed and soaked in hot water

2 small shallots, peeled and cubed

170 g or 6 ounces minced prawns (shrimps)

¼ teaspoon salt

spice paste

1 cm or ¼ inch galangal (*lengkuas*), skinned and julienned

1 stalk lemon grass (*seray*), upper stalks and outer layers removed, sliced thinly

1 clove garlic, peeled

6 shallots, peeled and cubed

6 dried chillies, soaked in hot water for at least 15 minutes

½ teaspoon *belachan*

gravy

1 tablespoon tamarind (*assam*), soaked in hot water for 30 minutes

2 tablespoons oil

1 stalk lemon grass (*seray*), top third and outer skin removed, the rest crushed

1 cup coconut milk

1 teaspoon salt

1.   Rinse the squid and discard the quill and ink sac. Retain the head and tentacles if preferred. Pat dry. Meanwhile, pound or grind the dried chillies and shallots and mix with the minced prawn and salt. Divide the mixture into equal parts and stuff into the cavity of each squid. If you wish to retain the head and tentacles, secure with a toothpick.

2.   Pound or grind the galangal, lemon grass, garlic, shallots, dried chillies and *belachan* into a fine paste. Add salt to taste.

3.   Strain the tamarind juice and discard the seeds and fibre. Reserve the tamarind juice.

4.   Heat a sauté pan and add the vegetable oil. When the oil is glistening, fry the spice paste until fragrant. Pour in tamarind juice and add the stalk of crushed lemon grass. Finally, pour in the coconut milk, bring this to a boil and add the stuffed squid. Lower the heat to a simmer until the squid cooked. Season the gravy with salt to taste.

Sambal Telor

Boiled Eggs with Chilli Gravy

Much like the prawn *sambal* (page 131) that goes with *mee siam* (page 133), this dish consists of hard-boiled eggs instead.

makes 6 servings

8 hard-boiled eggs

110 g or 4 ounces ounces red chillies

230 g or 8 ounces shallots,
    peeled and cubed

60 g or 2 ounces *belachan*, diced

60 g or 2 ounces tamarind (*assam*),
    soaked in 2 cups of hot water

6 tablespoons oil

1 cup coconut milk

3 tablespoons sugar

½ teaspoon salt

1. Peel the hard-boiled eggs. Set aside.

2. Pound or grind the fresh chillies, shallots and *belachan*.

3. Strain the tamarind juice and discard the seeds and fibre. Reserve the tamarind juice.

3. Heat a pan and add oil. When the oil is glistening, fry the spice paste over low heat until fragrant. Pour in the coconut milk and tamarind juice into the pan. Season with sugar and salt, according to taste.

4. Finally, add the hard-boiled eggs in.

Sambal Terong
Steamed Brinjal (Eggplant) with Chilli Paste

While many recipes state instruct the reader to fry the brinjal (eggplant), I vaguely recall that my mother steamed or boiled hers.

makes 4 to 6 servings

4 brinjals (eggplants)

60 g or 2 ounces dried shrimps,
  soaked in hot water

60 g or 2 ounces dried chillies,
  soaked in hot water

140 g or 5 ounces shallots,
  peeled and cubed

30 g *belachan*

Salt to taste

2 calamansi limes (*limau kesturi*)
  cut halfwise

1.   Rinse and pat dry the eggplants. Remove the tip. Slice into halves, lengthwise. Then slice into halves, crosswise. Prepare a steamer. When hot, lower the heat and uncover, place the eggplants in the steamer. Cover again and steam for 5 to 10 minutes until soft.

2.   Meanwhile, pound or grind the dried shrimp, dried chillies, shallots and *belachan*. The paste does not have to be extremely fine. Season with salt.

3.   Heat pan and add oil. Fry till fragrant.

4.   Remove the eggplants from the steamer and cool. Serve with the paste on the side. Spread some spicy paste on the eggplant and squeeze some lime over.

Ikan Sumbat

Fried Mackerel Stuffed with Chilli Paste

The word 'sumbat' or 'tersumbat' means 'gulp'. Whenever one of my baby nieces or nephews ate something chunky or had a mouth full of food, my mother could be heard screaming "*Pelan pelan, nanti tersumbat*". (Slow down or you will choke.) In some way, the same goes for the fish. It should be 'choked up' bulging with the chilli paste, then fried until the fish skin is slightly crispy. We had this fish often enough that it was a staple feature in our dinner menu. Sometimes, my mother would spread the same chilli paste on top of a fried steak of fish.

makes 6 servings

4 hardtail fish such horse mackerel or scad (*ikan selair*), otherwise Indian mackerel (*ikan kembong*)

1 cm or ½ inch turmeric (*kunyit*), skinned and chopped finely

1 stalk lemon grass (*seray*), upper stalks and outer layers removed, sliced thinly

5 shallots, peeled and cubed

3 cloves garlic, peeled

3 red chillies, deseeded if preferred

4 dried chillies, soaked in hot water for at least 15 minutes

1 teaspoon *belachan*

1 teaspoon tamarind (*assam*), soaked in ¼ cup hot water for 30 minutes

Oil for frying

1 teaspoon salt

2 calamansi (*limau kesturi*), sliced into halves

1. Rinse fish and pat dry. Scale fish and trim fins. Make a deep gash along the back fin, on both sides of the body.

2. Pound or grind the turmeric, lemongrass, shallots, garlic, red chillies, dried chillies and *belachan* into a fine paste.

3. Strain the tamarind juice and discard the seeds and fibre. Reserve the tamarind juice.

4. Heat a wok and add about 4 tablespoons of oil. When the oil is glistening, stir in the ground chilli paste. Fry over low heat until fragrant. Add tamarind juice to the paste. Dish out the spice paste and set aside.

5. Pat the sides of the fish with the salt. Using a teaspoon, scoop the spice paste and stuff each slit with the paste.

6. In the same wok, add more oil such that it reaches about 3 cm or 1 inch in depth. When the oil is smouldering, deep fry the fish, two at a time. Let the bottom side of the fish turn golden brown first, then using tongs, turn over the fish carefully to fry the other side.

6. Squeeze the lime halves over the fish and serve with plain rice.

Sambal Bendi

Stir-fried Ladies' Fingers with Chilli Paste

makes 4 to 6 servings

230 g or 8 ounces ladies'
   fingers (okra)

30 g or 1 ounce dried shrimps,
   soaked in hot water

60 g or 2 ounces dried chillies,
   soaked in hot water

140 g or 5 ounces shallots,
   peeled and cubed

60 g or 2 ounces *belachan*

Salt, optional

2 calamansi limes (*limau kesturi*),
   cut halfwise

1.   Rinse and pat dry the ladies' fingers.

2.   Bring a pot of water to boil. Also, prepare a large bowl of cold water beside the boiling pot.

3.   Meanwhile, pound or grind the dried shrimp, the dried chillies, shallots and *belachan*. The paste does not have to be extremely fine. Season with salt.

4.   Place some of the ladies' fingers on a strainer ladle and blanch in the pot of boiling water until the ladies' fingers are cooked. Shock the vegetable in the bowl of cold water to stop the cooking process. Trim off the tips of the ladies' fingers and arrange on a plate.

5.   Heat pan and add oil. Fry till fragrant.

6.   Serve with the spicy paste spread on the ladies' fingers and squeeze some lime over for taste.

Kang Kong Belachan
Fried Water Convolvulus with *Belachan* Paste

makes 4 to 6 servings

450 g or 1 pound water convolvulus
(*kang kong*)

20 g or ½ ounce dried shrimps,
soaked in hot water

3 dried chillies, soaked in hot water

4 red chillies

4 shallots, peeled and cubed

3 cloves garlic, peeled

¼ tablespoon *belachan*

Salt, optional

3 tablespoons oil

1.   Remove the roots of the water convolvulus. Then divide the stems and leaves. Cut them into 8-cm or 3-inch lengths. Soak all the vegetable in a large bowl of water to loosen any grit.

2.   Meanwhile, pound or grind the dried shrimps, the dried chillies, the fresh red chillies, shallots, garlic and *belachan*. The paste does not have to be extremely fine. Season with salt.

3.   Heat a sauté pan and add the oil. When the oil is glistening, add the spice paste and fry over low heat until fragrant. Remove the stems and pat dry. Toss into the pan and fry to soften. Repeat with the leaves. Continue to fry until the vegetable and paste are slightly crisp. Transfer to a plate and serve.

NOTE: This dish uses the basic *rempah titek* mentioned on page 26. In fact this dish is sometimes known as *kang kong masak titek*.

Sambal Titek

I came across the written recipe while rummaging through my mother's stash. It only listed the ingredients and did not state a method. My mother left it incomplete and I had to piece it together. When I asked my father for any recollection, he only urged me to cook it and see what it would end up looking like. *Sambal titek* actually refers to the spice paste made by combining *buah keras*, dried chillies, shallots and *belachan*. While this dish may be cooked with young papaya, my mother's recipe called for soft tofu beancurd and meatballs.

makes 4 to 6 servings

120 g or 4 ounces prawns (shrimps)

230 g or 8 ounces minced pork

1 piece soft beancurd

60 g or 2 ounces candlenuts
    (*buah keras*)

30 g or 1 ounce dried chillies,
    soaked in hot water

150 g or 5½ ounces shallots,
    peeled and diced

60 g or 2 ounces *belachan*

3 tablespoons oil

60 g or 2 ounces salted fish, rinsed,
    boned and cut into small cubes

4 cups water

Coriander leaves (cilantro)

1. Shell and devein the prawns. Chop coarsely, mix with the minced pork and form into meatballs.

2. Cut the beancurd into 2.5-cm or 1-inch cubes.

3. Meanwhile, pound or grind the candlenuts, dried chillies, shallots and *belachan*.

4. Heat a saucepan and add the oil. When the oil is glistening, add the spice paste and fry over low heat until fragrant.

5. Add the dried fish and fry until slightly crispy. Pour in the water and bring to a boil. Drop the meatballs into the pot and boil gently until the meatballs rise to the surface. Add the beancurd. Simmer for a few minutes until the beancurd is cooked.

6. Transfer to a serving dish and garnish with coriander leaves.

Pork Chops in Cinnamon Gravy

As with many mothers, mine considered Friday evening a casual night for cooking or dining out. In my mother's case, that meant that she would try a "Western" dish. For example, once, just when Kentucky Fried Chicken first opened and the novelty was strong, she borrowed a recipe for fried chicken with all the side dishes cooked and laid them out on the table.

Most times though, we relied on our old classics like chicken pie, chicken stew or pork chops. These pork chops reflect the colonial influence in Singapore, perhaps an outcome of British soldiers teaching Hainanese chefs to cook. Even today, I would inevitably order Hainanese pork chops when dining at the Singapore Cricket Club, an erstwhile bastion of the British Empire. The pork chops are seasoned, among others, in ingredients frequently used in Chinese cooking such as light soy sauce, star anise and white pepper. The sauce is also flavoured and coloured by dark soy sauce. Yet, the preparation can be unmistakably Western and the dish ends up unique and so proudly a reflection of a bygone era.

makes 4 to 6 servings

seasoning and batter
1.5 kg or 3 pounds 5 ounces pork chops
  (each slab 1.5 cm or ¾ inches thick)
1 teaspoon salt
1 teaspoon white pepper
½ teaspoon dark soy sauce
1 teaspoon light soy sauce
2 eggs, beaten, optional
1 cup flour
3 tablespoons vegetable oil

sauce
2 tablespoons butter or vegetable oil
2 potatoes, peeled and sliced into
  0.5 cm or ¼ inch thick pieces

1 medium onion, sliced into rings
2 tomatoes, seeded and cut
  into wedges
1 teaspoon salt
2 tablespoons dark soy sauce
1 teaspoon Lea & Perrins
  Worcestershire sauce
3 cups water
1 stick cinnamon
1 star anise
Slurry from 1 tablespoon cornflour
  and 3 tablespoons water
230 g or 8 ounces green peas, drained

1. Season pork chops in salt, pepper, dark and light soy sauce. Leave aside for at least half an hour.

2. Meanwhile, heat a Dutch oven and add the butter or vegetable oil. Saute the potato slices and the onion rings until the potatoes are brown around the edges and the onions soft. Stir in the tomato wedges. Add the salt, dark soy sauce and Lea & Perrins sauce. Pour in the water and add the cinnamon and star anise.

3. Bring to a boil and lower to a simmer. Add the slurry a bit at a time. Stir until the sauce thickens to your desired consistency before adding more slurry. Alternatively, turn up the heat to boil down the sauce. Throw in the green peas. Set the sauce aside.

4. Heat frying pan and add some oil. Dip each pork chop in the beaten eggs. Then dredge the pork chops in a bowl of flour.

5. When oil glistens, fry the pork chops, a few at a time, in the pan until they are cooked. Turn over the pork chops to brown both sides. Transfer the pork chops to a plate lined with paper to absorb the excess oil.

6. The pork chops are usually served with white rice or French loaf bread (baguette), covered with the sauce which includes the potatoes, onions, tomatoes and peas.

Roti Babi

Bread Toast topped with Minced Pork and Prawn (Shrimp)

My all-time favourite sinful sandwich is *roti babi*, especially delicious when the bread is crispy yet drenched in oil, top heavy with a tasty pork and prawn (shrimp) stuffing. We sometimes had it at tea-time and I still can recall the warm fried aromas in the middle of a hot afternoon.

makes 6 to 8 servings

12 square slices white bread

450 g or 1 pound minced pork

230 g or 8 ounces prawns (shrimps), minced finely

2 eggs

1 yellow onion, diced finely

1 red or green chilli, deseeded and diced finely

1 bunch coriander leaves (cilantro), stems removed, chopped finely

1½ teaspoons cornflour

1 teaspoon salt

1 teaspoon light soy sauce

½ teaspoon Lea & Perrins Worcestershire sauce

4 cups vegetable oil

1. Toast the bread slightly to stiffen the bread. Then spread some butter on each side.

2. Meanwhile, combine the minced pork, minced prawns, egg, onion, chillies, coriander leaves, cornflour, salt, light soy sauce, and Lea & Perrins sauce. Knead into a fine mixture.

3. Scoop a tablespoon of the pork topping on each slice of bread and spread the topping with the back of the spoon.

4. Heat a sauté pan over medium heat and add the oil until it reaches about 4 cm or 1½ inch deep. When the oil is hot, use a slotted spatula to transfer three to four slices of bread to the pan. Do not overfill the pan with too many slices of bread. Use the spatula to gently press down the topping on the bread to ensure that the meat is fully fried in oil. When the bread turns light brown, turn it over. Flip back to the top again and transfer to a plate lined with absorbent paper. Best served when warm. For children, a simpler topping would include just minced pork, cornflour, salt and light soy sauce.

Chicken Pie

We ate our chicken pie on Friday nights, with gobs of Maggi tomato ketchup and Lingham's chilli sauce. It was always a hearty meal and very much a part of our family ritual. My dad would finish off the gravy with French loaf bread (baguette). Again, like paper-wrapped chicken, it was always a surprise to see what chicken part we would dig out of the pie. Sometimes, my mother also made chicken pie for after-school lunch.

Like an old-fashioned mother, she made her pie crust from scratch. She used Knorr chicken cubes for her stock flavouring. I prefer chicken stock. To simplify, you can buy frozen puff pastry for the crust top in place of the short crust pastry listed below.

makes 6 to 8 servings

pie crust
310 g or 11 ounces flour
½ teaspoon salt
¼ teaspoon baking powder
230 g or 8 ounces butter, cut into cubes
4 to 6 tablespoons ice cold water

pie filling
1 Kg or 2½ pounds chicken, cut up into parts; or chicken thighs
1 teaspoon salt
½ teaspoon pepper
3 tablespoons butter
½ carrot, peeled and chopped into 2.5 cm or 1 inch chunks
1 big onion, cut into 8 cubes
2 cups chicken stock

1 piece star anise
1 stick cinnamon
115 g or 4 ounces button mushrooms
115 g or 4 ounces green peas
3 hard boiled eggs, optional
½ cup milk

Slurry from 3 tablespoons cornflour and 1 tablespoon water
1 egg beaten with a pinch of salt, for eggwash

pie crust

1. First prepare the pie crust if you wish to make your own crust. Mix flour, salt and transfer to a table surface. Create a hole in the middle, hence forming a ring of flour on the table surface. Rub in the cut butter using your fingertips, until the mixture feels like fine bread crumbs.

2. Add cold water, a little at a time, kneading the flour and water into dough. Wrap with clear plastic film and refrigerate for at least an hour.

pie filling

1. Season chicken pieces in salt and pepper, leave to marinate for at least an hour.

2. Place the butter in a Dutch oven or pot and bring to heat. When the butter has melted, fry carrots and onions until they turn soft. Sweat them over low heat, do not burn. Remove and set aside.

3. Add the chicken pieces and turn occasionally to brown all sides. Toss the onions and carrots back into the pot, followed by the chicken stock. Add the star anise and cinnamon stick. Bring to a boil and lower heat to simmer, covering the pot partially. Simmer for about 30 minutes until the chicken is tender.

4. Add the green peas and button mushrooms and eggs (optional). Stir in the milk and some slurry, a bit at a time, until the gravy thickens to your desired consistency.

5. Turn off heat and set aside.

baking

1. Preheat your oven to 200 degrees C or 400 degrees F. Take out the pastry dough from the refrigerator and let it thaw for about 15 minutes. (If you choose to use ready-made puff pastry, read the instructions for thawing and use accordingly.)

2. Transfer the chicken pie filling to a deep oven-proof bowl.

3. Dust some flour on a table surface and dust the rolling pin with some flour. Roll the round mound of dough by using the pin to press down on the dough, turning 45 degrees and repeating. Continue this until you press the dough flat into a flat round piece with a surface area large enough to cover the bowl of chicken pie filling. Place the rolling pin on the middle of the dough and flip one side over, transfer and place on top of the bowl of chicken pie filling. Crimp and brush some egg wash on the pie surface. Some ready-made puff pastry comes flat and folded into three slabs, all you need to do is unfold into one large flat piece of pastry dough.

4. Bake in the oven for about 20 minutes, then reduce the oven heat to 150 degrees C or 300 degrees F and bake for another 30 minutes until the pie crust turns golden brown.

Ginseng Chicken Soup

Desperate to do better in my physics test, I asked my classmate how she retained such great mental agility. Her secret was the weekly home brewed pig's brain soup that her mother prepared for her. It sounded somewhat oxymoronic that one could have better brains by consuming those of a pig. Yes, I was desperate, but I still could not stomach (excuse the pun) this Chinese tonic of last resort. Nonetheless, my mother sympathised with my plight and made me ginseng chicken soup. This ginseng soup is an age-old brew that Chinese wives and mothers lovingly prepare for their family to strengthen them physically and mentally. It is a common tradition especially around school exams. I continue to cook this soup once in a while when everyone seems too lethargic.

makes 4 servings

700 g or 1½ pounds chicken thighs, about 4
4 knobs ginseng
1 teaspoon black peppercorns

6 cups cold water
½ teaspoon salt
½ cup dark soy sauce

1. Remove any excess skin from the chicken pieces.

2. Combine the chicken, ginseng, peppercorns in a large saucepan and cover with enough cold water, about 6 to 8 cups.

3. Bring to a boil, covered. Then lower to a simmer for at least an hour until the chicken meat is tender and about to fall off the bones. Add salt to the soup for taste. Serve the soup and chicken in a bowl, with an accompanying dipping bowl of dark soy sauce and a plate of plain rice.

NOTE: My mother always preferred that we drank the soup just before bedtime, almost like a midnight snack. For her, it was more essential to drink the soup than consume everything. We ate the meat separately, dipped in soy sauce.

Bubor

Porridge

Porridge was a staple if someone was ill. It would normally be plain porridge, often served with *tauk yu bak* (page 235) and an omelette, garnished with *chai po* (preserved radish). Then again, we also had porridge as a meal of its own. This type of porridge my mother made was heartier and less refined than the smooth Hong Kong-style *congee*. You could still feel the texture of the rice grains and she would throw in small prawns (shrimps), diced firm soy bean cakes, slivers of streaky pork and soft peanuts.

makes 6 to 8 servings

1 cup peanuts, optional

2 cups rice

10 cups water

230 g or 8 ounces streaky pork
(*samchan bak*)

230 g or 8 ounces small prawns
(shrimps), shelled and deveined

1 teaspoon salt

½ teaspoon white pepper

2 teaspoons light soy sauce

2 pieces firm soy bean curd;
seared and cut into
1-cm or ½-inch cubes

3 red chillies, sliced finely

1. Soak peanuts in water for an hour. Rinse out water and add fresh water. Bring to a boil for half an hour over low heat. Drain with a colander.

2. Rinse rice grains and place in a large pot. Add the water, enough such that the depth of water is two to three times the depth of the rice. Bring to a boil, uncovered. Lower the heat slightly and watch the pot to ensure the water does not spill over. Cook for at least half an hour until the rice is soft and you achieve a porridge consistency.

3. Meanwhile, slice the pork into thin strips about 0.5 cm or ¼ inch wide and into pieces about 2.5 cm or 1 inch in length.

4. Toss the pork and the shelled small prawns into the porridge. Season with salt, white pepper and light soy sauce according to taste.

5. Garnish with bean curd cubes, peanuts and sliced red chilli and serve in individual bowls.

Sandwiches from the Can

Sardines, Corned Beef or Luncheon Meat

Now, my children's idea of a blessed breakfast treat is to go to the diner round the block. One of us would order corned beef and hash, which the children would share with us. Basically, it is a pan-fried mush of corned beef and potatoes, accompanied by golden potato hash browns and two fried eggs. I hope that someday, my children will appreciate also another joyous way of having corned beef—the way their grandfather (my dad) did ... with the aroma of Libby's corned beef served up with slices of fresh chilli. Indeed, these three breakfast sandwiches below are simple, substantial, yet somewhat creative and reflect the kind of meal we had in the morning.

makes 6 to 8 servings

sardine sandwich filling
1 can sardines in tomato sauce, preferably Ayam brand
1 yellow onion, sliced into thin rings
2 red chillies, sliced finely
1 lime, squeezed for juice

corned beef sandwich filling
1 can corned beef, preferably Libby's brand

1 yellow onion, peeled and cut into thin rings
1 tablespoon oil
2 red chillies, sliced finely

luncheon meat sandwich filling
1 can corned beef, preferably Spam brand
1 tablespoon oil
2 eggs, beaten

sardine sandwich filling

1. Combine all the ingredients and mash with the back of a fork. Remove any fish bones or spine. Serve with white bread.

corned beef sandwich filling

1. Remove the corned beef from the can and crumble with a fork.

2. Heat oil in a frying pan. When the oil is glistening, fry the onion rings until they are soft and translucent. Stir in the crumbled corned beef until slightly brown and crispy. Transfer to a plate and top with the sliced red chilli. Serve with white bread.

luncheon meat sandwich filling

1. Remove the luncheon meat from the can and cut into square slices about 1 cm or $1/2$ inch thick.

2. Heat oil in a frying pan. When the oil is glistening, add the slices of luncheon meat. Pan fry until each side is slightly crispy along the edges. Pour the beaten egg mixture over the luncheon meat and fry until cooked. Transfer to a plate and serve with white bread.

Sweet Rewards

Nonya cakes, or kueh-kueh, are traditionally a labour of love because of the meticulous preparation needed before cooking.

A fastidious Nonya like my mother would have spent afternoons picking out the broken rice grains so that her glutinous desserts would look perfect. Key ingredients for Nonya cakes, in addition to glutinous rice or rice flour, include coconut, *pandan* leaves, and *gula melaka*. In the past, many of the recipes required first and second *santan* (coconut milk).

The first was the extraction from squeezing grated coconut and water; while the second was a more diluted extraction obtained from using the same grated coconut and additional water. The flour was often derived from a lengthy process of soaking and rinsing rice grains and then grinding them using the granite mill (*batu boh*). The fermentation process also steered clear of baking soda, using traditional ingredients such as coconut water. The challenge, these days, is to replace age-old methods by substituting with time-saving methods and ingredients with the right precision so that the *kueh* remains the same in taste and texture.

In primary school, I was one of the very few Nonya girls around. It was bad enough that I had a hard time mastering the compulsory Chinese language well because we did not speak it at home. Therefore, I became embarrassed by what I then considered my odd heritage. So when my mother made all these colourful *kueh-kueh* to give to the teachers, I would be too shy to bring them around.

My mother often told me that many decades ago, especially after the war, Nonya ladies could support their families financially by making *kueh* to sell. They would prepare a few and display them on a tray lined with banana leaves, then go from door to door to sell. I think of it as an entreprenuerial way to leverage one's limited but valuable skills when hard times had befallen the family. The Nonya mother was doing what she could to supplement a struggling husband's income.

I vividly recall a Nonya *bibik* (or elderly lady) who ran a home-based operation of supplying many hotels and shops with her delectable variety of *kueh*. She recruited sons and daughters-in-law to manage this for her. The outdoor kitchen had several charcoal stoves used to bake *kueh ambon* (page 283) and *kueh bolu* (page 113) while the indoor kitchen had steamers filled with *kueh lapis* (page 271) or *putri sarlat* (page 265). These were later arranged at the dining table into large rectangular metal trays with lid covers, then swiftly moved into vans for delivery. The operation seemed to churn all these goodies throughout the day and night. I remembered dropping in to get a few pre-ordered boxes one evening, and witnessing this flurry of activities while the *bibik* sat right in the middle of the living room on a wooden settee, collecting the cash and tabulating them in a metal tin box.

These days, it is all too easy to buy *kueh* from a kiosk, be it in a mall, the airport or a bus terminal. Yet most of the *kueh* are made in modern-day factories and never quite taste the same as the homemade ones of yore.

When my mother was in hospital, we had a special tea-time with my father, my sister Maggie, and my two aunts. We asked for permission to buy some of the *kueh-kueh* from the cake shop in the hospital café—an assortment of Nonya cakes. My mother eyed her favourite *kueh lapis* (page 271) and consumed it, much to her delight. Apparently, she relished it so much that she secretly sent the maid for a few more of these. We also comfort ourselves in one thing—in those last days, we did not deny our mother of some of the sweet rewards that made her so happy—the *kueh-kueh* represented the joys of her cooking, the sweetness of her life and the love of her family.

Kaya Egg Jam
Pandan-Infused Egg Custard Jam

My best friend Angele, whose mother is from Malacca, learnt a while back that Malaysian *kaya* is golden while the Singapore version is green. The golden tinge derives from adding a dose of caramelised sugar while the green could stem from the egg yolks or *pandan* essence. The home-made *kaya* I grew up with was green and custardy. *Kaya*—bought in stores or served in chain cafes—is nowadays often golden and runny. Those of the older generation also remember *kopi tiam kaya* (served in coffee shops) made of duck eggs instead of chicken eggs. It was a cheaper ingredient. The *kopi tiam kaya* was also runnier so that it could be spread faster and allow for quicker service. Hence the origins of runny jam.

makes 12 servings

10 eggs, room temperature
(allows for sugar to dissolve
more quickly)

3 cups sugar

¾ cups thick coconut cream

4 *pandan* leaves, tied into a knot

1.   Add water in a saucepan and bring it to a gentle boil. Break the eggs into a heatproof bowl that sits nicely on the saucepan and whisk. Add sugar a little at a time and continue to whisk to dissolve sugar. Stir in the thick coconut cream. Stir continuously until the mixture thickens.

2.   Add the knotted *pandan* leaves to the mixture.

3.   Place a metal stand in a large or Dutch oven pot. Fill the pot with cold water, almost up to the height of the stand. Bring to a gentle boil. Wrap the lid with a kitchen towel to absorb water condensation droplets which may fall on the *kaya* jam and impact the texture. Transfer the heatproof bowl of *kaya* mixture onto the metal stand.

4.   Whisk or stir mixture often for the next quarter to half an hour to break up any clumps. At this point, skim the top of the mixture with a slotted spoon to remove lumps.

5.   When the mixture begins to thicken, cover and simmer for another half an hour to an hour. Replenish more hot water to the pot if necessary.

6.   Turn off the heat when the jam mixture becomes firmer. Do not overcook or the jam will have a knobby texture. Leave the jam to cool completely before storing in an air-tight container. Discard the *pandan* leaves. Refrigerate the jam if you wish to keep it for a few weeks.

NOTE: For Step 1, it is important to stir and use a gentle heat to ensure that the eggs do not cook into scrambled eggs, hence the need to use the double boiler method.

Putri Sarlat

Steamed Glutinous Rice topped with Coconut and Egg Custard

This quintessential Nonya dessert goes by many names: *serikaya, serimuka, kueh sarlat*. I grew up knowing it as *putri sarlat* which one of my best friends, Karen, would jokingly call 'Putrid'.

The name for *kaya* (egg jam, page 263) stems from *serikaya* as these two desserts are related. Both being egg-based, atypical of Asian sweets, there is some speculation that these were influenced by the Portuguese who colonised parts of South East Asia. Indeed, there is a Portuguese dessert called 'sericaia' which combines eggs, sugar, milk and cinnamon of which the taste and texture resemble *kaya* and *putri sarlat*. The same Portuguese influence lends itself to the famous tan tarts found in the former colony of Macau, the tarts being the originator of all those we find in *dimsum* restaurants.

I recall my mother making the custardy kaya top in either green or yellow. The glutinous rice base was always laced with blue rice, very much like the blue rice grains in Nonya *kueh chang*. Before serving, you need to cool the *putri sarlat*. To do so, you can let the tray rest on a rack. My mother used to put the tray in a larger tray filled with water (just enough not to spill into the cake tray). This quickened the cooling process so that the rice would not overcook. More importantly in the olden days, the moat of water also prevented ants from climbing into the sweet tray of *putri sarlat*.

makes 12 servings

- 450 g or 1 pound glutinous rice (*pulot*), to be soaked for at least 3 hours
- 1½ cups coconut cream
- ½ cup coconut milk
- ¾ teaspoon salt
- 1½ teaspoons sugar, to add to part of the coconut cream
- 3 to 4 drops blue food colouring, or extracted from ½ cup of clitoria (*bunga telang*) blossoms soaked in hot water

- 8 eggs
- 300 g or 10½ ounces sugar
- 6 *pandan* leaves, tied into a knot
- 1 tablespoon rice flour
- 1 tablespoon plain flour
- 3 to 4 drops green food colouring

prepare rice

Rinse the rice three times. Place the rice in a pot and cover with enough water, at least 2.5 cm or 1 inch above the level of the rice. Soak for at least 3 hours before steaming the rice, preferably overnight.

prepare coconut cream and milk

1. Divide the cream into two portions: ½ cup for cooking the glutinous rice, and 1 cup for the egg mixture.

2. Set aside the ½ cup of coconut milk for the rice.

bottom layer of glutinous rice

1. Place a metal stand in a large or Dutch oven pot. Fill the pot with cold water, almost up to the height of the stand. Bring to a gentle boil to create your steamer.

2. Drain the glutinous rice and place it in round tray. Use a baking tray that could be round, 20 cm or 8 inches in diameter. You could also use a square tray with sides of 20 cm or 8 inches. Brush the tray with a little oil. Place the tray in the steamer pot that you have set up.

3. Steam the rice until it turns translucent, about 30 to 45 minutes. Remove the tray from the steamer, stir in the ½ cup of coconut milk and place it back in the steamer. Continue to steam for another 15 minutes.

4. Meanwhile, add in the salt and the 1½ teaspoons of sugar to the 3 ounces of coconut cream. Divide the cream into 2 bowls. In one of these bowls, add the drops of blue food colouring.

5. Remove the rice from the steamer. Mix half of the rice into the bowl of plain coconut cream, and the other half into the bowl with the cream with the blue food colouring. Transfer the two batches of rice back to the original bowl, making sure the two batches lay side by side. Do not stir them together as yet. Place back in the steamer and continue to steam the rice for a further 30 minutes.

6. Remove the tray. Now use a scoop to stir the rice. Alternate the white and the blue rice so that you achieve a marbled layer of blue and white rice. Fold a double layer of tin foil and line it on the rice. Press down with something heavy, such as a pestle so that the layer of rice is tightly packed.

7. Bring back to steam for another 15 minutes. Leave it to rest while you work on the *kaya*.

top layer of kaya custard

1. Add water in a saucepan and bring it to a gentle boil. Break the eggs into a heatproof bowl that sits nicely on the saucepan and whisk. Add the sugar a little at a time and continue to whisk to dissolve it. Stir in the thick coconut cream. Stir continuously until the mixture thickens.

2. Add the knotted *pandan* leaves to the mixture.

3. In the meantime, place the rice flour and plain flour in a bowl. Add 1 cup of the coconut cream reserved for the egg mixture, to the bowl and whisk to remove flour lumps. Then pour the remaining cream, whisking again to remove any additional lumps. If necessary, strain the flour mixture. Then add to the egg mixture in the heatproof bowl, along with the drops of green food colouring. Continue to stir until the mixture thickens.

4. Remove from heat. Discard the *pandan* leaves. Pour the custard through a strainer, over onto the tray of pressed rice.

5. Cover the tray with a wet cloth hanging over the edges and put back in the steamer on low heat for approximately an hour until the kaya custard sets. The cloth lining absorbs the condensation from the steam. Otherwise, the droplets will fall back on the surface of the custard and spoil the intended smooth finish.

6. It is necessary to use a gentle heat. Turning the heat up would no doubt cook the custard faster, but it will cause ridges to form in the layer of custard. Aim for a nice smooth surface.

7. Cool the dessert before serving.

NOTE: While making the *kaya* custard at Step 1, it is important to stir and use a gentle heat to ensure that the eggs do not get cooked into scrambled eggs, hence the need to use the double boiler method.

Kueh Wajek

Steamed Glutinous Rice drenched in *Gula Melaka* Syrup

Sometimes, my mother made this *kueh wajek* and would serve this with mashed durian. It is not easy to make as it seems, judging from the simplistic recipe found in many cookbooks. The sticky rice does not stay moist for long, made all the more difficult when the thick sugary syrup begins to harden like toffee. This is tricky and some people in the past were supposedly resigned to chewing the grainy rice and spitting it out. I have tried to modify the recipe so that you get the best chances of keeping this *kueh* as moist as you can.

makes 12 servings

600 g or 1 pound 5 ounces glutinous rice (*pulot*)

1¾ cups coconut milk

90 g or 3 ounces *gula melaka*, scraped

230 g or 8 ounces sugar

½ teaspoon salt

4 *pandan* leaves, tied into a knot

1. Rinse rice in water three times. Place rice in a pot and cover with water at least 2.5 cm or 1 inch above the level of the rice. Soak for at least 3 hours, preferably overnight. Drain.

2. Spread the rice in a bamboo basket (the type used for steaming *dimsum*) lined with cloth. This allows the rice grains to cook evenly—glutinous rice sticks together, which may result in some grains remaining uncooked. Alternatively, place cloth in a metal cake tin (but that requires that you turn the rice a couple of times during the steaming process). Place a metal stand in a large or Dutch oven pot. Fill the pot with cold water, almost up to the height of the stand. Bring to a gentle boil to create a steamer. Place the tray of rice on the stand and steam the rice for an hour.

3. Meanwhile, pour coconut milk into a saucepan and place on low heat. Add *gula melaka* to coconut milk, along with sugar and salt. Add knotted *pandan* leaves. Stir occasionally to ensure the sugars dissolve in the coconut milk to form a thick and brown syrup. Remove from heat and let cool. Discard *pandan* leaves.

4. Check on rice—it should look translucent when cooked. If rice has been cooking on the cloth, transfer to a metal tin 20 by 20 cm or 8 by 8 inches that has been brushed with oil. Use a spoon to stir syrup into the rice. Mix well, ensuring rice is drenched in syrup. Continue to steam rice until mixture becomes thick and moist. Then, press the rice down in the tray to form a layer about 4 cm or 1½ inches thick. Cover tightly with plastic wrap pressed down on rice. Allow to cool. Best to store in an airtight container. If the rice hardens, steam briefly before serving.

Kueh Ko Swee

Steamed *Gula Melaka* and Rice Flour Cake served with Grated Coconut

To make this *kueh* requires several Chinese teacups. My mother's teacups were smaller and hence the *kueh ko swee* was dainty. To appreciate a good *kueh*, it has to have the right chewy texture which at the same time, allows one to bite into it more firmly. This is brought about by the use of *abu* water. For a long time, I thought *abu* water was a mystic potion because my mother kept it in large Horlicks bottles and we were not allowed to touch them. Just the word *abu* incited anxious fears because *abu* could also mean ashes or something related to religious rituals. Recently, I have discovered that this same water, also called "potassium carbonate and sodium bicarbonate water" or simply, alkaline water, is the same ingredient used to make *cha siew pao* and is also responsible for its beautiful springy texture.

makes 8 servings

250 g or 8¾ ounces *gula melaka*, scraped
170 g or 6 ounces white sugar
10 *pandan* leaves, tied into a knot
3¼ cups water
230 g or 8 ounces rice flour

70 g or 2½ ounces *sago* flour (or substitute with tapioca flour if not available)
1 teaspoon alkaline water (*ayer abu*)
1 coconut without skin, grated
½ teaspoon salt

1. Combine the *gula melaka*, white sugar, knotted *pandan* leaves and the water in a large saucepan. Bring to a boil and stir until the sugars dissolve, about 10 minutes. Remove from heat and let cool. Discard the *pandan* leaves.

2. Combine the rice flour and *sago* flour together in a bowl. Make a well in the centre and pour in the alkaline water and cooled sugar syrup. Using a metal spoon, mix well together to form a smooth mixture, pressing out any clumps.

3. Place a metal stand in a large or Dutch oven pot. Fill the pot with cold water, almost up to the height of the stand. Bring to a gentle boil to create your steamer.

4. To prepare the grated coconut, toss with the salt and steam for about 2 minutes. Remove and allow to cool.

5. Prepare a tray that will fit on the wire rack, line the tray with several little Chinese teacups. Place the teacups in the steamer for about 5 minutes to warm the teacups.

6. Use a ladle to pour the mixture to fill each of the teacup to a level of three quarters in depth. Cover the steamer for about 15 to 20 minutes until the *kueh* cooks through.

7. To serve, use a paring knife or fork to tip out the *kueh* from each teacup. Arrange the *kueh* on a serving plate and scatter the grated coconut to toss the kueh evenly on all sides.

Kueh Lapis Kukus

Steamed Rainbow Layer Pudding

Children love this *kueh* for the simple reason that they can peel off each coloured layer. I used to discard the white-coloured layer which was my least favourite. We often called this *kueh* the "colour-colour" or rainbow *kueh* and it invariably appeared as a vibrant complement to other *kueh-kueh* my mother made that looked less cheery but no less delicious, like *kueh ko swee* (page 268) or *kueh ambon* (page 283).

makes 6 servings

3 cups coconut milk

300 g or 1½ cups sugar

5 *pandan* leaves, tied into a knot

170 g or 6 ounces *sago* flour

65 g or 2 ounces rice flour

3 drops red food colouring

2 drops blue food colouring

2 drops green food colouring

2 drops yellow food colouring

1. Combine 2¼ cups of the coconut milk, sugar and knotted *pandan* leaves in a large saucepan and bring to boil. Stir gently until the sugar dissolves. Remove from heat and let cool. Discard the knotted *pandan* leaves.

2. Meanwhile, combine the *sago* flour and rice flour in a bowl. Make a well in the centre and pour the remaining coconut milk, stirring with a metal spoon to smooth out clumps. Pour the cooled sugar mixture in and stir.

3. Divide the mixture evenly among five different bowls. Add a different colouring to each bowl and stir. Leave the fifth bowl without any colouring, this will be the white layer.

4. Place a metal stand in a large or Dutch oven pot. Fill the pot with cold water, almost up to the height of the stand. Bring to a gentle boil to create a steamer.

5. Place on the stand, a 15 cm by 15 cm or 6 inch by 6 inch square tin. Brush the tin with a little oil.

6. Pour a few spoonfuls of the red mixture to the bottom of the square tin. Spread evenly to form a thin layer, about 2 mm or ⅛ inch thick. Steam until the layer is cooked through. Repeat the process, using any coloured mixture. Continue to do so until the mixtures are all used up or the tin is filled to ¾ of its level.

7. Allow the *kueh* to cool down before slicing to serve. You can cool this by placing the tray on a baking sheet tray and filling cool water in the sheet tray to surround the *kueh* tin.

Kueh Talam Hijau
Green and Brown Layered Coconut Custard

makes 12 servings

sugar syrup

300 g or 10 ounces *gula melaka*,
    scraped into fragments

1½ tablespoons sugar

2½ cups water

brown bottom layer

110 g or 4 ounces *sago*
    (or tapioca) flour

370 g or 13 ounces rice flour

1¼ cups coconut cream

green top layer

1¼ cups coconut milk

280 g or 10 ounces sugar

20 *pandan* leaves, tied into a knot

110 g or 4 ounces *sago*
    (or tapioca) flour

370 g or 13 ounces rice flour

2 cups coconut cream

Green food colouring, optional

1. For the sugar water, combine all the ingredients in a saucepan and bring to boil.

2. Let cool.

3. For the brown layer, combine the *sago* and rice flour in a bowl. Make a well and pour in the coconut cream and the sugar syrup. Stir well to remove any clumps.

4. For the green layer, combine the coconut milk, sugar and knotted *pandan* leaves in a small saucepan and bring to a boil. Stir to dissolve the sugar. Let cool. Discard the *pandan* leaves.

5. Combine the *sago* and rice flour in another bowl. Make a well and pour in the coconut milk mixture, along with the coconut cream. Add a few drops of green colouring if necessary.

6. Place a metal stand in a large or Dutch oven pot. Fill the pot with cold water, almost up to the height of the stand. Bring to a gentle boil to create a steamer.

7. Place on the stand, a 20 cm by 20 cm or 8 inch by 8 inch square tin. Brush the tin with a little oil.

8. Steam the brown layer mixture in the tray until it is firm. Then pour the green layer mixture onto the brown layer and steam until cooked.

9. Allow the *kueh* to cool down before slicing to serve. For extra firmness, I prefer to chill it in the refrigerator briefly before serving.

Kueh Lompang

Steamed Rice Flour Cake served with Grated Coconut

This *kueh* also requires the Chinese teacups used to make *kueh ko swee* (page 268). The grated coconut used in both this and *kueh ko swee* are kept fresh by steaming it with a little bit of salt.

My mother served this *kueh* at children's parties, along with the rainbow-layered steamed *kueh lapis kukus* (page 271).

makes 12 servings

255 g or 9 ounces white sugar

3¼ cups water

5 stalks *pandan* leaves,
    tied into a knot

230 g or 8 ounces rice flour

½ tablespoon *sago* flour (substitute with
    tapioca flour if not available)

1 teaspoon alkaline water (*ayer abu*)

2 to 3 drops red food colouring

2 to 3 drops blue food colouring

2 to 3 drops green food colouring

2 to 3 drops yellow food colouring

1 coconut without skin, grated

¼ teaspoon salt

1. Combine the sugar, water and knotted *pandan* leaves in a saucepan and bring to a boil until the sugar dissolves. Remove from heat and let cool. Discard the *pandan* leaves.

2. Combine the rice flour and *sago* flour together in a bowl. Make a well in the centre and pour in alkaline water and sugar syrup. Using a metal spoon, mix well together to form a smooth mixture, pressing out any clumps.

3. Divide the mixture into 4 portions and add a different colouring to each.

4. Place a metal stand in a large or Dutch oven pot. Fill the pot with cold water, almost up to the height of the stand. Bring to a gentle boil to create a steamer.

5. To prepare the grated coconut, toss with the salt and steam for about 2 minutes. Remove and allow to cool.

6. Prepare a tray that will fit on the wire rack, line the tray with several little Chinese teacups. Place the teacups in the steamer for about 5 minutes to warm the teacups.

7. Use a ladle to pour the different coloured mixture to fill each of the teacup to a level of three quarters in depth. Cover the steamer for about 15 to 20 minutes until the *kueh* cooks through.

8. To serve, use a paring knife or fork to tip out the *kueh* from each teacup. Arrange the *kueh* on a serving plate and scatter the grated coconut to toss the *kueh* evenly on all sides.

Kueh Ko Chee

Glutinous Rice Flour Cake with Mung Bean Filling

My sister Nancy loves this one. Yet, I rarely saw my mother make this. Now, I understand the reason why and remember exactly when she even ever made it. *Kueh ko chee* was served up for ancestral worship. My older sisters got to eat a lot more of this *kueh* while growing up, when my mother prepared offerings for the ancestral table. She did away with all that when she became a Christian. Back then, she took her duties seriously. She once caught me eating something off the table and it left her aghast that I had stolen a share from our ancestors. She made me apologise at the altar for being such a greedy girl.

The recipe below, however, is completely different from what we know as *kueh ko chee* with the white and blue pastry on the outside and the *gula melaka*-drenched grated coconut filling inside. When we tested it, we were left befuddled by the fact that we had never seen such a Nonya *kueh* and were puzzled by the existence of such a recipe clearly titled '*Kueh Ko Chee*'. The recipe bears testament to the fact that among the hundreds of recipes which my mother left behind, there are simply those that I will never be able to ask her if they were wrongly labelled or hard-to-explain strange concoctions.

To obtain the conventional *kueh ko chee*, you could substitute the mung bean filling with the coconut filling from *ondeh ondeh* (page 279), and leave out the black glutinous rice for the pastry dough. You also have the option of adding some blue colouring from *bunga telang* (blue peaflower) to the dough.

makes 6 servings

2 tablespoons black glutinous rice

13 banana leaves

½ cup peanut or coconut oil

450 g or 1 pound green mung beans
   (*kachang hijau*)

2 cups water

450 g or 1 pound sugar for mung
   bean filling

1½ cups coconut milk (or milk derived
   from squeezing 2 grated coconuts)

600 g or 1 pound 5 ounces white
   glutinous rice flour

¼ teaspoon salt

2 tablespoons sugar for pastry

1. Wash and soak the black glutinous rice for 3 hours, preferably overnight.

2. Prepare a saucepan of boiling water. Cut the banana leaves into semi-circles about 18 cm or 7 inches in diameter. Dip each leaf into the saucepan of boiling water. Brush the oil on one side of each leaf.

3. Rinse the mung beans. Add the beans and water to a saucepan and bring to a boil. Lower heat and continue to simmer until the beans soften. Then pour in the sugar and stir continuously, mashing gently until the sugar dissolves and you form a smooth bean paste. This will take about 2 hours. Remove from heat and cool the bean paste. Then shape into round balls about 3.5 cm or ½ inches in diameter.

4. Drain the black glutinous rice and have it ground wet. Leave on a large tray lined with a cloth to dry. When it is dried, mix with the white glutinous rice flour, coconut milk until the mixture is well blended. Add the salt and sugar. Take a pinch of this dough mixture and flatten into a disc and place the bean paste filling in the middle, fold into a ball.

5. Roll each semi-circular banana leaf into a cone. Drop a rolled ball of mixture into the cone and fold over to seal and form a flat base. Arrange on a round steamer tray or plate.

6. Place a metal stand in a large or Dutch oven pot. Fill the pot with cold water, almost up to the height of the stand. Bring to a gentle boil to create a steamer.

7. Place the plate of *kueh* on the rack. Cover the steamer for about ½ to 1 hour until the *kueh* cooks through.

277

Ondeh Ondeh
Glutinous Rice Flour Balls with *Gula Melaka* Filling

My sisters used to send my nieces over to my mother's home so that these young girls could learn cooking techniques from *mama* (maternal grandmother). Recently, one of these nieces gave an account of these lessons. The only thing my mother taught them was *ondeh ondeh* which she considered was the first and easy step to Nonya cooking. Because my mother was so fastidious and impatient, they never ventured beyond *ondeh ondeh*. Moreover, my mother simply used her fingers to do 'everything'. In that, she measured ingredients by pinching the ingredients, to kneading the dough and to tasting the final product by licking her fingers. This practice was highly common of Nonyas. They simply *agak agak* (approximate) everything without the need for any fancy kitchen tools.

makes 6 servings

garnish
230 g or 8 ounces grated,
    skinned coconut

1 teaspoon salt

pastry
230 g or 8 ounces sweet potato

230 g or 8 ounces glutinous rice flour

1 teaspoon salt

1 tablespoon green food colouring

1 tablespoon *pandan* essence

¾ cup water

filling
230 g or 8 ounces *gula melaka*,
    scraped into fragments

1. Prepare a steamer and steam the grated coconut with some salt for about 5 minutes. Remove and let it cool. Reserve the steamer.

2. Peel the sweet potatoes and steam until soft. Mash with a wooden spoon.

3. Combine the mashed sweet potato, glutinous rice flour, salt, green colouring, *pandan* essence in a bowl. Use your fingertips to knead into a mixture. Add the water, a little at a time, until you achieve a doughy consistency.

4. Pinch and divide the dough into balls, each about 2.5 cm or 1 inch in diameter. Press each ball flat into a disc and add a teaspoon of the *gula melaka* in the middle. Fold and roll back into a ball.

5. Prepare a pot of water and bring to a boil. Add a few balls at a time and boil until these balls rise to the surface. Scoop them out with a slotted spoon. Toss in the grated coconut and transfer to a serving tray.

Kueh Dadar

Coconut Pancake with Grated Coconut Filling

I learnt to make this at my very first Home Economics lesson in school. It illustrated the fact that Katong Convent, which my mother and my sisters also attended, was highly influenced by the Nonyas who formed a significant part of the community.

makes 6 servings

filling
300 g or 11 ounces *gula melaka*
2 tablespoons white sugar
3 tablespoons water
6 *pandan* leaves, tied into a knot
600 g or 1½ pounds grated coconut

coconut sauce (*santan*)
60 g or 2 ounces rice flour
2 tablespoons plain flour
1 teaspoon salt
3 cups coconut milk
60 g or 2 ounces sugar
6 *pandan* leaves, tied into a knot

crepe skin
230 g or 8 ounces plain flour
1 tablespoon *sago* flour
   (or tapioca flour)
1 teaspoon salt
4 eggs, beaten
7 to 8 *pandan* leaves, pounded
   for essence
2½ cups coconut milk
2 teaspoons red food colouring
1 tablespoon green food
   colouring

filling

1.   Place *gula melaka*, sugar, water and knotted *pandan* leaves in a pot. Bring to a boil for 5 minutes until the sugars dissolve. Turn off heat. Add the grated coconut. Toss and coat until the sugar mixture is completely absorbed by the coconut mixture. Let cool. Discard the *pandan* leaves.

coconut sauce (*santan*)

1.   Combine the rice flour, plain flour and salt in a bowl. Add half of the coconut milk and stir to remove clumps.

2.   Combine the remaining coconut milk, sugar and knotted *pandan* leaves in a saucepan and bring to a boil. Pour into the flour mixture. Combine and bring back to boil gently, stirring continuously until the mixture thickens. Remove from heat and let cool. Discard *pandan* leaves. Chill.

crepe skin

1.   Combine the plain flour, sago flour and salt in a bowl. Make a well in the middle and whisk in the beaten eggs, a little at a time. Add the *pandan* essence, followed by the coconut milk, a little at a time. Remove any lumps and whisk to obtain a smooth batter. Strain to remove *pandan* fibres.

2.   Leave the batter for half an hour before frying.

3.   Divide into 3 portions. Add the red food colouring to one portion to obtain a pink batter. Add the green food colouring to the second portion. Leave the third portion as is.

4.   To prepare the *kueh dadar* skin, heat a nonstick frying pan, about 20 cm or 8 inches in diameter. Pour a ladle full of the batter and use a spatula to spread out the batter across the pan. The underside is cooked when it detaches from the pan. Flip the pancake over. Remove from the pan and set aside. Repeat with the rest of the batter.

5.   Spread 1 to 2 tablespoons of the filling in the middle of one layer of skin. Fold the lower half of the skin over the filling, then fold the left side over followed by the right side. Roll up to the top.

6.   Serve the *kueh dadar* with the chilled coconut sauce (*santan*).

Kueh Ambon

Baked Honeycomb Cake

My sister Angela and I love this *kueh* because it reminds us of rubber bands, made all the more appealing because they are edible!

This *kueh* has to proof before baking for the yeast to do its magic. It was traditionally baked on a charcoal stove. The recipe here uses the conventional oven. In my mother's recipe, there was no indication of *pandan* leaves. I had added it here as an ingredient for enhanced flavour.

Kueh ambon can be baked in a round baking tray or in a mould with several small oval cavities. The mould would produce ovoid-shaped *kueh ambon* like those in the photograph. For simplicity, the method below calls for the baking tray.

makes 12 servings

yeast mixture
30 g or 1 ounce dry yeast
140 g or 5 ounces plain flour
2 teaspoons sugar
1 cup warm water (about 40 degrees C or 105 degrees F)

kueh
1½ cups coconut milk
4 *pandan* leaves, tied into a knot
6 eggs
400 g or 14 ounces sugar
200 g or 7 ounces *sago* flour (substitute with tapioca flour if not available)

1. Combine the yeast, plain flour and sugar in a bowl. Add the water, a little at a time, and stir the batter until smooth. Cover the bowl with a cloth and let it rest for 2 ½ to 3 hours.

2. Place coconut milk and knotted *pandan* leaves in a saucepan and bring to a gentle boil. Turn off the heat and let cool. Discard the *pandan* leaves.

3. Place the eggs and sugar in a mixing bowl and use an electric mixer to whisk. Pour in the coconut milk. Fold in the *sago* flour and then beat in the yeast dough. Leave the *kueh* mixture to rest overnight, covered.

4. Preheat an oven at 180 degrees C or 350 degrees F. Brush tin with a little oil. Line a round tray, about 30 cm or 12 inches in diameter, with parchment paper.

5. Pour the batter into the round tray and bake in the preheated oven. After 10 minutes, turn down the oven temperature to 150 degrees C or 300 degrees F. Bake for another 30 minutes until the *kueh* is cooked. You can test this by inserting a paring knife (or *satay* stick) into the *kueh*, it should come out clean.

Kueh Bengka Ubi Kayu
Baked Tapioca Cake

My mother made this frequently. Each time she baked this, she would never fail to mention that during the Second World War, they all survived on yam (*keladi*) and tapioca (*ubi kayu*). There is a saying in our home: "*tanam keladi*", which means to bury in soil along with yam—a metaphor for meeting one's passing.

makes 12 servings

1.5 kg or 3¼ pounds fresh
   tapioca, skinned
115 g or 4 ounces grated coconut
450 g or 1 pound white sugar
½ teaspoon salt

1 egg
1 teaspoon vanilla essence
1½ cups coconut milk (or milk
   squeezed from 2 coconuts)
2 to 3 tablespoons butter, softened

1. Grate the tapioca and squeeze dry to extract the liquid. Discard the liquid.

2. Preheat the oven at 200 degrees Celsius or 400 degrees F.

3. Combine the grated tapioca, grated coconut, white sugar, salt, egg, vanilla essence and coconut milk. Mix well.

4. Grease a baking tin, 20 by 20 cm or 8 by 8 inches, with half of the butter. Line with parchment paper. Pour the batter into the tray. Dot all over the surface with the remaining butter.

5. Bake for 10 minutes until the top layer is light golden brown. Cover the top with a tin foil and lower the oven temperature to 180 degrees Celsius or 350 degrees F. Bake for another hour or until a paring knife inserted into the *kueh* comes out clean.

6. Remove the baking tin and leave on a wire rack to cool completely before serving.

Kueh Pisang
Chilled Mung Bean Flour Pudding with Banana

This is a refreshing dessert, especially after a spicy meal. Each kueh is individually wrapped in banana leaf. It is also portable and can be packed off for a picnic. My family never fails to remind me that I missed their golden era of the 1960s when Changi still meant the beach, not the airport. My parents would often cart the whole family off for a weekend outing there.

makes 12 servings

20 banana leaves, trimmed into squares of 8 cm or 3 inches wide

150 g or 5 ounces sugar

4 *pandan* leaves, tied into a knot

3 cups water, divided into 2 cups and 1 cup

100 g or 3½ ounces mung bean flour (*tepong hoen kueh*)

2 cups coconut milk

4 to 6 bananas, peeled and sliced into 0.5 cm or ¼ inch pieces

1. Pour boiling water over banana leaves to soften. Wipe and leave aside.

2. Combine the sugar, *pandan* leaves and 2 cups of the water in a saucepan and bring to boil for 5 minutes. Turn off heat. Let cool. Remove the *pandan* leaves.

3. Place the mung bean flour in a separate saucepan and make a well in the centre. Pour in the remaining 1 cup of water. Stir well to remove lumps. Add in the coconut milk, followed by the warm sugar mixture, again stirring to remove lumps. Bring the entire mixture to a boil over low heat for a minute until it makes bubbles, making sure that it does not boil over. Remove from heat.

4. Scoop one tablespoon of the mixture and dab on one cut piece of banana leaf. Place a slice of banana on top, followed by another tablespoon of the mixture. Fold the two edges over each other, and then fold the left and right sides over to form a little packet.

5. Chill all the little packets in the refrigerator for at least 2 hours before serving.

Goreng Klodok

Banana Fritters

makes 12 servings

6 large bananas (*pisang rajah* variety, preferably)

2 large eggs, beaten

120 g or 4 ounces sugar

270 g or 9½ ounces flour

1 teaspoon baking powder

90 g or 3 ounces grated coconut, without skin

3 tablespoons coconut milk (best squeezed from freshly grated coconut)

¼ teaspoon salt

2 cups oil

1. Peel and mash the bananas into smaller chunks. Beat the eggs and sugar together until the sugar dissolves and the batter is thick.

2. Sift the flour with baking powder. In a large bowl, put the grated coconut with the peeled banana and half of the flour mixture. Rub the mixture with the fingertips. Pour in the beaten eggs, along with the rest of the flour, the coconut milk and salt. Stir lightly to get mix the batter evenly.

3. Heat a wok and add in oil. When the oil is smouldering, lower the heat to moderate. Using a tablespoon, drop a few spoonfuls of batter into the hot oil. When one side of each *klodok* is light brown, use a spatula to turn them over.

4. When both sides have browned evenly, scoop them out, preferably with slotted scoop and leave on a platter lined with absorbent paper.

5. Do not stack the *klodok* when hot, otherwise they will turn flat and soggy.

Kueh Bongkong

Rice Flour Pudding wrapped in Banana Leaves

My sister Molly and I love this dessert. It is a creamy *gula melaka* and coconut concoction and is very refreshing when served chilled. The appealing part also is the boat-shaped banana leaf wrapping that it comes in. I remember sitting in the "factory line" helping my mother spoon grated *gula melaka* and pinning the leaves together with sharp toothpicks. Years back, I expressed my regret that I did not know how to fold those boats for *kueh bongkong*. Immediately, Aunty Paddy whipped out a piece of paper and taught me.

makes 12 servings

- 30 banana leaves, trimmed into rectangles 15 cm by 20 cm or 6 inch by 8 inch
- 5 to 6 cups of coconut milk (can be obtained by squeezing 600 g or 1 pound 5 ounces of white grated coconut with 4 cups of water)
- 3 tablespoons white sugar
- 5 *pandan* leaves, 3 leaves tied into a knot, the rest cut into 1.5-cm or ½-inch pieces

- 180 g or 6 ounces rice flour
- 1 tablespoon *sago* flour (substitute with tapioca flour if not available)
- 1 teaspoon salt
- 250 g or 9 ounces *gula melaka*, scraped into fragments
- 10 toothpicks

1. Prepare a saucepan of boiling water. Dip each leaf into the saucepan of boiling water and set aside.

2. Set aside ¾ cup of the coconut milk for later use.

3. Combine the remaining coconut milk, 1 tablespoon of sugar and knotted *pandan* leaves in a saucepan and bring to a boil. Turn off heat. Let cool.

4. Combine rice flour, sago flour and salt. Add half of the coconut milk.

5. Stir and with a metal spoon to remove any clumps. Whisk slowly until thick. Add the remaining coconut milk to dilute if the mixture is too thick. Transfer back to the saucepan and bring back to a gentle boil. Cook until you obtain a white glue-like paste. Remove from heat and discard the *pandan* leaves.

6. Place a metal stand in a large or Dutch oven pot. Fill the pot with cold water, almost up to the height of the stand. Bring to a gentle boil to create a steamer.

7. Line a piece of banana leaf. Dab 2 tablespoons of the mixture on the leaf, top with 1 tablespoon of *gula melaka*. Dab another tablespoon of mixture on top, followed by a cut piece of *pandan*. Then add another tablespoon from the ¾ cup coconut milk previously set aside. Fold along the middle of the banana leaf. Then, lift and invert both ends of the midline upwards in the shape of a boat. Crimp the two edges of each end by folding backwards so that the eventual flaps lean against the 'boat'. At this point, line another piece of banana leaf at the bottom and lift both ends to fold around the middle of the boat. Pin all the leaves together by inserting one of the toothpick across in the middle, about 1 cm or ¼ inch from the top edge. Repeat till ingredients are used up.

8. Place the *kueh bongkong* on a tray (with some depth) and steam, covered, for about 10 minutes. The *gula melaka* will melt into a syrup, hence the tray to catch any spillage. Let them cool before chilling in the refrigerator.

Apom Bokuah

Pancakes with Banana Gravy

In the olden days, *apom bokuah* was made from ground wet glutinous rice (*pulot*). The glutinous rice grains had to be soaked overnight, then ground using the heavy *batu boh* (round stone mill for grinding). The ground rice, still wet, would be wrapped in cloth, pressed down by heavy weights to extract excess water. These days, processed glutinous rice flour is used instead.

   In researching this much cherished Nonya dessert, I spent nights deciphering the mind-boggling method. All the various recipe versions had confusing distinctions for No. 1 coconut milk and No. 2 coconut milk, subdivided, recombined, with split portions of the different types of flour. It was a mathematical challenge. I hope that this version below does justice to what seemed like the most elaborate dessert recipe I have ever encountered.

makes 6 servings

yeast mixture
4 tablespoons plain flour

¾ ounce dry yeast

1 tablespoon sugar

150 ml or 5 fluid ounces warm
  coconut water (about 40 degrees C
  or 105 degrees F)

batter
1¼ cups coconut cream

1 teaspoon baking powder

340 g or 12 ounces rice flour

2 tablespoons glutinous rice flour

¼ teaspoon salt

1¼ cups coconut water

1¹/₃ cups coconut milk

Coconut oil

Blue food colouring

Red food colouring

Green food colouring

sauce
60 g or 2 ounces rice flour

170 g or 6 ounces plain flour

5 cups coconut milk

675 g or 1½ pounds *gula melaka*,
  grated or scraped into fragments

3 tablespoons sugar

2½ cups water

8 *pandan* leaves, knotted

½ teaspoon salt

½ cup coconut cream

12 bananas (*pisang rajah* variety,
  preferably), sliced then steamed

1. For the yeast mixture, mix the plain flour, dry yeast, sugar and warm coconut water. Stir until smooth. Leave overnight until the mixture is frothy and double in volume.

2. For the batter, heat the coconut cream until it thickens, about 5 to 7 minutes. Turn off heat and set aside.

3. Sift the rice flour and glutinous rice flour. Combine the rice flour, glutinous rice flour and salt in a saucepan. Make a well and add the coconut water a little at a time. Heat for about 1 to 2 minutes.

4. With the flour mixture, pour in the coconut milk. Mix by hand until well-blended. Pour in the warm coconut cream and the yeast mixture.

5. Stir the entire batter and remove any lumps. Set aside in a warm place, covered for 2 hours, until the mixture is bubbly and frothy.

6. Scoop out some batter into a small bowl and add a few drops of blue food colouring. Repeat with the red food colouring and green food colouring.

7. Place the special pancake mould over a low heat. Brush with coconut oil. Scoop a ladle of the batter and pour it into the separate cavities of the mould. The batter is cooked when little holes appear. Using a satay stick, drizzle one of the three food colourings to put a little colour on each pancake. Use a fork to remove each pancake from the mould. Transfer to a plate.

sauce

1. Combine the rice flour and plain flour in a bowl. Stir in ¼ cup of the coconut milk and set aside.

2. Combine the *gula melaka*, white sugar, water and *pandan* leaves in a saucepan. Bring to a boil for 5 minutes until the sugars dissolve. Discard the *pandan* leaves. Pour in the remaining coconut milk. Boil over medium heat, stirring occasionally. Remove from heat and set aside.

3. Pour half of the hot sugar mixture to the bowl of flour. Stir to remove lumps. Then return the mixture back to the rest of the sugar mixture, simmer over low heat until the gravy thickens. Add the salt, coconut cream and steamed sliced bananas.

4. Serve the *apom bokuah* with this sauce.

NOTE: As an alternative, instead of steaming the bananas, you could add the slices while cooking the sauce.

Sweet Potatoes in Ginger Syrup

Ginger is thought to 'pukol angin' (beat the toxic gases and dampness out of you to relieve aches and pains). Hence, post-natal mothers were given lots of ginger to 'beat the wind'. In my case, a backache, especially in the winter, was often remedied with a knob of ginger, with the sliced surface dipped in brandy. The brandied ginger was used to rub my back and it left red streak marks, indicating the wind in my flesh and bones. It always worked.

The ginger flavour is strongest just beneath its skin. Therefore, leave the skin on to get the most of the flavour.

makes 6 to 8 servings

900 g or 2 pounds sweet potatoes

2 knobs ginger, sliced into 0.5-cm or ¼-inch thick pieces, skin intact

1 cup white sugar

6 cups water

1. Scrub the sweet potatoes. Cut into chunks 5 cm or 2 inches, skin intact. Steam them in a bowl for 15 to 30 minutes to soften.

2. Meanwhile, place the sugar in a pot. Add a cup of the water and bring to boil. Stir to dissolve the sugar. Dilute with the remaining water and add the ginger slices. Boil briefly. Turn off heat and set aside.

3. Remove the sweet potatoes from the steamer and let cool. Peel the sweet potatoes. Transfer to the pot of syrup and let sit for an hour to allow the potatoes to steep in the ginger-flavoured syrup before serving. The dessert is best served warm.

4. Serve in individual bowls.

Talam Agar Agar

Agar Agar with Coconut Milk Topping

This is a common dessert, it comes in a pink or green bottom layer and an opaque white top. Back then, we did not have the abundance of premium ice cream for dessert. So the closest we could get to a convenient after-dinner dessert was *agar agar*.

makes 8 servings

green layer
300 g or 10½ ounces sugar

1½ cups water

5 *pandan* leaves, tied into a knot

40 g or 1½ ounce *agar agar* strips, cut into 2.5cm or 1 inch pieces *

½ teaspoon green food colouring

white coconut layer
150 g or 5½ ounces sugar

2¼ cups of water

20 g or ¾ ounce *agar agar* strips, cut into 2.5 cm or 1 inch pieces *

¼ teaspoon salt

1¼ cups coconut milk

* Can be substituted with a similar amount of *agar agar* powder

1. For the green layer, combine the sugar, water and *pandan* leaves in a saucepan and bring to a boil. Add in the *agar agar* strips. Stir until the sugar and the strips are fully dissolved. Remove the knotted *pandan* leaves. Strain through a colander to remove lumps. Add the green food colouring. Pour the mixture into a round tray about 30 cm or 12 inches in diameter. Leave to set.

2. For the white coconut layer, combine the sugar and water in a saucepan and bring to a boil. Add in the *agar agar* strips. Stir until the sugar has dissolved. Stir in the salt and coconut milk and let it boil briefly. Gently ladle the coconut mixture over the green bottom layer in the round tray which by now should have set. Be careful not to break up the green layer.

3. Set aside to cool, then refrigerate for 4 hours before serving. Traditionally, *agar agar* is sliced into diamond shapes using a jagged knife to give it serrated edges.

Pandan Chiffon Cake

My mother had a lifelong consuming passion for achieving the lightest, fluffiest, spongiest, fresh-green shade of chiffon. Her obsession was manifested in the several egg beaters and cake mixers acquired during her jaunts to the CK Tang kitchen department. As a result, there were at least 10 to 15 drafts for pandan chiffon and I cannot claim that the version below reflects her desired result. But it surely reminds me of what had seemed like a long moment during my childhood when I had to taste slice after slice of pandan chiffon.

makes 8 servings

¾ cup coconut milk

4 to 5 *pandan* leaves, tied into a knot

10 tablespoons corn oil

110 g or 4 ounces cake flour,
    e.g. Softasilk

1 teaspoon baking powder

½ teaspoon salt

4 large egg yolks

200 g or 7 ounces sugar, divided
    into two equal portions

1 teaspoon *pandan* essence

1 teaspoon green colouring

5 large egg whites

½ teaspoon cream of tartar

1. Boil coconut milk and *pandan* leaves in a saucepan. Turn off heat and let cool completely. Discard the *pandan* leaves.

2. When about to bake, preheat the oven at 160 degrees C or 320 degrees F. Brush the sides of a round chiffon cake tin about 22.5 cm or 9 inches in diameter with some of the corn oil. Line the base with parchment paper.

3. Sift flour, baking powder and salt. Set aside.

4. Whisk the egg yolks and stream in one portion of the sugar, a little at a time. Continue to whisk until the sugar dissolves and the consistency is thick. Add the *pandan* essence, green colouring, corn oil and the *pandan*-infused coconut milk. Then fold in the sifted flour mixture.

5. Using a clean egg-beater bowl, beat the egg whites and cream of tartar. Pour in the second portion of sugar a little at a time. Beat until the mixture is stiff.

6. Fold the beaten egg whites into the egg yolk and flour mixture. Turn and fold until the cake mixture is well combined.

7. Pour the cake mixture into the greased tin. Bake in the oven for 50 to 60 minutes until the cake surface is golden brown and a stick comes out clean when inserted into the cake.

8. Let the cake cool. Place a wire rack over the top of the cake tin and turn over to get the cake out. Remove the paper lining at the base of the cake.

Pulot Hitam
Creamy Black Glutinous Rice with Coconut Milk

This is my favourite dessert. When I think of *pulot hitam*, I associate it with being at home on a lazy, balmy Sunday afternoon. Simmered long enough, the dessert takes on a oatmeal-like consistency, luxuriously sweetened with *gula melaka* (palm sugar), flavoured by *pandan* leaves, and served with a yummy drizzle of coconut milk.

Even though *pulot hitam* literally means black glutinous rice, the dry rice grains may look purplish. When you prepare this, as with most soupy Nonya desserts, it is best to use a stock pot, not too large in diameter, otherwise the *pulot hitam* will evaporate more quickly and end up too dry and thick.

makes 8 servings

230 g or 8 ounces black glutinous
    rice (*pulot hitam*)

10 cups water

4 *pandan* leaves, tied into a knot

230 g or 8 ounces *gula melaka*,
    scraped into fragments

2 tablespoons sugar

¼ teaspoon salt

½ cup thick coconut milk

1. Pick out empty husks and small pebbles, then wash and rinse the rice with water three times.

2. Place the rice in a pot and cover with enough water, at least 2.5 cm or 1 inch above the level of the rice. Soak overnight to soften the rice.

3. On the next day, drain the rice and soak it in the pot with the 10 cups of fresh water.

4. Add the knotted *pandan* leaves to the pot.

5. Place the pot over high heat. When the water begins to boil, turn down the heat to simmer for 1½ hours, partially covered.

6. Stir occasionally to ensure that the rice does not stick to the bottom of the pot.

7. Meanwhile, use the back of a spoon to crumble the *gula melaka*. Add the white sugar. (This helps to hold up the fine powdery consistency of the *gula melaka*.)

8. Stir the sugar mixture and salt into the pot.

9. Continue to simmer for another 30 to 45 minutes, adding water if necessary if the *pulot hitam* seems to thicken or dry up too fast. You can simmer longer if you like a thicker consistency. However, *pulot hitam* is best when it is neither too thick nor too watery. Discard the *pandan* leaves.

10. You can serve the dessert while it is warm.

11. I like to chill mine in the refrigerator first before serving. Bear in mind that the *pulot hitam* will get thicker when chilled. Also, ensure that the dessert has cooled down first before you refrigerate to prevent spoilage.

12. When serving, spoon *pulot hitam* into dessert or soup bowls, and drizzle 1 to 2 teaspoons of coconut milk over each serving.

Kachang Hijau
Green Mung Beans in Syrup

My mother may seem crass for cooking this *kacang hijau* hawker-style. Most Nonya cookbooks list the refined version with coconut milk. I have decided to stick to what I remember we ate, the green beans cooked in the simple syrup which was simpler to prepare. These are the same green beans that I was preoccupied with throwing into our garden to watch them grow into bean sprouts.

makes 6 to 8 servings

340 g or 12 ounces green mung beans, whole and with shells on

340 g or 12 ounces white sugar

10 cups water

5 to 6 *pandan* leaves, knotted

1. Pick out tiny pebbles among the beans. Soak the beans in water for at least an hour. Drain.

2. Meanwhile, combine the sugar, water and knotted *pandan* leaves in a stock pot and bring to a boil. Stir to dissolve the sugar. Turn off the heat and discard the *pandan* leaves.

3. Add the beans to the pot. Boil the beans over medium heat, partially covered, until the beans are swollen and soft. Most likely, the skin would be coming off. Discard the *pandan* leaves.

Tau Suan

Mung Beans in Syrup

This is also especially delicious for young children and if parents worry about the amount of sugar, you could always cut back on that.

makes 12 servings

450 g or 1 pound mung beans
   (shelled and split)

1½ to 2 cups sugar

10 cups water

5 to 6 *pandan* leaves, knotted

3 tablespoons cornflour

¼ cup water

Crispy crullers (*yu char kway*),
   optional, sliced into 2.5-cm
   or 1-inch chunks

1.   Check the beans and remove tiny pebbles and blackened or broken grains. Soak the remaining beans in water for at least 2 hours. Drain with a colander and steam for 30 minutes.

2.   Meanwhile, combine the sugar, water and knotted *pandan* leaves in a large saucepan and bring to a boil. Stir to dissolve the sugar. Turn off the heat and discard the *pandan* leaves.

3.   Combine the cornflour and ¼ cup of water to form the slurry. Stir in a bit of the slurry to the saucepan to thicken the sugar syrup. Add more if necessary until you get a syrupy consistency. Add the steamed mung beans to the large saucepan.

4.   Serve in individual bowls, garnished with chunks of the crispy crullers.

Bubor Cha Cha
Sweet Potato and Sago in Coconut Milk

My husband and I love to roll up our sleeves and make these bright lengths of dough. We wear our blue and red stained hands with pride. *Bubor cha cha* is a joyful burst of coloured sago 'jewels' and can be served either warm or chilled with crushed ice.

makes 8 servings

600 g or 1¼ pounds sweet potatoes

600 g or 1¼ pounds yam

450 g or 1 pound white sugar

6 cups coconut milk, separate the top layer of cream and set aside

3 *pandan* leaves, tied into a knot

230 g or 8 ounces tapioca flour, set aside 30 g or 1 ounce for dusting

6 tablespoons cold water

½ to 1 teaspoon green food colouring

½ to 1 teaspoon blue food colouring

½ to 1 teaspoon red food colouring

1. Skin the sweet potatoes and yam. Cut them into cubes of side 1 cm or ½ inch.

2. Prepare a steamer and steam the cubes for 15 minutes until they are cooked.

3. Meanwhile, combine the sugar, coconut milk and knotted *pandan* leaves in a pot and bring to a boil. Stir to dissolve the sugar. Turn off the heat and lelt cool. Discard the *pandan* leaves.

4. Bring a pot of water to a boil.

5. Meanwhile, place the 230 g or 8 ounces of tapioca flour in a bowl. Add enough cold water to form a fine paste. Press out lumps. Pour in some of the boiling water to make a thick starch paste with opaque consistency. (Leave the pot of remaining water boiling over low heat.) Stir to remove lumps. Transfer the starch to a clean table dusted with extra tapioca flour. Divide the starch into three portions and add enough colouring to make one portion red, one portion green and the third, blue. Roll each portion into long strips, about 1 cm or ½ inch in width. Cut the strips into bits of 1-cm or ½-inch squares or triangles.

6. Remove the sweet potato and yam cubes from the steamer and allow to cool.

7. Turn up the heat for the pot of boiling water, adding more water if necessary. When there is a rolling boil, gather the starch bits and drop them into the pot. When the bits start to float to the surface, gather them up with a slotted spoon and plunge in cold water to stop the cooking process. Leave in the cold water so that they do not clump together.

8. Combine the bits with the yam, sweet potato and coconut milk.

9. You can serve *bubor cha cha* warm or chilled. If chilled, refrigerate for at least 4 hours, adding the coconut cream to each bowl just before serving.

Apom Balek
Pancakes made with *Gula Melaka*

This recipe was included at the very last minute, on the last day of our cookbook photoshoot. My sister Angela and I felt that we would not do justice to our mother's memory by not including this. She had made *apom balek* very frequently in the later part of her life. The recipe kept resurfacing in her files but I was discouraged from testing it because I did not think I would know how to. Thankfully, Angela had the gumption to just try it out.

makes 8 servings

50 g or 1¾ ounces light brown sugar
250 g or 8½ ounces *gula melaka*
    (scraped or grated)
10 tablespoons coconut water
300 g or 2 cups plain flour
½ teaspoon baking powder

2 cups coconut milk
½ egg, beaten
Coconut or vegetable oil
    for brushing pan

1. Place the light brown sugar and *gula melaka* in a small saucepan. Stir in the coconut water. Bring the mixture to a gentle boil.

2. Add brown sugar and stir to dissolve. Then leave syrup aside to cool.

3. Combine the plain flour and baking powder, then sift into a mixing bowl. Make a well in the centre. Pour in the syrup, a little at a time, followed by the coconut milk and the beaten egg. Whisk to a smooth consistency.

4. Heat a nonstick pan and add some of the coconut or vegetable oil. Turn down the heat. Scoop a ladle of the batter and pour on the pan, enough to form a pancake about 6 cm or 2.5 inches in diameter. Cook the pancakes until bubbles appear on the surface. Remove the pancakes from the nonstick pan and fold each one over into half. Repeat.

5. You can serve the *apom balek* pancakes with the banana sauce that goes with *apom bokuah* (page 290).

"She gets up while it is still dark; she provides food for her family...

She watches over the affairs of her household
and does not eat the bread of idleness.

Her children arise and call her blessed; her husband also and he praises her:

'Many women do noble things, But you surpass them all'."

Proverbs 31:15, 27-29

Acknowledgements

My sincere thanks to the team at Marshall Cavendish who took this manuscript and ran away with it so professionally—Lydia Leong, Sanae Inada, Lynn Chin and Violet Phoon. Thanks to my editor Brenton Wong who was such fun to work with. Thanks also to Joshua Tan who photographed the dishes. After photographing *sambal belachan* so many times, we succeeded in making Joshua an honorary Baba.

I am also indebted to Dorothy Wong, Shirley Wong, Cheryl Francisco and the late James Tan, for testing the recipes and preparing several of them for the photos in this book. *Kamsiah* to Linda Chee for contributing kind words for this book.

This book would not have been completed without the input of very special friends and relatives who were dear to my mother: Mrs. Paddy Chou, Mdm. Mabel Cheang and the late Mrs. Tan Eng Leong (*kohpoh* Beng Neo).

I am blessed with many friends who have encouraged me. Thank you all for your prayers. In particular, my children's godparents Angele Lee, Shu Chiu, Shujaat Islam, Stacey Tay and Stanley Peck; and my dinner buddies Lynette Shek in Singapore and Peggy Tan in New York. *Gracias* too to Erika and Yolany Barahona who looked after my children while I typed away.

I thank my sisters for the memories they gave me. I can never thank Maggie enough for caring for my children whenever I needed to work on the project while in Singapore. And to Angela for assisting me with the recipes. I am also grateful to Maggie and Angela for preparing some of the dishes for the photos. I hope that this book will also be a source of pride and joy for our father, Mr. Wee Hoon Leong.

This cookbook memoir is a legacy for my nieces and nephews as well as for my children—my little Nonya Lizzie and my handsome Alex. Mama would have wanted this for all of you.

Most of all, my sincere love to my dear husband Tracy for his enduring patience with me. Words and action cannot fully express my gratitude. God bless you always, sweetie.

Weights and Measures

Quantities for this book are given in Metric, Imperial and American (spoon) measures. Standard spoon and cup measurements used are: 1 tsp = 5 ml, 1 Tbsp = 15 ml, 1 cup = 250 ml. All measures are level unless otherwise stated.

LIQUID AND VOLUME MEASURES

Metric	Imperial	American
5 ml	$^1/_6$ fl oz	1 teaspoon
10 ml	$^1/_3$ fl oz	1 dessertspoon
15 ml	$^1/_2$ fl oz	1 tablespoon
60 ml	2 fl oz	$^1/_4$ cup (4 tablespoons)
85 ml	$2^1/_2$ fl oz	$^1/_3$ cup
90 ml	3 fl oz	$^3/_8$ cup (6 tablespoons)
125 ml	4 fl oz	$^1/_2$ cup
180 ml	6 fl oz	$^3/_4$ cup
250 ml	8 fl oz	1 cup
300 ml	10 fl oz ($^1/_2$ pint)	$1^1/_4$ cups
375 ml	12 fl oz	$1^1/_2$ cups
435 ml	14 fl oz	$1^3/_4$ cups
500 ml	16 fl oz	2 cups
625 ml	20 fl oz (1 pint)	$2^1/_2$ cups
750 ml	24 fl oz ($1^1/_5$ pints)	3 cups
1 litre	32 fl oz ($1^3/_5$ pints)	4 cups
1.25 litres	40 fl oz (2 pints)	5 cups
1.5 litres	48 fl oz ($2^2/_5$ pints)	6 cups
2.5 litres	80 fl oz (4 pints)	10 cups

DRY MEASURES

Metric	Imperial
30 grams	1 ounce
45 grams	$1^1/_2$ ounces
55 grams	2 ounces
70 grams	$2^1/_2$ ounces
85 grams	3 ounces
100 grams	$3^1/_2$ ounces
110 grams	4 ounces
125 grams	$4^1/_2$ ounces
140 grams	5 ounces
280 grams	10 ounces
450 grams	16 ounces (1 pound)
500 grams	1 pound, $1^1/_2$ ounces
700 grams	$1^1/_2$ pounds
800 grams	$1^3/_4$ pounds
1 kilogram	2 pounds, 3 ounces
1.5 kilograms	3 pounds, $4^1/_2$ ounces
2 kilograms	4 pounds, 6 ounces

OVEN TEMPERATURE

	°C	°F	Gas Regulo
Very slow	120	250	1
Slow	150	300	2
Moderately slow	160	325	3
Moderate	180	350	4
Moderately hot	190/200	370/400	5/6
Hot	210/220	410/440	6/7
Very hot	230	450	8
Super hot	250/290	475/550	9/10

LENGTH

Metric	Imperial
0.5 cm	$^1/_4$ inch
1 cm	$^1/_2$ inch
1.5 cm	$^3/_4$ inch
2.5 cm	1 inch

Index

Project Manager: Sanae Inada-Wallwork
Editor: Brenton Wong
Designer: Lynn Chin
Photographer: Joshua Tan, Elements By The Box
Recipe Testing & Food Preparation: Dorothy Wong

Photo Credits

Singapore Heritage Society: page 10, image of Cheang Hong Lim from the book *One Hundred Years' History of the Chinese in Singapore* by Sir Song Ong Siang

Cornell University Library: page 10, image of Mrs Cheang Hong Lim

Chan Eng Thai (great grandson of Madam Chia Gin Tee): page 10, images of Cheang Jim Chuan, Chan Kim Hong Neo and Chia Gin Tee

Singapore Press Holdings: page 12, newspaper article

All other images courtesy of author

Published by Marshall Cavendish Cuisine
An imprint of Marshall Cavendish International

Other Marshall Cavendish Offices:
Marshall Cavendish International. PO Box 65829, London, EC1P 1NY, UK • Marshall Cavendish Corporation, 99 White Plains Road, Tarrytown NY 10591-9001, USA • Marshall Cavendish International (Thailand) Co Ltd. 253 Asoke, 12th Flr, Sukhumvit 21 Road, Klongtoey Nua, Wattana, Bangkok 10110, Thailand • Marshall Cavendish (Malaysia) Sdn Bhd, Times Subang, Lot 46, Subang Hi-Tech Industrial Park, Batu Tiga, 40000 Shah Alam, Selangor Darul Ehsan, Malaysia

Marshall Cavendish is a trademark of Times Publishing Limited

National Library Board, Singapore Cataloguing-in-Publication Data

Wee, Sharon (Sharon Beng Ling)
Growing up in a Nonya kitchen : Singapore recipes from my mother / Sharon Wee.
— Singapore : Marshall Cavendish Cuisine, 2012.
p. cm.
Includes index.
ISBN : 978-981-4346-36-8

1. Cooking, Peranakan. 2. Cooking, Singaporean. I. Title.

TX724.5.S55
641.595957 -- dc22   OCN775289868

Printed in Singapore by KWF Printing Pte Ltd